Managing Your Communication
In and For the Organization

William I. Gorden
John R. Miller
Kent State University

Waveland Press, Inc.
Prospect Heights, Illinois

For information about this book, write or call:

Waveland Press, Inc.
P.O. Box 400
Prospect Heights, Illinois 60070
(312) 634-0081

Copyright © 1983 by William I. Gorden and John R. Miller
Second Printing

ISBN 0-88133-007-8

Printed in the United States of America.

Contents

Acknowledgements

Major corporations and their advertising agencies seek noble ways to create goodwill. Often sponsorship of some good work far removed from its own products or services demonstrates corporate goodwill. Such nonprofit oriented ventures by business might be thought of as long term investments in building communities in which those who live and work can do so in healthy, beautiful, safe and stimulating environments. Gambles for good have payoffs in goodwill.

Business is noted for its philanthropic support to the arts. Famous works of art adorn such cities as Chicago, in which, thanks to business headquartered there, one may enjoy giant works by Picasso, Chagall and Calder.

Business also competes to sponsor very fine media events. This is fortunate indeed. Texaco has long sponsored weekly broadcasts of the opera. Diamond Shamrock sponsored the televised celebration of Cleveland's Playhouse Square Renovation. IBM sponsors CBS's *Face the Nation.*

Occasionally, a company finds a creative way to inspire goodwill by providing a desired service which also demonstrates the need for its product. The "Power of the Printed Word" series financed by the International Paper Company is an example of this type of goodwill-advertising venture.

International Paper Company directly links itself with knowledge-based organizations such as the schools, libraries, textbook companies, and newspapers by sponsoring essays on reading skills, use of the library, vocabulary improvement, appreciation of the classics, writing and speaking skills. These people in such knowledge-based industries (teachers, professors, librarians, book publishers, and journalists) have a natural self-interest and good feeling toward a company that demonstrates its goodwill by such campaigns.

The business community also is attracted and grateful to a company that sponsors the "Power of the Printed Word" series. Why? Essays on communication skills: fast reading, comprehension, vocabulary development, how to read an annual report, how to write a business letter and resume, and how to make a speech.

All this International Paper did with flair and verve by its choice of nationally known personalities such as Bill Cosby, James Michener, Tony Randall, Kurt Vonnegut, George Plimpton, Jane Bryant Quinn and Malcolm Forbes.

The short essays throughout this book are to be read as informative asides. Talk about the ideas and suggestions. Try them.

Preface

Careers in preindustrial society were largely agriculture, hunting and mining. In the industrial age, the odds increased that much of one's life would be linked with a machine and that one would live in the city rather than on the farm. In this day, which some are calling the postindustrial era, theoretical knowledge and technical applications have again shifted the kinds of careers for new entrants to the job market.

The name of the game has changed. Whereas in preindustrial society, the game was man pitted against nature, in the industrial age the game was man against fabricated nature, and in the postindustrial era, the game is between persons.* The odds are that those of you who read these words will enter careers in which communication competencies are essential to job accomplishment and to the functioning of the organization which you enter. And like it or not the odds are you will be employed by an organization. Ours is a complex society and only a very few of us will be self-employed.

Not only is communication the means by which business is conducted, but it also is the means by which the company tells its story to potential investors, stockholders, consumers, environmentalists and legislators.

In 1977, we authored *Speak Up for Business*, our first business and professional speaking book. That text during two printings was used by students in over 70 classrooms. Also it was the textbook used in Executive Speaking classes which is a requirement of our Masters of Business Administration curriculum. Because we have learned so much from these teaching experiences and our many business consulting and training experience, we have endeavored to encapsule all this in a very practical book we are entitling *Managing Your Communication — In and For the Organization*.

Our new book is written for those who have elected careers in business and the professions. The text is designed to acquaint them with face to face communications of a formal and semi-formal nature: including preparation for presentations in-house and to the public, interviewing and group interaction.

The text approaches communication with equal value placed upon both competence and commitment. That is we believe that business needs and our country needs young people who are skilled, articulate and honest.

We are pleased to have Carole Barbato, Instructor of Speech Communication at Kent State University, guest author most of Chapter Four, "Using Written Channels and Technical Media." We trust that the materials presented in this chapter will make our book even more practical to those of you who will complete your college education in this media-minded decade.

*Daniel Bell, "Welcome to the Post-Industrial Society," *Physics Today,* Vol. 29 (February 1976), pp. 46-49.

At the close of each chapter, we include a number of addresses by executive officers of major corporations, excerpts of speeches by individuals at various levels in business, and manuscripts and outlined speeches by students headed for careers in business. In Chapter Four, we have projects on resume writing and on use of media. In Chapter Six, we include many hypothetical role play situations. We believe these project activities with cases and speeches provide first-hand information and insights into the work of the business world. More importantly, they also serve as models.

To aid the student, Projects ask questions designed to teach specific communication concepts and to guide skill development. For Project Five-1, which focuses on a Thesis and Behavioral Objectives, answers have been included to the questions. The purpose of this is to provide yet another approach to learning — one in which the student may compare his thinking to the authors.

We recommend that the study guide for each project be detached from the text and placed along side the model being studied. The student may fill in the answer as he reads. The instructor may use the Project study guides as a springboard for class discussion or as assignments to be handed in. Whether the instructor does either of these things or not, we recommend that you, the student, do the Projects. If you genuinely want to develop your own communication skills to aid a career in business or the professions, these models will be helpful.

Yet another feature of this text are the Performance Profiles included in the Appendix. These serve as criteria for assignments and when used by the instructor as a record of feedback to the student. These Performance Profiles also are made to be detached at the time of the presentation of an assignment.

This is a book of action. Its very title suggests that learning is doing. We become articulate by articulating our thoughts and feelings. *Managing Your Communication* will call forth your best efforts to articulate your ideas and to test them in the marketplace. It is only when we see how others respond to our messages that we really know what we have said. The activities of this text beg for interaction. It is through feedback that we learn to monitor and to improve our communicating.

Finally, we ask a favor of those who read this book and who take our courses. We like to collect the business cards of those of you presently employed while enrolled in the course. If you are now employed and have a business card, that card symbolizes that you are a communicator in and for your work organization. If you don't have a business card yet, please do send us your first business card when you have them made up. We like to know where you are *Managing Your Communication*.

1

Who Needs Communication Skills?

Chapter Outline

Top Management Speaks
Marketing Speaks
Internal Communications
Careers and Communication Competencies
Employees Speak
Associations
Recap

    Project One-1:   *Identification*
    Project One-2:   *Communication Skills*
    Project One-3:   *Thesis Personalized*

Chapter Objectives

Those who complete this chapter should better understand:

1. the importance of communication competencies for those who elect careers in business and other complex organizations;

2. that the quality of communication depends upon the clarity of communication, persuasiveness of communication and the interpersonal climate of the relationship;

3. that business is concerned about its relationship with its public.

"Communication has proven as elusive as the Unicorn."
— Peter Drucker
Dean of Management Consultants

"People will talk more with machines and less with people. There will be less opportunity for what a sociologist might call 'casual non-work-oriented verbal interfacing among work peers'..."
Jeremy Main, "Work Won't Be the Same Again,"
Fortune, June 28, 1982, pp. 58-65

In 1886, a young man sold watches to railroad station agents in his spare time. Richard W. Sears' business prospered and within seven years he moved his business from Spring Valley, Minnesota, to Chicago, where he advertised for a watch repairman. Alvan C. Roebuck answered the ad. That was the beginning of the firm that operates out of the 110-story Sears Tower, does business in over 835 retail stores and three times that many catalog outlets, and has subsidiaries or affiliates in Latin America, Spain, Belgium and Canada, with an annual sales volume in the billions.[1]

Some sixteen years before Sears began his watch business, a company which soon specialized in canned soup began its climb to well over a billion in annual sales and many millions in net profit. The Campbell Soup Company does not operate out of a gleaming skyscraper as does Sears but its headquarters for years has been as simple as its apple-cheeked cartoon kids. Everything is institutional green, offices are just cubicles—nobody has an ashtray on his desk![2]

America is made up of success stories like Sears' and Campbell's. More recent tales of growth include companies like Texas Instruments, which grew from 1,700 to 17,000 employees and from $2 million to over $200 million in the decade of the 1950s.[3] Assets of the three largest U.S. banks is incomprehensible to the average person: Citicorp, Bank America and Chase Manhattan total nearly 300 billion dollars.

Today's story of corporate America reflects more than mom and pop operations. Managing to make a profit and to survive entail much more than minding the store and hustling sales. Communication is so essential to pulling it all together that it seems preposterously simple to ask the question: Who in business needs communication know-how? It's preposterous because almost every corporation has a division concerned with internal training and communication. In addition, business purchases communication know-how. Great sums are annually invested in advertising and promotions of products.

Hundreds of industries have public relations departments or employ outside firms to enhance their images. Company speakers' bureaus are common, from public utilities to drug firms, to carry their company's message. One drug firm alone has sent out more than 500 employees to speak some 20,000 times to over a million listeners—at a cost of about $3 for each delivery.[4]

But for those of us who are employed in business and industry or who are in training for business careers, the question "Who needs it?" is asked out of a need to know. We need to know in what ways we, personally, will need communication skills. Therefore, in this chapter, in answering this question we will deal with both the obvious answer—that is, those at the top need communication know-how—and with less obvious answers which grow out of answers given by representative personnel in many different careers.

Top Management Speaks

The Chief Executive Officer. The foremost person in business who needs communication skills is the chief executive officer. Consider for a moment the constituencies he must face: the board of directors and his own executive committee, shareholders and prospective investors, unions, militant consumers, and environmentalists, Wall Street analysts, government agencies, Congress, foreign affiliates and their governments, civic and charitable organizations. His task seems particularly formidable at a time when the large majority of Americans believe big business is too big and that it does not have the consumer's interest nor the environment at heart.

Leadership Depends on Communicating

"You may be a brilliant technician, but if you can't communicate, you won't succeed."

Herbert Hidebrandt and colleagues at the University of Michigan graduate school of business asked 1,158 newly promoted chairmen, presidents, and vice presidents in a variety of businesses: "Which courses best prepare one for business leadership? Their answers:

Business Communication	71.4%
Finance	64.7%
Accounting	57.9%
Business Planning	47.7%
Marketing	38.1%

Business Communication scored highest. "Today's [Business Communication] classes take a practical approach — offering training in preparing reports, making presentations and running meetings."

— Report paraphrased from *Nation's Business,* April 1982, p. 17.

Today the number one spokesman for the American corporation is its chief executive officer (CEO). In the past, this individual spent the majority of his time managing his business but today the average CEO is spending 40 percent of his time arbitrating conflicting claims upon his company brought by consumers, shareholders, workers, management, government at all levels, and even the heads of foreign nations.[5] "It's an odd world we're living in," says Frank A. Nemec, former Chairman of the Youngstown Sheet & Tube Co., "We're sitting on a volcano of conflicting interest." American Motors Corporation Chairman, Roy D. Chapin, Jr., says that "the added dimension of social responsibility, or whatever it is, has to some extent always been our responsibility, but that has now become so almost overwhelming that if I wanted to, I could spend my entire time being civically and governmentally not just active but hyperactive." He adds that, "How you interpret to the public the fact that you are a company concerned about people is a very important assignment of the Chief Executive Officer." Others echo this concern. First Chicago Corporation's Chairman, Gaylord Freedman, states: "The Chief Executive must take a position on the issues. It just isn't practical for the CEO to have a junior officer make those decisions by which a corporation affects society. That's the Chief Executive's role."

The Chief Executive must be a political being. By this we do not mean he must donate to political campaigns. (In fact, such patronage has proven disastrous for many firms.) Nor does it mean that CEOs must be active in campaigns although some have been such as C. Peter McColough, Chairman of Xerox, who took on the treasurership of the Democratic Party. Rather it means that one must present the case for business before government regulatory agencies and congressional committees. Gulf Oil Corporation Chairman Bob Dorsey says that in the recent past the amount of time spent speaking to government bodies by the average CEO has increased fivefold; and William B. Johnson, Chairman of Illinois Central Industries, Inc., says that he now spends half of his time speaking to the government and the public. Certainteed Products Corporation President Byron C. Radaker observes, "The amount of work necessary to prepare yourself and keep yourself informed about the political situation, the world situation, and how investors are reacting is terrific. And it keeps getting bigger." The schedule book of A. W. Clausen, President of the Bank of America Corporation, records that he spent 28 days in Washington, D.C. in one year making presentation after presentation before major government conferences and committees.

CEOs increasingly find that they must concern themselves with the general public. Lawrence E. Fouraker, Dean of the Harvard Business School, says there are a few CEOs who do an excellent job of representing their companies—such men as David Rockefeller, Chairman of Chase Manhattan Corporation; C. Peter McColough, Chairman of the Xerox Corporation; and Gaylord Freeman, Chairman of First Chicago Corporation—but they are a relative few. According to Dean Fouraker, "Visibility for chief executives has almost always been associated with disasters, but there are relatively few heroes in the business community. Most businessmen would prefer to remain anonymous." Anonymity, however, is a luxury few CEOs can afford today. American Telephone & Telegraph Chairman John D. de Butts, for yet another example, participated in several press conferences in one year and was a frequent visitor on network TV talk shows.

During the fuel crisis of the 70s, Shell Oil Company of America President Harry Bridges, felt the pressure of the public. So he took a two-day course in how to appear on television and meet reporters. "I'm not a natural to appear on the television set or to be publicly interviewed, but it was a job that suddenly had to be done that you couldn't in all honesty just pass on to someone else." Like most CEOs, Bridges had very little training to prepare him for his public speaking role.

One answer to the tremendous pressures of the CEO's time schedule is to redefine his role. Some major CEOs have reorganized their role so as to place the internal management of the company in the hands of the President, allowing them to spend the majority of their time on outside image-developing activities. Thus, the role of the CEO becomes that of an ambassador, as opposed to his traditional role of manager. Bob R. Dorsey, Chairman of Gulf Oil Corporation, said that he learned his public speaking skills on the fly, but he states that the new generation of CEOs must be prepared to face these experiences. Lester B. Korn, Chairman of Korn/Ferry International, a large executive search firm, asserts that the "Assignments for chief executive officers are beginning to specify that the candidate be someone whose appointment would enhance the image of the company with the public."

Being seen in the ceremonial role is one of the most important tasks for a CEO, says C. Peter McColough, Chairman of the Xerox Corporation. McColough indicates that, "A company's reputation, good or bad, is made not only by the quality of its products and services but also by its people, especially its top people." He spends at least two months a year speaking and traveling in foreign countries. He adds, "A company like Xerox can't live in a stockade. I've spent more and more time on things that might affect society here and abroad because I think they affect Xerox and all our lives." A former General Mill's Chairman is a great believer in personal communication with operating units. In fact, he found himself on the road speaking to company plants about three days a week. He believed so much in getting the facts via the spoken word that he met with eighteen of his middle managers every ten days and had them deliver a ten-minute presentation on their operation.

Who needs communication know-how? In short, the "boss needs it." The authors of this text have consulted with many businesses, and one of the most frequently voiced opinions of middle management is that the top executives need to speak up more forcefully for the company. One vice-president, for example, who is in charge of corporate training for a multinational firm that does billions of dollars of business annually, told us in words that could not be mistaken: "Our top executives can't make a speech. We have a great speech writer but our men can't deliver. They stink! They're smart enough to earn six figure salaries, but their presentations are deadly." This head of corporate training then put it to us squarely: "How long would it take you to train our seven top men to deliver an effective speech?"

> *"You don't save the company significant money by being your own spokesperson. In my old company we checked out who had the greatest believability and found it was Walter Cronkite—and he didn't want to do ads for us. And then we got Bill Cosby.*
>
> *"To guys like that you have to give more than a couple of cars. You pay a lot of money, maybe a couple hundred thousand. So you could save that. But listen, when you're spending maybe sixty or seventy million on TV, what's a hundred thousand among friends?"*
>
> —Lee Iacocca,
> Chief Executive Officer
> Chrysler
> *Forbes,* August 16, 1982

How to read faster

By Bill Cosby

International Paper asked Bill Cosby—who earned his doctorate in education and has been involved in projects which help people learn to read faster—to share what he's learned about reading more in less time.

When I was a kid in Philadelphia, I must have read every comic book ever published. (There were fewer of them then than there are now.)

I zipped through all of them in a couple of days, then reread the good ones until the next issues arrived.

Yes indeed, when I was a kid, the reading game was a snap.

But as I got older, my eyeballs must have slowed down or something! I mean, comic books started to pile up faster than my brother Russell and I could read them!

It wasn't until much later, when I was getting my doctorate, I realized it wasn't my eyeballs that were to blame. Thank goodness. They're still moving as well as ever.

The problem is, there's too much to read these days, and too little time to read every word of it.

Now, mind you, I still read comic books. In addition to contracts, novels, and newspapers. Screenplays, tax returns and correspondence. Even textbooks about how people read. And which techniques help people read more in less time.

I'll let you in on a little secret. There are hundreds of techniques you could learn to help you read faster. But I know of 3 that are especially good.

And if I can learn them, so can you—and you can put them to use *immediately*.

They are commonsense, practical ways to get the meaning from printed words quickly and efficiently. So you'll have time to enjoy your comic books, have a good laugh with Mark Twain or a good cry with *War and Peace*. Ready?

Okay. The first two ways can help you get through tons of reading material—fast—*without reading every word*.

They'll give you the *overall meaning* of what you're reading. And let you cut out an awful lot of *unnecessary* reading.

1. Preview—if it's long and hard

Previewing is especially useful for getting a general idea of heavy reading like long magazine or newspaper articles, business reports, and nonfiction books.

It can give you as much as half the comprehension in as little as one tenth the time. For example, you should be able to preview eight or ten 100-page reports in an hour. After previewing, you'll be able to decide which reports (or which *parts* of which reports) are worth a closer look.

Here's how to preview: Read the entire first two paragraphs of whatever you've chosen. Next read only the *first sentence* of each successive paragraph.

"*Learn to read faster and you'll have time for a good laugh with Mark Twain—and a good cry with War and Peace.*"

Then read the entire last two paragraphs.

Previewing doesn't give you all the details. But it does keep you from spending time on things you don't really want—or need—to read.

Notice that previewing gives you a quick, overall view of *long, unfamiliar* material. For short, light reading, there's a better technique.

2. Skim—if it's short and simple

Skimming is a good way to get a general idea of light reading—like popular magazines or the sports and entertainment sections of the paper.

You should be able to skim a weekly popular magazine or the second section of your daily paper in less than *half* the time it takes you to read it now.

Skimming is also a great way to review material you've read before.

Here's how to skim: Think of your eyes as magnets. Force them to move fast. Sweep them across each and every line of type. Pick up *only a few key words in each line.*

Everybody skims differently.

You and I may not pick up exactly the same words when we skim the same piece, but we'll both get a pretty similar idea of what it's all about.

To show you how it works, I circled the words I picked out when I skimmed the following story. Try it. It shouldn't take you more than 10 seconds.

My brother Russell thinks monsters live in our bedroom closet at night. But I told him he is crazy.

"Go and check then," he said.

I didn't want to.

Russell said I was chicken.

"Am not," I said.

"Are so," he said.

So I told him the monsters were going to eat him at midnight. He started to cry. My Dad came in and told the monsters to beat it. Then he told us to go to sleep.

"If I hear any more about monsters," he said, "I'll spank you."

We went to sleep fast. And you know something? They never did come back.

Skimming can give you a very good *idea* of this story in about half

"Read with a good light—and with as few friends as possible to help you out. No TV, no music. It'll help you concentrate better—and read faster."

the words—and in *less* than half the time it'd take to read every word.

So far, you've seen that previewing and skimming can give you a *general idea* about content—fast. But neither technique can promise more than 50 percent comprehension, because you aren't reading all the words. (Nobody gets something for nothing in the reading game.)

To *read faster and understand most*—if not all—of what you read, you need to know a third technique.

3. Cluster—to increase speed and comprehension

Most of us learned to read by looking at each word in a sentence—*one at a time.*

Like this:

My—brother—Russell—thinks—monsters...

You probably still read this way sometimes, especially when the words are difficult. Or when the words have an extra-special meaning—as in a poem, a Shakespearean

play, or a contract. And that's O.K.

But word-by-word reading is a rotten way to read faster. It actually *cuts down* on your speed.

Clustering trains you to look at *groups* of words instead of one at a time—to increase your speed enormously. For most of us, clustering is a *totally different way of seeing what we read*.

Here's how to cluster: Train your eyes to see *all* the words in clusters of up to 3 or 4 words at a glance.

Here's how I'd cluster the story we just skimmed:

My brother Russell thinks monsters live in our bedroom closet at night. But I told him he is crazy.

"Go and check then," he said.

I didn't want to. Russell said I was chicken.

"Am not," I said.

"Are so," he said.

So I told him the monsters were going to eat him at midnight. He started to cry. My Dad came in and told the monsters to beat it. Then he told us to go to sleep.

"If I hear any more about monsters," he said, "I'll spank you."

We went to sleep fast. And you know something? They never did come back.

Learning to read clusters is not something your eyes do naturally. It takes constant practice.

Here's how to go about it: Pick something light to read. Read it as fast as you can. Concentrate on seeing 3 to 4 words at once rather than one word at a time. Then reread

"Preview, skim, and cluster to read faster—except the things you want to read word for word."

the piece at your normal speed to see what you missed the first time.

Try a second piece. First cluster, then reread to see what you missed in this one.

When you can read in clusters without missing much the first time, your speed has increased. Practice 15 minutes every day and you might pick up the technique in a week or so. (But don't be disappointed if it takes longer. Clustering *everything* takes time and practice.)

So now you have 3 ways to help you read faster. <u>Preview</u> to cut down on unnecessary heavy reading. <u>Skim</u> to get a quick, general idea of light reading. And <u>cluster</u> to increase your speed *and* comprehension.

With enough practice, you'll be able to handle *more* reading at school or work—and at home—*in less time.* You should even have enough time to read your favorite comic books—and <u>War and Peace</u>!

Marketing Speaks

A second common answer to who needs communication skills is the sales force. An engineer in a small company which manufactures cables and pulleys talked with one of the authors at a dinner party about the fact that their sales force had to compete with the major companies and he said, "Our men are green. They've never had any formal training. So last month we brought them in from the field for an address by a professor of marketing." He added, "That professor gave a speech which I could have given. In fact, I could have done a better job and he charged us five hundred bills!"

Both the head of corporate training and the engineer had right answers. The top men do need communication know-how. And the sales force must be able to sell. The harsh realities of the world of business dictate that minimum communication skills be had by core personnel. It is a matter of survival. For the over four million companies in this country, the average life is only seven years. In a recent year, about 450,000 went down and nearly 375,000 went inactive.[6]

Internal Communications

What is it that conveys information necessary to transform raw materials and human resources into new products and services? Obviously, the quality of cooperation is directly related to the adequacy and accuracy of information about scheduling and processing.

Be they downward, upward, or horizontal, communications are integral to the life of most businesses. The accuracy of a supervisor's instructions obviously is directly related to the quality of the product. The accuracy of the orders translated into manufacturing and distribution is a matter of communication. The vitality of research and development depends upon both internal and interdepartmental communications. Negotiations between labor and management are yet another place where communications may either break down or hammer out a mutually-acceptable contract.

The success of most organizations depends upon many factors including working conditions, fairness and adequacy of wages, responsibility and achievement. Whether these factors become dissatisfiers or motivators directly relates to interpersonal communications. The satisfaction or unhappiness of any employment begins with the job interview. Personnel selection, to be successful, depends upon more than intuition. It is only when, and if, the communications are open, honest, and thorough, that the interview enables both the prospective employer and the employee to determine job placement wisely.

On the job communication relationships spell either production or any host of problems such as absenteeism, slowdowns, stealing, interdepartmental strife, and other difficulties. Think for a moment about these many relationships: employee to employee, employees to supervisors, between supervisors and supervisors, supervisors and the next level of management of another division, between upper division and the board members, between the board members and the stockholders and, finally, and most important, between the company and the consumer and community.

The quality of any of these relationships depends upon the *clarity* of the communication, the *persuasiveness* of the communication, and the interpersonal *climate* of that relationship. A message thus functions on two levels: "The Word Level," that which is stated in words and graphs and "The Interpersonal Feeling Level," that which is expressed in nonverbal behavior such as the tone of the voice, the gesture, facial expression and eye contact. The feeling level depends upon the liking and respect held by those within the relationship. Even the simplest communications between one person and another is complex; and within an organization, and between an organization and its constituency, the potential for communication breakdown is manifold greater.

Careers and Communication Competencies

One of the evidences of being educated is the ability to articulately communicate one's ideas and feelings, both on and off the job. Those lacking much formal education also must communicate, and sometimes do so publicly. A survey of blue collar workers in a medium sized city asked how many times they spoke to an audience of ten or more persons in the last year. Almost half (46.5 percent) said that they had delivered at least one speech and 31 percent indicated that they had made four or more speeches. These presentations were given in churches, to union meetings, clubs, etc.[7]

Our research into who needs communication know-how has led us to the unmistakable conclusion that personnel at all levels within the business community practice and depend upon communication skills, both their own and those of the people with whom they deal. Consider these examples from varied occupations:

Clothing Buyer. First, let's look at a young woman named Jamie R. She has one year's experience as an assistant buyer for a retail clothing business in West Virginia. She worked part time for the company at the store level and, as a result of an interview, she received a promotion to the job she now holds. She works at both the store level with the public and at the office level, bargaining with salesmen and manufacturers. She is responsible to seventeen managers of stores.

She describes her job as giving and following instructions and orders, buying and selling face to face and working with committees and small groups. Clarity is probably the most important characteristic needed in her communication. Next to this she mentioned responding and corresponding on a level the other person understands.

Advertising Manager. Orlando H. is an advertising production manager in Miami, Florida. He has sixteen years' experience. He stated that his employer hired him after an interview and that it is his belief that unless a person communicates effectively he cannot be evaluated objectively no matter what his work abilities may be. His work entails giving and following instructions, written reports and oral briefings, staff meetings, buying and selling face to face, working with small groups, speaking to larger audiences within the company, to business conferences, and to community audiences.

He stressed the importance of tailoring messages to a particular audience level. He advises persons interested in a career like his to develop more than the average working vocabulary, to be conscious of one's diction and not to allow any regional accent which would tend to reduce one's image.

Dentist. A dentist, Dr. Dale D., with sixteen years' experience, related that an interview has nothing to do with him getting into business, but that his ability to communicate certainly had a lot to do with his occupation. "Dentistry is oriented toward person-to-person communication where we must sell the patient on the desire to want excellent dental health. I communicate with individual experiences, chalkboard, and models presentations. I find one of the most overlooked modes of communication, and to us the most important, is the ability to *listen.* So much information can be gained if only people would develop this talent."

Medical Technician. Helen M., a medical technologist in a small Ohio town with twenty years' experience, said, "I am employed in a private laboratory where the patient's only contact for the necessary service is through me to the doctor. Proper communication is vital!"

Potato Chip Manufacturer. A potato chip manufacturer, Don M., also in Ohio, built his business from the idea up. He put it bluntly, "To build a manufacturing organization and market your product, you must be able to influence people to believe like you do." And this prosperous businessman, who is truly in the chips, advised that persons who would succeed should develop their communication skills: "The ability to communicate is a must, the number one prerequisite for accomplishment in our crowded world. This is what moves people. Technicians can be hired to handle all the details."

Executive. Robert H., the President and General Manager of an automotive firm in Windsor, Canada, with seventeen years' experience, said he was expected to convey objectives and instructions to subordinates in an unambiguous way. He also makes periodic presentations to customer groups and to officers of the parent company. Mr. H. was of the opinion that "The ability to organize data and present results and recommendations as oral or written reports is second only to a job speciality like law, engineering, finance, or marketing. One's knowledge and ideas are largely ineffective unless one can convey them to others."

Aerospace. Jack B., who describes his job as an Engineering Administrator-Planner with twenty-seven years' experience, states he must present "ideas, plans, figures, charts, graphs, ect., to other members of management with clarity, but briefly." He adds, "Learning to speak and gaining confidence to do so is a must in climbing the ladder of success. This ability, learned or natural, is a must—concentrate on it!"

Technical Careers. An architectural draftsman told the authors, "Today people want answers *fast.* Selling a fair idea at short notice in many cases is better than stumbling over a brilliant one." A public engineer, in reference to his job of selling the public on city planning, wrote, "People should be able to express themselves so that they may be able to direct others or get ideas across to others." An engineer with eleven years' experience said much of his work involves explaining the project requirements to draftsmen and manufacturing personnel, and that he also has to talk with customers and venders. Another who described himself as a design specialist with ten years' experience wrote, "In designing prototype machinery like I do, I must be able to be precise and concise on drawings and in instructions to the machinists who perform the fabrication."

Employees Speak

In a survey of engineers, some fifty-six percent of 7,000 questionnaires were returned. The questionnaire asked the engineer in which of some 123 subjects was he in need of more training.

Public speaking was ranked number four in needed training areas by sixty percent.[8] In a second survey of 2,090 practicing engineers in Pennsylvania, approximately three out of four declared they needed more training in conference leadership, public speaking and technical reporting.[9]

Speakers' Bureaus. General Motors Corporation representatives make over 2,200 speeches annually. Its middle managers present the bulk of these 2,000; senior level managers present 130; and the Chief Executive Officer makes 30 major speeches each year. Let's look at what several other of the biggest companies and corporations report.[10] Western Electric Company has over 100 employees who make some 2,000 presentations annually. Kaiser Aluminum and Chemical, in the words of their public relations department, give "hundreds." A competitor company in describing its program used nearly identical language: "Our people—plant managers, top executives, technical and sales personnel, and middle managers—deliver hundreds of speeches each year on a wide variety of topics." Standard Oil has between 50 to 100 employees presenting some 500 speeches annually. Dow Chemical estimates its people give 1,000 addresses each year. Georgia Pacific has some 300 employees that present approximately 1,500 per year. Timken averages between 200 to 250 presentations. Republic Steel, 600. Champion Spark Plug has a team of auto race drivers who give over 600 talks annually on safety. 3M has about 400 employees involved in over 1,000 presentations. Eaton Corporation began its speakers' bureau in 1972 and it soon grew to involve over 100 members of its staff who annually deliver more than 1,000 speeches. The survey discovered that 30 of our nation's major businesses make 100 or more presentations annually. Six said they make over 1,000.[11]

The Public Affairs Department of Phillips 66 Petroleum Company began a crash program in 1973 to speak about the energy crisis. Several days of training were designed to prepare those who would take part in the "Stand Up-Speak Out" campaign. Group discussions were conducted on such subjects as "The Selling of American Business," "Free Enterprise," "How to Develop Resources and Facts," "How to Make Presentations," and "How to Answer Questions." There were practice sessions in which all participants were able to review their presentations on "instant replay" video tape equipment. Some 2,000 speakers' kits were distributed to employees who made between 8,000 to 10,000 presentations the first year.[12] A sister company, Conoco Oil, reports approximately 200 employees engaged in their speakers' bureau, which has been active for over five years. Middle management delivers 375 presentations and the chief executive officer averages 30 to 40 appearances. The annual total for all personnel is 600 speeches.[13]

You be the judge. Did Lowell Thomas, Sr., the world famous traveler and news commentator, overstate the importance of communication skills when he said: "The ability to speak is a short-cut to distinction. It puts a man in the limelight, raises his head and shoulders above the crowd?"[14]

The 3M Director of Research and Development wrote:

> We do not publish a directory of speakers, by subject, for this reason: I have seen such a policy destroy the vitality of several otherwise effective Speakers' Bureaus. If any expert, already quite busy with regular duties, finds himself on a list of free offerings, and finds himself being called frequently, directly and willynilly by many outside organizations, he soon withdraws his cooperation in sheer self-defense.
>
> By controlling demands made upon our various speakers to ensure they are not unduly overworked, we can maintain a loyal crew of enthusiastic 3Mers who are willing to talk about their favorite subjects, the subjects they know best.

One final note: We don't wait to be asked. We actively seek public forums to articulate 3M's point of view concerning vital issues (free trade is one case in point).

Such speaking engagements are coordinated with corporate publicity efforts to help achieve company objectives. The Speakers' Bureau cannot function in a vacuum.[15]

The Director of Communications for Dow Chemical told us that each of their five regional headquarters is responsible for developing its own communication activities. He added:

We provide qualified speakers when requested. We initiate speaking engagements where we feel our interests can be well served. An example would be speaking to financial analysts. Presentations at "in house" business meetings and sales meetings would number in the hundreds if not thousands. We expect our people to be able to present ideas to groups. We have an extensive audiovisual department and provide coaching if needed or desired. We have closed circuit and television cassette facilities available "in house" and use this facility quite extensively to make presentations to our sales offices and manufacturing locations.[16]

The survey also revealed that many of the top companies are very poorly organized in their communication program and do very little to tell their story of business. Sixty-two indicated that they had no speakers' bureaus, forty-six had no formal program and three quarters of the companies did not respond to the questionnaires. One director of public relations, who stated that their middle and senior management each delivered more than ten presentations annually, wrote, "Unfortunately, our chief executive is not a prolific public speaker, as are many chief executive officers of major companies around the nation."[17]

As with gaining skills for any activity, communication skills come from coaching, practice, motivation and experience.

Employees are interested in what goes on within their place of work. Nearly all want to know about the future plans of management and the effects of external events on their job. They need and want job-related information, personnel policies, and job advancement opportunities. They want to know about profits and how their organization fares against competition. Employees want news of other departments and divisions. They also are curious about where their organization stands on current issues and its involvement in the community according to an extensive survey of over 45,000 employees in 40 different work organizations.[18]

In addition, this survey provides a picture of where employees get their information and where they'd prefer to get information. From these rankings, we can see that employees perceive considerable discrepancy between current practice and how they prefer to get organizational information. What conclusions might you draw from this comparison below?

How Employees Get Information

Current Ranking		Preferred Ranking
1	Immediate supervisor	1
2	Grapevine	15
3	Employee handbook and other sources	4
4	Bulletin board(s)	9
5	Small group meetings	2
6	Regular general employee publication	6
7	Annual business report to employees	7
8	Regular local employee publication	8
9	Mass meetings	11
10	Union	13
11	Orientation program	5
12	Top executives	3
13	Audio-visual programs	12
14	Mass media	14
15	Upward communication program	10

Employees see their immediate superior as their current first source of information and that's the way they prefer to get information about their job and organization. Fifty-five percent indicated that their superior was their first source, and 90 percent indicated they want that to be their first source. The grapevine was their second current source of information. Ironically, the grapevine was their least preferred source! What they'd prefer second and third would be to get information in small group meetings and from top executives. They do not discount the importance of handbooks, bulletin boards and annual reports, but they do prefer information in face to face channels.

Associations

Nonprofit Organization. Communication is the chief product of the nonprofit organization. Think about it. The health and effectiveness of such organizations depend upon their ability to win and retain members, to solicit funds, to influence public opinion and to lobby legislatures. Their product must be communication.

One way to realize how essential good communication is may be to consider for a moment the various categories of nonprofit organizations:

Nonprofit Organizations	*Examples*
Professional Associations	American Bar Association
	American Library Association
	National Educational Association
Trade Associations	U.S. Chamber of Commerce
	American Hotel and Motel Association
	American Bankers Association
	Agricultural Institute of Canada
Government	U.S. Postal Service
	U.S. Civil Rights Commission
Public Service	American Red Cross
	Sierra Club
	Salvation Army
Schools	University of Utah
Hospitals	Scripps Memorial Hospital
Miscellaneous	Junior Achievement
	Boy Scouts
	Carnegie Hall
	San Diego Zoo

Personal interviews of 81 chief executive officers of these orgnizations and others like them[19] resulted in such statements as the following:

"I feel that about 80 percent of my job really is public relations in the total communication sense."

— Head of a 126,000 member Canadian Association

"We are all communicators. So although I am not personally on the communication budget, I spend a hell of a lot of my time communicating."

— Head of a 93,000 member U.S. organization

"I think the economics of supporting nonprofit associations is going to be a very, very painful concern during the next 10 years."

— Executive Director of a U.S. association

Many answers were short and direct to the question: What would happen if your association was forced to abandon your communication program? "Disaster." "We'd collapse." "I can't even imagine that." "We'd be out of business." The general response to the important role of communication for these executives may be represented in this one answer, "I really believe that there are very few problems that you can't correct through a good communication program with your members or with your employees. The majority of problems I run into result from poor communication."

Recap

Communications, that process of conveying and interpreting information, is the sin qua non (without which) for transforming raw materials and human resources into new products and services. Much of top management's work involves communication. The chief executive officer and many others frequently must speak for the company. The sales and marketing division must persuasively communicate with output wholesale and retailers. Those within a company who plan, coordinate and deliver, interdependently exchange information.

Young people interested in business should expect their communication to be influential in their careers. The following observations summarize these influences:

1. The live job interview is usually expected. In that half hour or so (sometimes a day-long introduction to the organization) a job candidate must communicate his competence and interest in the job. He must, in addition, discover whether the work, the working conditions, wages, and the climate will suit him.

2. Most careers involve both giving and taking instructions, both receiving and translating information.

3. Most careers involve both written and oral reports. Even many production line workers, whose work is more thing-centered than people-centered, must confer with immediate supervisors and fellow workers.

4. An employee's or a manager's "liking" for his work relates to his ability to describe his responsibilities in terms of his relationship to others.

5. Active, discriminative listening is one communication skill which is very important to a career.

6. Most persons-on-the-job advise young people to develop and perfect their communication skills.

7. Interpersonal communications are directly related to job satisfaction and company morale.

8. Persons with job competence do not necessarily possess the ability to present messages accurately or humanely.

9. Many people believe that their upward mobility and market ability are related to communication skills.

10. Employees at all levels speak about their companies and can become an effective or damaging voice for their firms and for business generally.

11. Core personnel in management have a particular responsibility to reach the public with the story of the business community.

NOTES

1. *The Washington Post,* December 30, 1973, G 1.
2. *Ibid.*
3. Scot Myer, "Who Are Your Motivated Workers?" in *How Successful Executives Handle People, Harvard Business Review,* special edition, 1970, p. 31.
4. Gerald M. Goldhaber, *Organizational Communication* Dubuque, Iowa: Wm. C. Brown Co., 1974), p. 257. .

5. "The Chief Executive," *Business Week,* May 4, 1974, pp. 37-85. This feature article so well supports our contention that the CEO must carry high competence in communication skills that we will extensively quote from it in subsequent paragraphs.

6. George Odiorne, "The Trouble With Sensitivity Training," *Training Directors Journal,* Vol. (September-October, 1963), p. 54; Robert N. McMurry, "Clear Communications for Executives," *How Successful Executives Handle People, Harvard Business Review,* special edition, 1970, pp. 1-15.

7. "Education in Industry: Synopsis of the Joint ECAS-RWI Feedback Committee Report," *Journal of Engineering Education,* Vol. 55 (May, 1965), pp. 254-56. Abstract in Harry E. Hand, *Effective Speaking for the Technical Man* (New York: Van Nostrand-Reinhold Co., 1969), p. 3.

8. Samuel S. Dubin and H. LeRoy Marlow, *Survey of Continuing Professional Education for Engineers in Pennsylvania* (Pennsylvania: Continuing Education Office, Pennsylvania State University, 1964); Abstract in *Effective Speaking, Ibid.,* p. 4.

9. John R. Miller and William I. Gorden, "Survey of the Fortune 500 Speaker's Bureau," Unpublished, 1974. Subsequent data were gathered in this survey.

10. *Ibid.*

11. *Ibid.*

12. "Stand Up-Speak Up." *Philnews* (Bartlesville, Oklahoma: June 1974), pp. 16-20.

13. Dale Carnegie, *How to Win Friends and Influence People* (New York: Pocket Books, 1935, 1970, 82nd Printing), p. 6.

14. Miller and Gorden, "Survey," 1974.

15. *Ibid.*

16. *Ibid.*

17. *Ibid.*

18. "45,000 Employees Judge Effectiveness of Internal Communication," *Journal of Organizational Communication*, 10, 1981, 3-11.

19. "CEO's of Nonprofit Organizations Agree: Communicate or Perish," *Journal of Organizational Communication*, 10, 1980, 4, 9-19.

Identification

In the last century communication was thought of as oratory. This image pretty much has faded. In its place is the image of identification. Spokespersons want to further an appreciation of their organization. They desire to be a part of an organization with which they are proud to be identified.

It is a two way street. An audience, likewise, wants to be recognized, to have their identities acknowledged. Keep this image foremost as you pursue your communication skill development.

Study the process of identification in the model speech which follows.

Please **print** your answers to the following questions after you have scanned the introductory paragraphs and proceed into the body of his speech in the space allotted.

1. In what specific ways does the speaker acknowledge his audience?

2. In what ways does he establish the identity of his corporation?

3. In what ways does he use illustrations personal to his audience and himself to support his theme?

Notice how skillfully D.C. Burnham, a former chairman of Westinghouse Electric Corporation, in an address to the Indiana Chamber of Commerce, builds common ground with his audience. See how he intertwines his acknowledgement of the several publics in his audience from various locations in the state with his corporation stake in their communities. Also consider how he, in this rich farm state, develops his theme.

Thank you Mr. Blanchar. Members of the Indiana State Chamber of Commerce, fellow Hoosiers:

I can qualify as a Hoosier if you overlook the fact that my parents neglected to move from Massachusetts to Indiana until I was five years old. Why it took them so long to see the obvious wisdom of that move, I do not know. But I count it my good fortune that I grew up in Lafayette and benefited from an education at Purdue University—an institution with which I still maintain close association.

Any trip to Indiana is always a homecoming for me because the strong home-state ties are never completely severed, no matter how distant you travel or how long you may be gone.

Fortunately for me, Westinghouse provides excellent excuses for occasional homecomings. As I'm sure you know, we have manufacturing plants in Muncie, Bloomington, and Union City. Our construction subsidiary, Cebor Construction Corp., is headquartered in Fort Wayne, and our fine radio station WOWO in Fort Wayne comes in loud and strong, even at my home in Pittsburgh. Some of you might not be aware that 7-UP Bottling of Indiana is a wholly-owned subsidiary of Westinghouse or that our Learning Corporation has operated the Atterbury Job Corps Center for almost seven years. We maintain a small engineering laboratory at Purdue. The district headquarters of Westinghouse Electric Supply Company is here in Indianapolis. And we have other distributors, dealers, and sales offices throughout the state—all of which establishes us, I hope, as a solid corporate citizen of Indiana.

I see a table down front, which is surrounded by familiar faces, so I know this meeting has not been neglected by Westinghouse. Either that, or a committee was hurriedly organized to make sure Burnham doesn't say the wrong thing in Indianaopolis.

You can relax, gentlemen. A Hoosier is always on his good behavior when he comes back home.

Even on good behavior, however, I want to speak plainly today about one or two things that are uppermost on my mind as I view the national and world scene from my position in American industry.

One of these subjects has been in big headlines recently . . . the energy crisis. But the other—equally important—is a "silent crisis," so I'll talk about it first.

The silent crisis is productivity and the need to improve it. Productivity is a word that, unfortunately, may still be strictly academic to a lot of people . . . something they think only economists talk about. But how wrong they are.

That word holds the key to our standard of living and to the solution of a lot of our problems today. It can help us solve the problem of inflation. It can maintain our balance of payments in world trade. It can provide more jobs and good wages. And yet it is one of the least understood concepts of our modern society.

But ask the Indiana farmer what it means. He'll tell you. On the farm it means more acres plowed per day of work, more bushels of corn per acre or more pork per pound of feed. And that means more dollars per year for the farmer. And, of course, that means a new dress for his wife, a new tractor for the farm, and perhaps college tuition for his son or daughter. To the farmer, improving productivity is an essential part of his business . . . a way of life.

In fact, American agriculture has provided the greatest example of continuous productivity improvement that the world has seen over the past 100 years.

It was a century ago that the government began setting up land-grant colleges and initiating a long-range program to improve farming. Better seeds, better farm equipment, soil enrichment, crop rotation, all added up to a basic productivity improvement program. Averaging about six percent a year for the past century, this productivity improvement program has been so successful that now it only requires a little over four percent of the work force in this country to raise the food needed to feed all the rest of us. In 1870, nearly 50 percent of the people were needed to do that job.

Indiana has played a major role in this productivity improvement program on the farm. It is no accident that this state ranks near the top of the list in the production of corn, soybeans, hogs, and many other agricultural products.

And fortunately, Indiana has achieved great balance through its equal attention to productive industry. The importance of a productive auto industry and steel industry in this state are just two examples.

I'm getting a signal from my friends to mention the electrical industry as a third example.

It was through productivity improvement that the United States became the greatest industrial nation in the world. By productivity improvement please understand that I am *not* talking about getting people to work harder or put in longer hours. I'm talking about getting people to work smarter, use better methods, better tools, greater skills. I don't think the American farmer today works any harder than he did 100 years ago; probably not as hard in terms of physical effort. He has new tools and machines to do a lot of the hard work for him. Likewise, in American industry, much of the back-bending effort has been eliminated through the application of modern machinery and methods. And the American workman is the benefactor—along with the American consumer.

But at this point let me insert the first word of warning. While it is nice to sit back and contemplate our great progress and accomplishments, there is no room for complacency. The fact is that other countries in the world are catching up with us. My friends in the auto and steel industries in recent years have felt the keen edge of competition from companies abroad. Some of my friends down at the Westinghouse table can tell you things about worldwide competition in the electrical industry that will shatter any illusions about America having an insurmountable lead in industrial productivity. We manufacture electric power transformers at Muncie. In recent years we have been engaged in an all out productivity improvement race with manufacturers overseas to meet their competitive challenge. And it has been a real struggle.

Look what has happened to industrial productivity in other nations. From 1965 to 1970, productivity in Japan rose more than 14 percent a year. In the United States during that period it went up only a little over two percent a year. In the past decade in Europe, productivity gains ranged from five to eight percent a year.

Of course other nations are beginning to encounter some of the same sort of problem we encountered earlier. Sharp wage boosts in some of the European countries and currency realignments are now causing problems for manufacturers there. Japan also is feeling the effects of inflationary pressures.

But, as a result, businessmen overseas are stepping up their productivity efforts, too, and the competition they will provide in the years immediately ahead will be intense. What goes on tomorrow in Tokyo, Frankfurt, Stockholm, and even Moscow, will affect what goes on in Indianapolis, Muncie, Bloomington, and Gary. I understand Weir Cook Airport in Indianapolis is negotiating for international status in passenger service to augment its existing international freight capability. That's good news. This state is engaged in worldwide business, competing for worldwide markets and we had better be prepared.

I've mentioned agriculture and manufacturing, but there is another area which is crying out even more for productivity improvement—that's the services. If you have had a long illness lately, or if you have a couple of children in college right now, you know what I'm talking about. The cost of hospital care or a college education is sky high compared with what it used to be a few short years ago. Why? Because so little has been done over the years to improve productivity in these services. The service industries offer the greatest opportunity for productivity improvement in the years immediately ahead . . . and also the greatest need.

A century ago, there was about an equal number of Americans in manufacturing and in the services. By 1970, however, 58 percent of our work force was employed in the services with 38 percent in the manufacturing industries. We have become a service job society to a great extent. And yet we have done less to improve productivity in these occupations than anywhere else. But, at last, efforts are under way.

Let me tell you just one personal experience to illustrate the point. Not long ago I had to have some root canal work done on a bad tooth. My regular dentist sent me to a specialist, and I was fascinated to see how this professional man has worked to improve his productivity.

He has three rooms, each a different color, with a girl technician in charge of each room. I went into the Blue Room and the young lady seated me in the chair, put the napkin around my neck, got out my x-rays, and positioned them behind the viewer. Then she placed all the dentist's tools in position and even put the rubber framework around my tooth.

Only then did the dentist step into the room. He took a look at the x-rays, picked up the drill, and went to work. When he finished drilling, he packed some temporary material into the cavity, and in less than five minutes he was gone. The young lady disassembled all the gear, told me when to come back and, meanwhile, the dentist had gone on to the Pink Room and I could hear him already drilling on someone else.

I would guess that his productivity is about three times as great as that of the average dentist.

My company is actively engaged in bringing productivity improvement to the services. Several years ago, our engineers joined with physicians at the Johns Hopkins School of Medicine in a program aimed at improving the productivity of pediatricians. The doctors and the engineers worked together to study precisely what the Johns Hopkins clinic pediatricians were doing with their time. They analyzed the whole clinical process. Without going into the details, let me simply report that that clinic now serves about 50 percent more patients a day than before. Patient waiting time has been cut in half and budget levels are either unchanged or reduced. And this has been done with no reduction in the quality of the care provided.

Another example. Several years ago, Allegheny County, in which Pittsburgh is located decided it needed to improve the effectiveness and efficiency of many of its County government functions. We have worked with them on a productivity improvement program that has won the County a national achievement award.

One of the things done, for instance, was to automate the voter registration file. Formerly a new voter filled out a form with all of the vital information about himself—age, sex, party affiliation, address, and voting district. And this then set off a long chain of clerical work with paper going from one person to another and the opportunity for clerical error increasing each time the information was handled.

Today the job is done faster, cheaper, and more accurately through computer techniques. There is just one manual typing performed and then the computers take over. As a result of fewer errors and reduced effort, this new system is saving Allegheny County more than $300,000 a year and its effectiveness is immensely improved.

(This ends this extended excerpt of D.C. Burnham's address.)

Project One-2

Communication Skills

Circle the 1 to 5 scale.

How important do you believe the following skills are to employee effectiveness?

	Very Little				Very Great
1. Interviewing skills	1	2	3	4	5
2. Variety in vocabulary	1	2	3	4	5
3. Parliamentary procedure	1	2	3	4	5
4. Skillful use of informal channels	1	2	3	4	5
5. Nonverbal expressiveness	1	2	3	4	5
6. Assertiveness	1	2	3	4	5
7. Legible handwriting	1	2	3	4	5
8. Group leadership skills	1	2	3	4	5
9. Effective management of conflict	1	2	3	4	5
10. Making decisions cooperatively	1	2	3	4	5
11. Skillful use of formal channels	1	2	3	4	5
12. Correct pronunciation	1	2	3	4	5
13. Correct grammar	1	2	3	4	5
14. Persuasiveness	1	2	3	4	5
15. Sensitivity to others	1	2	3	4	5
16. Clear distinct voice	1	2	3	4	5
17. Organizing ideas clearly	1	2	3	4	5
18. Credibility	1	2	3	4	5
19. Personal confidence when speaking	1	2	3	4	5
20. Accurate listening	1	2	3	4	5

Dr. James Crocker surveyed businesses in greater Cincinnati. His findings are reported below—those factors considered most needed in employees ranked from most to least important.

> Accurate listening
> Credibility
> Organize ideas clearly
> Clear distinct voice
> Personal confidence while speaking
> Sensitivity to others
> Correct grammar
> Persuasiveness
> Correct pronunciation
> Skillful use of formal channels
> Making decisions cooperatively
> Effective management of conflict
> Skillful use of informal channels
> Group leadership skills
> Legible handwriting
> Assertiveness
> Nonverbal expressiveness
> Interviewing skills
> Variety in vocabulary
> Variety in vocal intonation
> Ability to use parliamentary procedure

Crocker concludes:

- Listening and other interpersonal skills are very important.
- Basic communication skills must be emphasized for a career in business and industry
- Skills in organization and orderly thinking are highly valued by employers.

Thesis Personalized

A well crafted message links a theme with a target audience interests and values. In the Spring of 1981, C. Peter McCollough, Chairman and Chief Executive Officer of Xerox Corporation, addressed the National Leadership Business Conference of Junior Achievement Inc., in Washington, D.C. Please **print** your answers to the questions in the space allotted.

1. What was Mr. McCollough's thesis? What did he want his audience to believe, feel more strongly about or do? Try to put his thesis into one brief sentence.

2. What piece of evidence was most convincing that Xerox Corporation does, indeed, support the Spirit of Junior Achievement?

3. A well crafted message links a thesis to an audience by a variety of supporting material.
   a. Jot down here two quotations that compliment his audience.

   1.

   2.

b. Through what common analogy did he compliment the audience?

c. How does he link his message with the roots of the past?

d. While addressing his audience, in the seat of government, how does he disassociate himself from a federal solution to his theme?

"*In an attempt to modify a popular belief that corporations are interested in only one thing—making money—the Xerox Corporation announced in September 1971 that each year it would let about 20 employees have up to one year off with full pay and benefits to pursue social projects in their communities. In 1972, 21 employees set out to work in such fields as drug addiction, civil rights, literacy, and penal reform. The program is now in its 11th year and still going strong. Robert Schneider, vice-president of public affairs at Xerox, says that over 270 employees have had leaves since 1972, at an average annual cost of $400,000 in replacement salaries.*"

—Richard Haitch in New York *Times*

Following is a speech by C. Peter McColough, Chairman and Chief Executive Officer of the Xerox Corporation. Mr. McColough delivered the speech on March 5, 1981 before the National Business Leadership Conference in Washington, D.C.

The American writer and historian, Henry Adams, has told us, "a teacher affects eternity...No one can tell where his influence stops."

The core of any educational experience is the student/teacher relationship. As I look out at you Junior Achievement volunteers, I see teachers, and I envy you your job. In envy you your student/teacher relationship. You have it all year—the pleasure of time spent with outstanding young people. I have that opportunity all too rarely.

It is said that the reward of teaching is the privilege of assisting discovery. And that's exactly what you dedicated volunteer men and women are doing for our young people in Junior Achievement. You give Junior Achievement direction, like a lens on a powerful flashlight. Without the lens, there is no focus. A flashlight with the same amount of energy and brightness—but with no lens—scatters its light. With a lens, it illuminates the path ahead.

You Junior Achievement volunteers are guiding our youngsters down the path of free enterprise, a revolutionary idea born more than 200 years ago, in the incredible notion that it is better for all men to live decently at the expense of no one than it is for a few men to live lavishly at the expense of others.

You have nurtured that idea with your volunteer work in Junior Achievement. By your own example, you've lighted the way. You've given scope and meaning to the workings and the benefits of the economic system our young people will one day inherit. I'm confident in what I say next. Today's young Junior Achievers will take your places as tomorrow's Junior Achievement advisers. They'll keep the spirit of volunteerism alive, as you have in Junior Achievement.

The tradition of volunteerism in our country is even more American, if anything, than the tradition of free enterprise. There are many free economies among the industrialized nations of the world. But not one of them relies as heavily on the volunteer efforts of individual citizens as we do here in the United States.

Let me give you an example. We have a social service leave program at Xerox. We give our employees time off at full salary for as long as a year, to do volunteer service work in their communities. About 300 of our people have gone on social service leave. We're very proud of the program. In fact, we're marking its 10th anniversary this month.

We tried to start that program in Europe through our Rank Xerox organization, with only limited success...very limited. There are small programs with just a few employees involved in three countries. We think the effort is worthwhile. But it taught us something. We found that products can be exported with relative ease. Exporting ideas, however, requires a degree of receptivity based on historical attitudes. In the case of social service leaves, we learned that they just do things differently over there.

To understand why America has become such a public spirited bastion of volunteerism is to understand the tenacity of the American nature. Don't forget, America is a nation born out of hardship and struggle. The moment the first settlers arrived on these shores, they were confronted by a vast and largely hostile wilderness, the likes of which they'd never experienced.

But they had strength and vision. In 1628, Captain John Smith wrote in his diary in Virginia: "I would rather be a settler in America than Good Queen Bess on the throne of England. Here, one can spread his wings and soar like eagles. These are the times for men to live."

Indeed, America was a great adventure our forefathers survived and in which they prospered. Through ingenuity and hard work, they carved out a new society. They knew that failure was out of the question. There would be no government to step in and make things right. The government was an ocean away, and these people were on their own.

The first settlers learned quickly that to survive was to cooperate. They relied on each other in times of personal hardship and crisis...and there were many of those times. They worked voluntarily and cheerfully, family with family, neighbor with neighbor, to build their communities in the new land. Along the way, they became an extraordinarily resourceful and self-reliant breed of men and women.

So, volunteerism took roots in American soil out of social necessity and human need. As the pioneering families spread out across the continent, they relied even more on their own resources—and on the resources of their neighbors—to keep them whole.

The American volunteer evolved from necessity. Today, it is an important part of the American way of life. Our society simply could not exist without it.

Without the American volunteer, there would be no Junior Achievement. Without the American volunteer, there would be no United Way, an organization I've been involved with for a number of years. Imagine for a moment the crises our cities would face if people stopped giving their time and their money to United Way agencies. If government had to assume the cost of those services, the cost would triple, and many of those services would cease to exist.

Many of us don't realize that a large share of social responsibility in America rests with agencies supported primarily by voluntary contributions by private citizens. And I believe that that large share is going to have to get larger.

The problem is that ranks of volunteers are beginning to thin. The number of homes with two working parents is increasing dramatically, which robs communities of the largest block of ready volunteers—housewives. The problem is compounded, because it is happening at a time when inflation is cutting into the ability of the public sector to provide public services. Local government cannot bear the burden alone, and our federal government is clearly in a budget-cutting mood.

What that means, then, is that someone has to pick up the slack. People like yourselves, and more of you. More people from the business community, from large corporations, all the way down to the thriving small businesses that are the keystone of our economy. John Gardner once said that the values we cherish as people will not survive without the constant attention of the ordinary citizen. Well, neither will our society. As on a ship, everyone should be prepared to take the helm.

America's free enterprise is clearly the most efficient economic system mankind has yet to devise to meet the material needs of people. We need only compare our standard of living with that of the Soviet Union—a thoroughly-controlled economy that can amass a great military machine, but has the lowest standard of living of any industrial nation in the world. The Soviets cannot even feed all their own people.

But for all its efficiency, the American free enterprise system is not without its flaws. Our government has created and contributed to many of its problems, but as your national chairman and my colleague, David Kearns, likes to tell people...''We cannot walk away from our economic problems and assign them to the government for fixing...The government isn't them. It's us, and we must all share the burden.''

So, the spirit and great tradition of the American volunteer—that sense of individual commitment to society—is needed now as never before. The ranks of volunteers must grow as government's involvement lessens. There is still much to do, and we have not done enough—we have never done enough—so long as there are things to be done that we can do.

Nathan Hale said that, ''every kind of service necessary to the public good becomes honorable by being necessary.''

That is precisely why you're here in this room today. When you were asked to contribute to Junior Achievement back in your hometowns, you didn't send a check. You sent yourselves.

That's also why David Kearns—one of the busiest men I know—served as your chairman for the past two years.

That's why I'm pleased to be with you today.

David, my congratulations on a job well done...a job that needs someone like you to do it. As Nathan Hale said...''it's an honorable job by being necessary.''

2

Characteristics of Communication Within the Organization

Chapter Outline

Communication Dimensions
Communication Awareness
Internal Communication
Nonverbals in Organizational Life
Primary Language
Interpersonal Competencies
Listening
Credibility
Recap

Project Two-1: *A Look Into Your Future*
Project Two-2: *Whistleblowers vs. Informers*

Chapter Objectives

Those who complete this chapter should better understand:

1. the nature of the communication transaction;
2. a systems' view of communication within an organization;
3. the special characteristics of nonverbal communication within organizations;
4. how internal communication may become more effective within the organization;
5. the need for ethical commitment within business and government organizations.

> "There's a problem in this country that has cost American business billions of dollars in losses: we don't understand how important it is to listen."
>
> — J. Paul Lyet
> Chairman, Sperry Corporation

> "A 1980 survey of presidents of Fortune 1000 companies identified the most anxiety-producing work situations for top management as: failure of subordinates to accept or carry out responsibilities and failure to get critical information."
>
> — Susan Mundale

The truck loads of letters delivered by the Postal Service annually are enough to convince most of us that communication is largely a matter of transportation. But reading and interpreting some of the letters which arrive in business offices from New York to Honolulu argue that sending a message from one head to another head is far more complex than mere transportation.

In a transaction, for example, between customer and company, we witness all the basic components in the communication process: Source, Encoding, Message, Channel, Decoding by Receiver, and Feedback. Communication, particularly face-to-face communication, is a complex process and cannot be accurately diagrammed because even the simplest exchange is a dynamic instantaneous happening. Admitting this, however, in order to discuss the implications of this complex exchange so much a part of the business world. Let's suppose we could stop the process long enough to draw a rough diagram of communication within a business organization.

The diagram seems simple, yet many concerns are triggered by such a simple transaction. The executive has myriad thoughts flash through his head, such as: Will such an inquiry be well received by my middle management? Will I be thought of as a crusader? Should I explain that my motives are in the best interests of avoiding racial conflict, getting government contracts—or argue that it is simply a question of morality? What words are currently acceptable to talk about these issues? A manager instantaneously upon receiving an announcement and agendum may have as many or more thoughts race through his minds such as: Are my records straight? How should I describe the recent problems in my division? Will the boss think I am prejudiced because we have few minority employees? At the meeting itself other questions may arise, such as: Does he simply want a report, or our real opinions? Why is this item last on the agendum? Does that smile mean that all is well?

People Feedback Loops

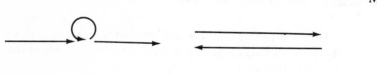

Self Modifying **Loop**

Examples: Manager, after thought, changes an order

Mutual Influencing **Loop**

Manager and secretary arrange their schedules

Indirect **Loops**

Manager orders work hours changed & annoys employees. This is turn results in lower output which then frustrates manager.

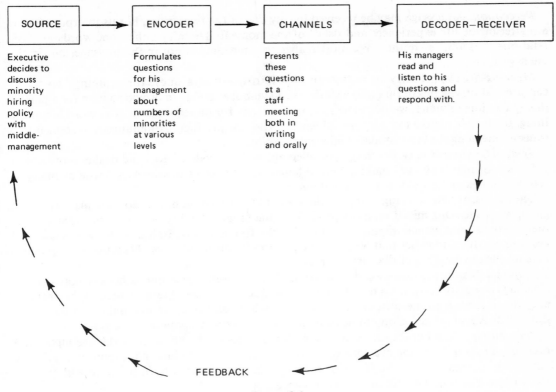

Figure 2.1

Communication Dimensions

Communication may be defined as the process of expressing ideas and feelings which are interpreted into more ideas and feelings. The following statements describe that process:

- Communication is irreversible and unrestrainable.
- Communication is a matter of perception.
- Communication is meaning-seeking.
- Communication is symbol-creating, picture-making and image-eliciting.
- Communication requests an affirmative response.
- Communication competes with noise and other attention-getters.
- Communication carries both logical and emotional dimensions.

Irreversible and Unrestrainable. Once said, something cannot be unsaid. A judge may order a jury to strike a certain piece of testimony from their minds, but that is easier said than done. It is also a truism that to say nothing is to say something. We cannot not communicate. Avoidance or silence may communicate very loud messages.

Perception. A message may be received by any one of the five senses, but its interpretation is a matter of the life experiences and "set" of the moment. Therefore, the same words may offend one, but amuse another. We must realize that meaning is not in the message, but in the message-user.

Meaning-Seeking. To try to phrase an idea into words is a quest for meaning. To try to capture reality which is in flux into a static word-symbol attempts to provide a map for a part of this space time in which we live. The *I* calls out to *you* for understanding. The word is not the thing; the map is not the territory; the blueprint is not the product. Communication seeks not to transmit meaning, but to stimulate and elicit meaning.

Symbol Creating-Image Eliciting. The telegraph with its code of dots and dashes represents a reduction of man's symbol making verbal language. Our large dictionaries house as many as 500,000 entries and provide some ten million meanings.

The aroma of bacon frying rising up the stairs to the bedroom in the morning may serve as a get-up message. Our minds take the pictures of the tangible reality we have known and apply them to the stimuli which impinge upon us like the frying bacon. So it is with these words and gestures we string together that we paint the pictures in our mind's eye. Then the word-pictures I create elicit in you, hopefully, similar images.

Requests. Rarely are one's words uttered to please himself alone, but rather his words are requesting cooperation from his target audience. Request is a general term, which in this instance may range from a subtle unspoken suggestion such as dinner by candle light to a command shouted by a drill officer. Communication in every case seeks a cooperative response.

Competitive. Communication competes with the states of the physical world, the high noise levels of our daily lives, the ever-present advertisements trying to buy our attention, and other competing communicators. So it is that messages can be distorted both by noise without and psychological overload within the target audience.

Logical-Emotional. The words we speak have a tonal quality and rate which carry emotional temperature. Our body rhetoric (eyes, gestures, movement, tension) communicates both the signs we intend and the emotional tensions we cannot easily hide.

Communication Awareness

An awareness of the nature of the communication process helps us have more realistic expectations. Foremost among these is the realization that messages are often misunderstood. Some writers have gone so far as to suggest that misunderstanding is the rule rather than the exception, and that being correctly understood is a happy accident. This may be putting it a bit too pessimistically. After all, we have seen the pyramids, the Great Wall of China, tunnels, bridges and skyscrapers built. There must have been many "happy accidents" for such marvelous human facts. Nevertheless, there are some guidelines which can help achieve greater understanding. These are:

- Organize a message as much as possible in visual terms. People understand and remember pictures.
- Organize a message, if possible, in chronological terms. We are used to time proceeding sequentially since before we could count.

- Preview and summarize a message. Use signposts to notify your listeners of where you are (i.e., first I will discuss equipment; next, I will describe the four steps in the smelting process). Repeat, where the message is very important.
- Ask for playback. Checking to discover what your listeners think you have said will help you know how clearly your message has been understood.
- Seek evaluative feedback. Morale can be assessed only if it is known. Remember only a thoughtless waiter pours the wine before he checks with you to see if you approve its aroma.
- Use more than one channel. The ears, eyes, touch and any other senses appropriate should be used to get across important messages. The concern of the company for the employee is often communicated by a dinner, a dance, a picnic as well as by a New Year's bonus.
- Speak in the language of your target audience. Link to his interest and goals.

Internal Communication

What do we find when we examine the communication within a business organization? Communication obviously is the means used to coordinate all the incoming goods and human resources and help the organization transform them into products and services. Accurate communication may be the *cause* for successful scheduling and meeting time tables. Inaccurate or inadequate communication may cause delays, conflict and dissatisfaction.

On the other hand, good communication may *result* from satisfied employees and poor communication from dissatisfied employees. Communications, good or bad may be either cause or effect of workers satisfaction or dissatisfaction. (See fig. 2.2) Rogers and Rogers define an organization as "an elaborate set of interconnected communication channels designed to impart, sort, and analyze information from the environment and export processed messages back to the environment."[1] Communication, thus, is the interactive informational process that links one system to other systems. The purpose of information is to change uncertainty to greater certainty.

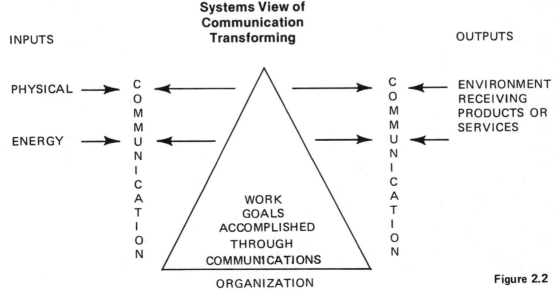

Figure 2.2

Researchers generally find, what the International Communications Audit-Teams found in studies of ten organizations:[2]

1. Most employees like their immediate work environment, but aren't that satisfied with their organization at large.
2. Most are receiving the information, they *need* to do their jobs, but not all the information they *want* related to organization-wide concerns.
3. Upward opportunities exist, but *follow up* is lacking, especially upward evaluation of supervisors.
4. Horizontal communication is weak, creating problems of mistrust, conflict/ competition.
5. Fact-to-face and written channels operate more effectively than other hardware.
6. Employees are least satisfied with distant information (top management) and most with closer sources (their boss, coworkers).
7. Messages originating from top management generally are clear, appropriate, believable, but timeliness is a problem.
8. Overall communication climate is more negative than positive for most organizations.
9. The most important communication employee problems are related to (a) inadequacy of information needed or wanted to do a good job, (b) misuse of authority, (c) mistakes in following procedures, and (d) interpersonal conflict.
10. In larger organizations (over 500) many employees are relatively isolated from both necessary and incidental information flow.

With these general principles in mind, in this chapter we will apply them first to communication within the organization, and in later chapters we will discuss communicating with wider audiences. We think too often in terms of public relations for our firm and of addresses made by top executives, and fail to realize that all personnel from top to bottom want to have a positive image. Good or bad, we all do communicate an image. Since organizational authority is structured from the top down, let's first examine how that downward communication might be more positive.

Downward Image. Those in supervisory positions, often by the nature of their jobs, are expected and are given the time and facilities to communicate company policy. Those in the line of command (to use a military analogy) have their daily or weekly staff meetings with subordinates. They control and may reward those who get the message down the organizational ladder.

In several businesses with which the writers are acquainted, the image of the top is that of a military command. In one, a young man in middle management described his general manager as a person who had to okay the smallest detail all down the line, even to the approval of employing a new secretary. He stated that this CEO could tolerate only "yes-men" below him. In that firm, the basic issue is to what degree does middle management wish to function under the authoritarian model. And apparently many didn't, because within a two-year period some twenty-one men at the middle management level made an exit from the company. Five of those who left started their own competing business.

Our assumption as we write is that communication within an organization must be two-way in order for that plant to be a productive, satisfying place of employment. This does not imply in any way that all policy decisions are a matter of referendum of the rank and file. Rather, it means that parties concerned about a matter know the thinking of each other, that they exchange information and opinions, and that each person feels a measure of responsibility for the welfare of his organization.

Input. The top men, of course, must make long-run policy decisions, and when these are announced they ought to be clearly stated. In short, when there is telling, it should be clear, and the telling should tell *why*. But one of the important rules of thumb which can rarely be over-emphasized is that before *telling, invite* reaction. One of the ways to communicate the image of "You-don't-count" is to fail to provide opportunity for input from those concerned. The core essential to any program within an organization is the communication of a genuine interest in the input of subordinates. And this must not seem to be patronizing, but rather with dignity a search for real input from those closest to an issue.

Availability. Yet another factor important to communicating a positive climate lies in availability. Distance and walls cut people off. Granted, managers need privacy for think-jobs, but they must not be too far from subordinates. Isolation communicates an image of aloofness. Thomas V. Jones, Chairman and President of Northrop Corporation, helped plan their home headquarters with much open space and glass panels between offices. He carries this openness into his communications. With disregard of channels, he arranges conference calls to examine an evolving situation or conflict. And his long-range planning bodies are ad hoc committees which cut across managerial levels.[3]

Resistance. The executive who wants a two-way climate must set the example and train his lower levels of management to cut resistance and delays. Just as distance and space can isolate, so can time delays, when handling employee concerns. Resistance, however, is more than the time it takes to send a problem up the ladder and to get an answer. It is an attitude. Some supervisors carry high resistance to employee input. They seem to blow a fuse at the slightest report of trouble or anything that might reflect poorly on themselves. And consequently, subordinates tend to hide their mistakes.

Appropriate Channels. Managers must select the most efficient and appropriate channels and, if a message is particularly important, more than one channel. What are these channels? Telephone, official directive, staff meeting, memo, individual conversation, letter, counseling session, bulletin-board notice, company newsletter, formal report and the grapevine. What, then, are the best channels? Obviously, the context of any situation governs the channel chosen, but here are some tips:

- Select an oral channel when giving instructions, and ask for feedback immediately. It also is helpful to provide visual examples of the desired format.
- Be direct and always put policies and procedures into writing.
- Invite oral feedback and questions before expecting a directive to be carried out.
- Handle grievances in person-to-person fashion, such as a personal counseling session. Do so in an off-to-the-side or, better still, a private place. Of course, more informal individual conversations are best for minor first offense violations such as not getting reports in on time.
- Set appointments by phone rather than memo.
- Use staff meetings to orient a number of new personnel.
- Use memos to reach a number of subordinates with the same message, such as notifying plant managers in different locations that they must increase production in the next month by twenty percent. The telephone is a good follow-up because it provides for feedback, but

also be sure to ask for a written response to important notices. Sometimes memos to a busy executive may be the best way to get his attention for a new idea and can set the stage for a conference to sell him on a new idea. Use individual conversations to get information on new procedures. Be specific with your questions. Also use conversation to trace down problems such as lost shipments.

More than any other factor the image of the Chief Executive Officer either hurts or helps the organization—both internally and externally. If he is viewed as competent, energetic, trustworthy, and concerned about his employees, those employees will sell their company to the community with pride. If, on the other hand, the image of the Chief Executive Officer and of one's supervisors are cantankerous, ruthless and inconsiderate individuals no employee will hold his head high when required to tell where he works.

It is the CEO who must decide how important communications are, and whether his firm needs professional help to set up a coordinated program to facilitate communicating *down, up, laterally,* and *externally.* The larger the corporation, the more a professional communication staff is needed. It is their job to see that management takes the concerns at the top to the lowest employee. It is their job to plan the best ways to announce policy and collect feedback on impending policy decisions. And it is their job to develop a program which encourages upward communication. How well this is done (through employee surveys, suggestion boxes, inside and outside committees, training of managers, etc.), ultimately will do much to determine whether the Chief Executive has a negative or a positive image.

Upward Communication. The key to getting and maintaining a positive image of top management within the organization lies in creating a structure for upward communication. One industrial photographer spoke to us in glowing terms about how the owner of a company in which he had worked treated him with respect, and how he would say, "It's your job. Tell us what you need." And for the boss, as busy and important as he was, to get out in the plant in his old clothes, the employee repeated again and again: "I could always talk to him. But when our plant was sold [a new firm], things were different."

This employee possibly had an old-fashioned image of what a superior-subordinate relationship should be. He thought in terms of personal attention, of respect for his abilities, and of a team relationship. The size of modern industry today makes such relationships pure nostalgia. The Chief Executive Officer obviously cannot frequently pass the time of day with the man on the line or the office staff. And since the Chief Executive and his senior managers are physically distant from both the rank and file and middle management, the need for an upward communication structure is paramount. Morale and production are directly related to the opportunity to be heard.

Only when top management understands the barriers and filters inherent in a hierarchy will they consider instituting a new structure. The barriers exist because first, the subordinate rarely comes into contact with the policy makers and second, when he does, he wants to put only his best foot forward. He does not want to reveal his own failures or those of his colleagues. "Keep your mouth shut and you won't get in trouble" all too often is the code of the factory, just as it was the code in the Army and in prisons. The greater the distance and the more levels through which a communication must travel, the greater is the likelihood that the message will be distorted, edited, or eliminated altogether—and the more impersonal it will be.

Designing Corporate Communication. Chuck Slocum, corporate manager of communication at Honeywell, makes the following seven suggestions in light of his experience working from corporate headquarters. Honeywell employs 97,000 persons in its 50 businesses and 500 branch locations.

1. Establish a working policy—one that assures that information is two-way, open, timely considers all sides, and presents the bad news as well as the good. The goals should be clearly articulated in written policy. Defining terms and securing agreement upon policy objectives is important in generating corporate commitment to developing effective communications.

2. Identify the staff function. Appointment of a staff and job descriptions define how corporate resources will be used. At Honeywell the employee communication function is staffed with a manager, specialist, assistant and intern. The team is assigned the responsibility to stimulate the communication process throughout the company by advising and coaching. One of their tasks was to prepare informative materials to explain the $430 million employee benefits provided by Honeywell and to provide advice to company managers in presenting this information at the local level. Communication coordinators of the 50 different businesses assist with such common projects. Some 40 editors of publications also extend the corporate communication network.

3. Recruit a broadly based steering committee. Communication co-ordinators at Honeywell establish ongoing five to seven member committees to advise them. Their advice is sought about such matters as how communication might aid in staffing, orientation, morale, productivity, product issues. They, therefore, provide opinions about newsletters, employee meetings, weekly breakfasts, recognition programs, communication training and audio-visual media.

4. Develop short-and long-range plans. General three to five year objectives may be worked out, such as "increased employee confidence in management," and then more specific measurable action items such as "prepare all-employee CEO report addressing work force concerns."

5. Use feedback to measure effectiveness. Pre-post audits of employee attitudes and a host of other evaluation techniques may be used to assess accomplishment of plans. Feedback may be obtained in small meetings, telephone surveys, hotlines, suggestion boxes. At least one anonymous method should be available to every work group so that fear of reprisal for complaints will be minimized.

6. Budget to solve organizational problems. At Honeywell some $5 million a year is devoted to employee communication activities. When presenting a budget it should be built around achieving such organizational objectives as improving co-ordination of organizational components, avoidance of confusion and duplication of effort and managing conflict.

7. Reassess, re-evaluate and revise as necessary. Sometimes some efforts need to be scrapped, others modified or expanded.

—Abstracted from "Employee Communication Is More Than Sharing Information With Employees," *Journal of Organizational Communication,* 1981, *3,* 6-8.

The reports by superiors sent up the organizational ladder often fall into this same trap. The negative is filtered out and only that which makes a supervisor's operation look good ascends. A design, then, that bypasses these barriers must (1) provide for contact with policy makers,

(2) provide answers, (3) assure anonymity when there are personally threatening situations, and (4) result in action. Suggestion boxes will not do the job.

How might such a plan be organized? The structure should be designed to handle questions either written, called in, or communicated in person. In short, a staff position(s) must be set up to handle questions, to first of all hear them and next to get the answers to those questions from the appropriate management level. Sometimes such a staff can be housed within various locations within a plant, provided that location can assure privacy. Some organizations have located such staffs off the premises.

Another aspect of the program may entail communication training for various units or, sometimes better still, personnel from various levels and divisions within the company. Such training may help employees to more accurately formulate their questions and direct them to the responsible company officer. Such interaction, moreover, helps employees to better see how their work relates to each other, information is shared and a broader perspective, if not a team spirit, may be generated.

In some such training programs individuals and/or teams are encouraged to submit proposals for improving working conditions, production and cutting costs. Interdepartmental committees must then review these proposals with a reasonable time frame, such as thirty days. Task teams have become an important means for job enrichment, cutting costs and providing that inter-personal component to job satisfaction. Some organizations have instituted such plans on their own. Others have employed consultants, some of whom guarantee that the cost of the training will more than pay for itself by employee proposals for cutting costs. A key aspect of such programs is the recognition given by a company. A personal letter of commendation rewards the team or individual. Somebody at the top knows he has made a sound proposal, that he has helped save the company money, or has increased productivity.

New England Telephone began its Upwards Communication Program by starting a "private lines" operation. All employees were assured that their identity would remain anonymous and that their questions which could be either mailed or called in would be forwarded to an appropriate official. In addition, key questions with answers are selected for publication in the company newsletter.

The coordinators of the Upwards Communication Program discuss sensitive personal situations with those who call in and, sometimes, request that the callers forego their anonymity in order to get some problems solved.

In the first year it was in operation, more than 2500 questions and comments were received. The topics of concern included working conditions, promotions, transfers, assignments, wages, benefits, etc. A survey of the employees showed that seventy-nine percent of those who used the program were satisfied with their responses and that almost all said they would use it again. Of those who used it, three out of four were nonmanagement and the other fourth were from management.

Vice President and General Manager of the Massachusetts area of New England Telephone, Bruce Harriman, concluded a report on their Upwards Communication Program by saying, "We think we have learned a few things about interpersonal communication in a structured situation and about making this knowledge work to our organization's benefit."[4]

Open communication channels will do much to minimize rumors so common in climates of distrust. Good formal communication will provide accurate information for the informal grapevine channels which every organization has and needs to infuse the messages of management.

Nonverbals in Organizational Life

Organizations are both consciously and unconsciously creating symbols and assigning meaning to the environment. Organizations exist in time and space and they build forms into which they have their being. Let us examine this environment in which business organizations and public organizations work.

Structure and Size. Just as man stands in awe of the size and order of his universe, so is he impressed by architectural triumphs. Massiveness, since the days of the pyramids, has spoken loudly of power and served as graphic evidence of permanence and position. Hitler, who thought of himself as the master builder, designed massive structures, and in so doing, told the world, "We are the super race." The site of the Nuremburg rally, for example, was 15 times the size of the standard football field. Hitler's stone viewing stand was backed by a colonnade of 170 stone pillars, 60 feet tall and illuminated by 1,200 spotlights. The nonverbal message of the physical setting added to the verbal and the roars of nearly a million voices reinforced their feelings of superiority.[5]

Harold Lasswell, the scholar, when writing about architecture said, "A completed structure influences both the symbolic outlook and the behavioral activities of the people who adapt to its existence."[6]

Boundaries. It is a law of physics that no two bodies may occupy the same space at the same time. Survival thus dictates that animals defend the territory which they inhabit. So it is that we come to set up territorial boundaries and to use personal symbols to mark our own space. Man's first bubble extends about as far as he can reach. To have this bubble invaded without permission causes discomfort, if not hostility. In close quarters, such as an elevator, we reluctantly reduce the size of our bubble, but we do not like to be crowded or pushed.

Since space and territory are in limited supply, the larger the territory under one's command, the greater one's status. Not only do prominent people often own large estates or office buildings, but they frequently travel with an entourage who protect their bigger bubble. The desk of the company president is usually larger, constructed of more expensive materials, and placed in a more spacious room than the desk of a clerk. Corner offices, which tend to be larger and contain more windows, therefore, are assigned to managers with higher status. Status also is assigned to what floor one's office is located; higher floors usually going to a higher level of management. And to be in an office with permanent walls indicates higher status than to be located inside movable partitions. The physical space in which one lives and works is frequently a rather telling message of one's income level and job ranking.

Focus. The focal structure of a place provides clues as to what people consider important. Was it not a round table that helped King Arthur change a motley, swarthy hoard of gluttons into responsible knights? Even today, the shape of a table will cause us to focus our eyes and attention on the leader. Such is the message of a long rectangular table with the chairman of the board at the end position. Or the authority may be more equally dispersed, as in a circular or horse-shoe arrangement.

Priests in primitive cultures knew well the impact of elevation. Sunlight and position focused all eyes toward the symbol of sacred authority. The rules of dominance grew out of the focus derived by structure, position, height, lighting and facial direction. No words have to be uttered to indicate who is king. Throne, height and focal structure tell all.

In our society, we know the effect of a conversation pit as contrasted to a TV lounge. In one

Organizations are pyramidal in structure. Even their buildings sometimes represent this authority structure.

instance, the strucure brings us together; in the other, it isolates by facing us all toward the tube. Observe the mood created by a classroom's arrangement. Is there a difference between a room where all chairs are in neat rows facing a desk as compared to one where chairs are clustered in small circles with no desk for the instructor?

How an organization arranges its space affects communication by making interaction either more difficult or easy. Fast food restaurants frequently are designed with only standing room in contrast to some lounges with soft and low lights. One hurries customer movement; the other invites customers to linger. Arrangement for such businesses as Burger King says economy, efficiency and uniformity. To linger even while ordering is discouraged both by the manner of the attendant at the microphone and by the posted menu and queue.

Consider another illustration. A vice president of a several billion dollar financial institution in Washington, D.C. showed one of the authors into their boardroom. He wanted a reaction to a triangular shaped table with slightly rounded corners. He told him that the Chief Executive did not sit at any of the corners but in the middle along one of the sides. There was a kind of symmetry about the setting in keeping with the office design of the institution's several floors below.

Next he escorted him through the open office landscaping which likewise had a triangular effect. Amid the many head-high partitions, cubicles were arranged so that each employee had an equal amount of space walled on two sides with an opening on an aisle. Only the top executives were situated in more spacious corner offices with a bit more privacy and window area.

Muted by deep carpets and music, a comfortable decorum seemed to pervade these work areas. With some pride, he was shown the latest collection of paintings and sculpture located about the place. Just as the plants were enjoyed by all and were selected, cared for and periodically replaced by a contracted florist, also the art belonged to everyone and was selected and periodically changed by an art consultant.

"So what do you think about this table?" asked the V.P. I surmised that it seemed to fit and reflected an effort on the part of the organization to break slightly from the traditional authoritarian administration, and appeared to symbolize an egalitarian work culture. The vice president, charged with corporate communications, then submitted that he was thinking of diagramming the organizational chart differently for the next annual report, perhaps in the form of overlapping circles instead of the traditional chain of command, and "What did I think of that? Or might overlapping pyramids be better?"

In this financial institution's effort to break from tradition, had it really? The reality of hierarchy was still there. There was a chief executive, five executive vice presidents, more vice presidents, directors, managers, et cetera. There was much specialization and differentiation within the walls of the corporate headquarters and in its several branch offices located in various geographical areas. There were controls over the expenditures in the various divisions and departments, and with rapid growth had come specialized integrative functions such as the vice president charged with various communication tasks.

The delta shape of the board meeting table, indeed, was quite appropriate. An organization, wherever it is located and regardless of efforts to treat everyone equally, nevertheless, is pyramidal in its structure and does treat some more favorably than others. Even in this financial institution, which had gone to such extraordinary effort to partition open space equally and fit it with like furnishings, favored treatment could be seen in the larger and more private accommodations assigned its officers.

Artifacts. As we noted in this detailed description of the office of the Washington, D.C. financial institution, status was rewarded by office location and size. The objects which surround an organizational member also provide signs of status. One way this may be illustrated is to answer three questions we have put to many thousands of employees who have attended our seminars: (1) What are the non-work objects in your work space? (2) How do they compare to non-work objects in your superior's space? and (3) What meaning likely is assigned these objects?

The list of objects include such things as plants, photos, slogans, flags, certificates, radios, candy, trophies, sports equipment, paintings, pet rocks, crafts. The meanings assigned provide clues of individual accomplishments, financial well-being, personality, degree of sociability, job seriousness, commitment to family, career path, sexuality, hobbies and life interest.

The location of these artifacts also provides a clue to one's sphere of activity. Sometimes a color scheme such as a royal blue decor: blue furniture, blue typewriters, blue phones, blue paintings, employees dressed in blue will signal where one sphere begins and another leaves off. Nonverbal artifacts communicate messages of territoriality, identity and degree of individuality or conformity.

Appointments. We live by the clock. The hunger for structure, so apparent in architecture and tradition, also shows up in our ability to fill days with dates, meetings and activities. So it is that we have watches, clocks and appointment books which order our day.

The time a communication takes place speaks loudly. Moreover, how early, late or on time we are conveys a message about how important we feel an appointment is. In some instances, to arrive early will seem crude, when the expectation is to come fashionably late. In some cultures, punctuality is not so rigidly prized. Mañana may not be tomorrow, but some indefinite time in the future—nor should one be offended to wait for several hours to see a high official. But even in this country, how long we wait is directly related to status. The higher the status of the other person, the longer one will wait.

Timing. A persuasive message may fall on deaf ears because the timing was off. A persuasion is the gradual process of securing cooperation, knowing "when" and "how long" is an essential part of the process. A salesperson who is conscious that time is money adjusts his message to the time of the customer. He not only does his best to find a suitable time, but he clearly estimates the time he needs, and then he scrupulously honors the time allotted. Whether it be a public address or a visit with a friend, it is wise to check out and honor the time expected for the communication event. The "how-often" and the "when" of a communication may sometimes influence opinion as much or more than the "what" of a message.

Body Messages. It is impossible not to communicate because of the many channels sensed by our bodies. That is to say, you cannot not communicate. Any communication event consists in a large part of reading nonverbal body messages. Indeed, how our nonverbal messages are interpreted has a great impact on what others think of our verbal messages. We may contradict a confident verbal statement with a nervous movement of hands and eyes. On other occasions, nonverbal clues amplify verbal messages as, for example, when a word of affection is accompanied by a hug or a squeeze of the hand. In all of our communicative acts, nonverbal messages give listeners important clues to our true inner feelings and thoughts.

Appearance. Like it or not, we tend to judge each other by appearance. There is general agreement within a culture, for example, about who is and who is not good looking. And in some cultures the greater a person's status, the taller he is perceived to be. Make-up, grooming and dress can influence the attitudes of an audience. And even though they are frequently wrong, people tend to judge others with a different physical appearance to have certain character traits.

The pretty as compared to the ugly do have an easier time of it. There are many instances of job discrimination toward people who veer too far from the norms set for acceptable height and weight. Many studies indicate what we all know, that people attractive to the opposite sex receive greater attention and exert more influence than those who are less appealing.

The way one dresses gives various clues about the individual. Conformity in dress, for example, has been found to correlate with conformity in other areas. One of the most effective signs of role is the uniform. It is widely used to provide readily visible signs of job classifications. In one trip to a hospital, we noted uniform and color differentiating practical nurses from registered nurses. There were ladies in gray, candy stripers, blue orderlies, green maintenance personnel, technicians in white pants suits, nurses in white gowns, surgeons in unironed green, and doctors in suits.

Dress conveys many meanings: decorative functions (fashionability or lack of style), sexual role (degree of concern for femininity or masculinity), formality (suitability for formal or informal occasions), conformity (uniforms or similarity of dress to others with whom one associates), and finally, but of less importance to many people, comfort and economy.

One's dress, like one's physical appearance, has much to do with self-image. A positive self-image of one's body appears to be directly related to feelings of security, and a negative image to insecurity. A prosperous cosmetics industry and plastic surgery practice thrive on the belief that looks influence how favorably one fares socially and vocationally. Make-up, clothing, hair style and glasses, if extreme, may detract from an individual's social and professional acceptability.

Body Placement. The placement of one's body tells us such things as who is in charge, who is the Chief and who are the Indians. Elected officials tend to sit in head chairs, such as at end positions at rectangular tables. People who are more influential tend to sit where they are able to see more people. Those with little influence tend to sit on the fringes and do not take head positions. People turn toward those with whom they wish to interact and turn away from those to whom they do not wish to speak or listen. Generally, we approach and come close to those things and people we like and keep our distance from those we dislike. Our body tends to be more open toward those with whom we feel comfortable and closed toward those with whom we feel discomfort.

People of higher status, as compared to subordinates, tend to take larger strides, to command larger territory, use larger, more definite gestures, to be less rigid, stand taller, be more open in posture and talk more loudly.[7] Do not infer that talking loudly means crudity and ill manner. People of higher status are not generally unsophisticated loudmouths.

Three crucial clues that appear to make nonverbal signs readable are (1) the degree to which positions permit much or little visibility, (2) the degree to which positional distance facilitates involvement or frustrates interaction, and (3) the size and strength of movement.

Movement and Gestures. We have a number of conventional gestures that signal such messages as come, stop, and approval (thumb and first finger touching). The vigor of descriptive gestures may convey messages of enthusiasm; the size of gestures correlates with power and status. Man has an inclination for symbolic gestures such as the forked fingers in a Victory or Peace sign; the raised, clenched fist signaling black power, or the upraised middle finger, indicating an angry, obscene response.

Gestures, just as body movement which precedes or accompanies words, may focus attention and emphasis on the verbal message. Gestures are extensions of thought and feeling into visual spatial symbols. When they appear to spring spontaneously from the message, they confirm. When they appear stilted and put on, they contradict the message. Gestures, therefore, at their best (1) express the mood of the speaker and listener, (2) assist communicators in depicting spatial relationships, and (3) aid in the dramatic account of human interaction.

Inappropriate vs. Body Appropriate Images. Inappropriate images usually fall into the problem of too much or too little. The person in business who is "read" as too aggressive tends to excess such as too much eye contact, invasion of another's space, too large a signature, too wide a gesture, too firm a handshake, too heavy an inflection and too loud a voice, too much interruption, too flashy a dress, and too much touching. The opposite behavior conveys a non-assertive message such as lowering eyes or looking away most of the time while another is speaking, yielding space, perhaps retreating in another's presence, tense or limp gestures, cluttered sentences, inaudible voice, withdrawal from a discussion, hands in pockets or folded tensely, avoidance of all touching.

Appropriate body activity, thus, is somewhere in between. How is it learned? Probably by observing and imitating those in the society and within organizations who are respected and liked.[8]

"Management style at Wal-Mart is as much press-the-flesh as watch-the-pennies. From Monday through Thursday Walton and his top executives travel in four company-owned planes, each aiming to visit a half dozen to a dozen stores every week. He chats with staffers — hundreds of whom he knows on a first-name basis — to find out what items and promotions are popular. He also helps managers exchange ideas and solve problems. On Friday and Saturday the boss is back at headquarters attending merchandise meetings and listening to plans for weekly and monthly sales budgets and promotional programs. Walton's 7:30 a.m. Saturday executive breakfasts — coffee and doughnuts — are strongly ingrained rituals."

Forbes, August 16, 1982

Primary Language

Some of the best speakers for organizations know the power of "primary language." What is primary language? The *immediate* impact on an audience — the message received which supersedes all other communication — is primary language.

To put it more simply — which do you believe most: the acts of a person or the words that person uses? We believe what we see — the nonverbals in any situation — more than words, probably because we know intuitively that it is easier to cover up the truth with words than it is to cover up emotions.

Words may even be incidental to many *live* messages. The feelings that come through in the voice and the feelings which are expressed in the eyes, gestures, and body movement count more.

Ad men know this. In commercials it is not so much the words that sell but the images which carry messages that are understood. Coca-Cola is acclaimed as the Real Thing. But the real thing is not explained in words. Rather it is explained by actors hugging, kissing, relaxing after an exciting activity and drinking a frosty cola. The whole picture is of the best that life can offer: the vigor of youth, affection, success, health and fun.

We understood the message even though our intellect may tell us that the message is contrived by ad men and actors and even though we may reason that coke does not cause those good things.

Geritol commercials tell a similar message for the J.B. Williams Company. Close-Up Toothpaste ads sing its praises for Lever Brothers.

Scholars of nonverbal communication explain that wordless sounds, body movements, signs and pictures constitute a primary language which is processed by special areas of the right brain—the system which is the seat of emotions.

Words and sentences,however, are processed in a more linear fashion, largely a left brain activity. Words derive much of their meanings from primary language such as the twinkle of an eye, the rate and stress of vocal intonation, the distance between sender and receivers.

A secretary who types ever so rapidly defines herself as a typist. The odds are that secretary will always be a secretary. On the other hand, the secretary who by her (or his) demeanor appears interested in managing and problem solving, will be "read" as management material. The nonverbals of dress also send primary messages of being serious about one's career.

Media consultants know how the reporters respond to "friendliness" and "sincerity of body language" and how these intangibles influence both who gets heard and who gets a fair hearing of their organization's story.

Interpersonal Competencies

Working with others is the nature of most careers. Perhaps that is why we place listening skills and sensitivity so high on our scale of values. Task accomplishment often depends upon interpersonal trust. We need to be able to count on each other. We need to be able to predict each other's behavior.

A Secure Base. How we interact with others on the job is related to our own mental and emotional well-being. Our stability and predictability cannot be a matter of·will but are a response to how secure is our personal base. For that base to be secure, we need: (1) a bonding with family, (2) an attachment to close friends, and (3) a supporting network at the place of work. We may get by with only two of these three for a time at the loss of some close friends, then the work network and family ties become more important. But we are on shaky emotional ground when two out of the three are disrupted such as loss of a spouse by death or divorce and moving at the same time so that we are separated from our close friends. Our stability in our job under such circumstances then may also be affected.

Managerial Interpersonal Skills. Interpersonal competencies are essential to managing people. An intensive study by McBer Associates (sponsored by the American Management Association) interviewed 1800 successful managers. The profile drawn of successful managers covers four crucial competencies: entrepreneurial, intellectual, social-emotional maturity and interpersonal abilities.

The AMA then constructed a curriculum for training managers under a certification program of the AMA. That curriculum included an interpersonal skills cluster and a socio-emotional maturity cluster.

An interpersonal skills cluster identified in successful managers included such attributes as self-confidence, developing others, concern with impact, use of unilateral power, use of socialized power, use of oral communication, positive regard and managing group process. The competencies under a socio-emotional maturity cluster point to the personal characteristics important in effective managers: self-control, spontaneity, perceptual objectivity, accurate self-assessment, stamina and adaptability. These too are directly related to interaction with people.

If then interpersonal competencies are recognized as essential to managing human resources, what approaches might be used to develop them? What models are appropriate for focusing upon interpersonal competencies? In recent times, Management and Employee Training has flirted with several interpersonal approaches with what might be called the self-disclosure, transactional and/or assertiveness schools. What are the underlying assumptions of these training approaches? Are they appropriate for the organizational setting? If not, what alternatives are there?

Windows and Onions. The self-disclosure approach to interpersonal competencies, we are told, is rooted in the ancient admonition to know thyself. Self-knowledge does not come from introspection, but by reciprocal self-disclosure. The standard model is Joseph Luft's Johari Window. The window is partitioned into four sections: the unknowable, the hidden, the blind to and the open. The educative experience comes from learning how others see those things about you to which you are blind and in revealing to others those aspects about yourself which you've kept hidden.

The open quadrant of the window, thus, grows larger and the blind and hidden sections shrink. The assumption is that transparency of self is so much easier to live with.

During the sixties and early seventies, the self-disclosure movement reached its peak. The National Training Labs prospered. It was "in" to have experienced the "here and now" of sensitivity training. In the microcosm of a small group of strangers and a psychologist, masks of pretense were torn away, guts were spilled, some people flipped out and others found they could express both positive and negative feelings.

The mecca for those who could afford it was the Esalen Institute on the rugged Big Sur country 300 miles north of Los Angeles. Workshops spawned in this setting were led by such persons as Gerald Heard, Alan Watts, Arnold Toynbee, S.I. Hayakawa, Paul Tilich, Carl Rogers, Abraham Maslow, B.F. Skinner, William Schutz and Fritz Perls. Experimentation and human potential were the bywords.

Intense self-awareness and intimate encounters became ok. The normal protective covering, like the skins of an onion must be torn off. From acquaintance, to friendship, to intimacy could happen quickly if the protective covering could be shed or penetrated. In the seventies, the human potential movement became a business in itself.

Hundreds of thousands have "experienced" such training as Transactional Analysis, est, and assertiveness training, and have become evangelistic about what it has done for them. One manager said that he had not faced up to what an SOB he was until he had taken the training. Such testimonials abound. The format of these seminars vary but the assumptions are similar; that is, by getting to know oneself, by monitoring one's feeling, and by expressing those feelings, we will become more authentic beings.

In a carefully couched attack on the sensitivity self-disclosure approach to interpersonal training several years ago, George Odiorne, the well-known management consultant, stated that these approaches were "based upon creating stress situations for their own sake which may go out of control and often do." He recommended that the "entire sensitivity training movement be sent 'back to the drawing board' until terminal behaviors could be more carefully defined and executed.'' His advice to business was to ''avoid the cult.''

We agree with Odiorne for two reasons: (1) self-disclosure training tends to focus on personal matters which if known to those at one's place of employment might adversely affect career progress, (2) self-disclosure training creates unrealistic norms for the work setting. The attention in self-disclosure is upon feelings. Managers sent away for sensitivity, transactional analysis and est type experiences too often return hooked on playing amateur psychologists. They have had an emotional purging — exhilarating experience. In its wake, they use the jargon such as ''where are you at,'' ''strokes and warm fuzzies,'' ''I am clear about,'' ''my space,'' and ''my child says'' — a jargon that isolates and alienates.

The self-disclosure approach to developing interpersonal competencies may strip away phoniness and game playing harmful to intimate relationships, but this is not what is appropriate in the work setting.

Investment. Another approach to interpersonal competencies is the investment model. In this model cultivation of good working relationships is viewed as an investment. Aristotle years ago observed that there are friendships of utility. Like it or not getting things done is easier when relationships are good. This is not to say that all is corporate politics. It is to say, as Peter Drucker has emphasized, that in an age of information overload, communication is all the more important. Communication is a process. It is transactive.

The investment in relationships focuses upon credibility rather than on self-disclosure. Training for credibility stresses the integrity, competence and goodwill.

Friendships within the work setting, of course, vary in intensity. Some are close. The pay-off for close friendships are more than utilitarian. Close friendships mean ego support: acceptance, appreciation and approval. A person who has close friends feels ''I am ok because someone besides my mother likes me.''

The investment approach to interpersonal competencies on the surface may strike some as manipulative and crass. We prefer to think of it as enlightened pragmatism. A network of people who like each other has much to contribute to morale.

Moreover, investing in credibility is not a matter of pulling strings. It rather is a matter of developing a secure personal base.

The social psychologists tell us that the payoffs of health, longevity and a kind of hardiness are the sum of a strong personal network and a genuine engagement in life.

Interpersonal investment training begins by helping the employee to see the linkage between a secure personal base and the welfare of the organization. A secure personal base is built by bonding with intimates, attachment with close friends and a supporting network at the place of work. The firm that believes in the interpersonal investment strategy approves of friendships.

Bureaucratic aloofness with its benefits of impartiality and even-handedness generates an aura of mystery. The investment strategy demystifies. Performance and appraisal must then be based on hard measures rather than on mystery and position.

Congruence. A third approach to training interpersonal competencies focuses upon symbolic congruence. Congruence trains superiors to ''read'' subordinates, and vice versa. Field studies have demonstrated that a subordinate's job satisfaction is higher when there is congruence between the way the subordinate describes the superior and the way the superior describes himself or herself. These studies also reveal that a manager's evelution of a subordinate's performance is more positive when he is cognizant of a subordinate's work-related attitudes.

Congruence training, thus, focuses upon reading the other person and being readable. Superiors learn the importance of giving feedback to subordinates and conversely subordinates learn to give feedback to the boss. Job descriptions are not left to chance. Ambiguity about job related matters are continuously sought out for clarification.[9]

When congruence happens in a work group across the unfolding of events there is a sharing of stories, rituals, traditions and sentiment. Community and commitment grow. Daydreams, fantasies and common visions are spun. These are the rewards of attention to interpersonal congruence.

The work organization has a real interest in discovery of employee preference for how he or she is managed. Compatibility between how a superior and subordinate feel about "bossing" and being bossed, about freedom and independence, is important to the satisfaction of both within their work situation. Congruence training acknowledges that employees differ in their life styles and values.

Three distinctive life styles have been identified: *formalistic, sociocentric* and *personalistic.*[10] Those with formalistic predispositions reflect a value system which indicates that actions should be guided by rules, regulations, policies and procedures established by authorities. Sociocentrics place high values upon interpersonal relationships, with collaboratively derived norms and consequently will function more compatibly in work units managed collaboratively. Those with dominant personalistic values are inner-directed. They value personal freedom, and fit best into a work organization which permits such independence. Usually, those with strongly personalistic values are most satisfied when self-employed or employed in temporary co-ordinated structures.

Most organizations are big enough to assign members to work groups based on their compatibility of life style, or at least to assign superiors based on their degree of compatibility with a work groups' personalistic life style dimension. This matching, however, usually is not as consciously done as might be beneficial.

What does this mean for the organization? Many companies recognize how important the physical and emotional well-being are by their diet and recreation programs, in their counselling centers for drug related and psychological problems, in their attention to hazardous work conditions, and in their demonstrated concern for creating and maintaining a pleasant work climate.

Indirect Communication. People often talk evasively. Sometimes such talk is designed to obscure what is really happening. Politicians and foreign diplomats have skillfully perfected their abilities to speak in abstraction, and even to convey hidden meaning in the subtleties of what they don't say.

Most of us speak indirectly for more personal reasons. We are afraid to present our real feelings, desires, ideas and opinions. We also speak indirectly in many different ways in order to try to manipulate and gain influence. Here are several ways people put messages indirectly.

1. Asking questions when we really want to give our opinion.
2. Seeking support by saying "don't you think that...," "Isn't it true that..."
3. Telling others what they think or feel saying things such as "You would or you wouldn't want that" and "I know you don't care."
4. By borrowing support interjecting another's position instead of giving your own such as "I think I speak for everyone when I say..." or "I agree with Dr. Brown when he says..." Debaters love this technique for gaining legitimacy for their own ideas.

5. Asking questions which expose weakness such as asking a beginner "How many times have you done so and so?" or unnecessarily asking an amateur for expert knowledge. Or saying "Have you done anything about . . ."
6. Asking for others' preference when hoping they'll suggest what you prefer.
7. Setting up the other person. Getting another to take a stand on ground you are prepared to knock out from under him. "Now I got'cha" is a cruel game.
8. Talking with cliches rather than describing in specifics.

Indirect messages keep others guessing. They cause attention to be directed to what is behind what is being said. Guesswork leads to misunderstanding and sometimes resentment. We don't like to be played with as though we are children or puppets. Indirect messages seem to beget negative responses: denial, deflection, and similar evasiveness. In short the attitude that "Two people can play the game you're playing."

Ineffective Coping With Stress On Self. Once we are of working age our self-concept is shaped by the dynamics of the work setting. In that interpersonal field, both positive and negative feedback interact with one's self-image. Feedback which is consistent with one's good image of self tends to increase one's feeling of self-worth. When one receives feedback which is inconsistent with a good self-image, feelings of self-worth are decreased. The individual who receives negative feedback must find ways of dealing with this stress upon his psyche. Under stress people may elect defensive and ineffective ways of coping. Virginia Satir suggests that four major ineffective methods of coping are: placating, blaming, distracting and computer-like responding.[11]

Placating. The placater tends to agree even when he does not agree. He wants so much to avoid disagreement and fighting that whatever another says is OK. He or she is forever blaming himself and apologizing so much that others feel sorry for him or feel guilty. He is passive, dependent, withdrawing, faceless, a people pleaser and a yes-man. He hides his own feelings by praising, agreeing, humoring and consoling. He counts himself out. "You count, I don't count." He plays underdog.

Blaming. The blamer is as disagreeable, bossy, and cantankerous as the placater is agreeable and phony. He finds fault, is aggressive and rebellious. He says, "I count, you don't count." He is judging, advising, dominating and puts others down. Almost every aggressive roadblock to communication is his: ordering, directing, commanding, threatening, moralizing, preaching, judging, criticizing, name-calling, ridiculing and shaming. He attends neither to the content or the feelings of other's messages, but rather discredits and devalues. He must be top dog.

Distracting. The distracter is always changing the subject. He is busy, busy, busy. In his hyperactivity he escapes discomforting feedback. He may take on a "live it up" or "who cares" posture. He ignores cues from others regarding their own needs. His roadblocks to communication are interrupting, diverting, and withdrawal. His frenetic flight behavior may be a plea for attention. He is not underdog or top dog but rather is a barking dog.

Analyzing. In a cool computer-like fashion the analyzer says, "Let's be reasonable." By analyzing he protects himself from his own hurt feelings. He has the right words and can find an intellectual explanation for everything. His head trip is so pronounced that he is boring, bland and devoid of emotion. His roadblocks to good communication are interpreting, diagnosing, lecturing, and logical arguments. He is the family psychologist, the little professor, the disqualifier. Gestures are absent or neutral. He is a cool poodle.

Direct Messages. Positive coping requires a riskier posture. The mask is cracked. He is real and he levels with others about his feelings, values and opinions. He can express either positive or negative feelings without trying to make points or put another down. He can criticize without blaming. He can shift subjects without trying to get off the hook. His messages are straight rather than circuitous, and yet not without tact. He can analyze without turning off his feelings. What he says is truth for him, without contriving ways to cover up feelings of weakness or help-lessness. His body is expressive and congruent with his words. He is open, alive, trustworthy and you know where he stands. He says, "I'm OK, you're OK," but he does not see the world through rose-colored glasses.

Effective coping begins with experiencing rather than covering up one's own feelings. Others do have their bad parts. A person who practices leveling communication may find the follow-ing steps helpful:

1. Describe specifically the behavior you dislike.
2. Express the feelings you have about that disliked behavior.
3. Suggest a better alternative,
4. Involve the other person by coming up with alternative solutions.

Levelers are essential to creating healthy environments. Feedback, to be really reinforcing of behaviors we like, must respond to other's good parts. Here are three simple steps to make that positive feedback more effective.

1. Describe the behaviors you like specifically.
2. Express the way the liked behavior makes you feel, and
3. Encourage the other person to keep doing those good things.[12]

Listening

Hearing and listening are related but not identical. Hearing refers more to the capacity or lack of physical capacity to perceive sound. Organizations must be concerned about hearing and auditory damage. Minimizing industrial noise level and requiring protective geat is a matter of federal safety regulation. So insuring individual capacity and suitable environments for message reception is a necessary requisite for listening.

Barriers to listening are also psychological. Perception is selective. Attention depends upon psychological readiness and the saliency of the message. Moreover, our cultural conditioning biases what we accept as worthy of our attention.

Memory reflects what we have determined is important. But it also reflects how much infor-mation we must process and how skilled we are at listening.

The listening problems we have just surveyed are not always present in every communicative experience. And as we noted earlier, we cannot be constantly thinking about how we are listen-ing or we will miss a good many of the messages being sent. But we can take stock of our listening habits and try to improve on them. What can we do to improve listening? Here is a list of suggestions that can help you improve your listening effectiveness in interpersonal settings as well as in more formal situations such as classroom lectures or public speeches.

Develop An Open Mind. Consider the advantages of knowing many things about many topics. In conversation, a broad knowledge of several topics can help you feel more comfort-able and make you a more interesting person to be with. One method of keeping an open mind is to ask honest questions, ones that reflect your own true interest about a subject and not ones that you think will appear intelligent, sophisticated or what others are interested in.

Proper Setting. Try to choose a place for your conversations as free from physical and psychological distractions as possible. Close out noise from surrounding areas and in interpersonal settings, choose a place to have serious discussions that will allow for full concentration by you, your partner, and friends.

Bias. Be aware of your biases and guard against letting them prejudice the message. Although you may have held a certain opinion for a long time, each new speaker deserves the chance to tell you what they know about a topic. The advantages of listening without bias are similar to those of having an open mind. New insights may be available to you, and you may discover someone whose company and support you appreciate.

Take Notes. In public and formal settings, do not be afraid to take notes. Taking notes can help you focus on the main points of the message. Later, when referring to your notes, it will help you organize the message so you can remember it more accurately and evaluate it more objectively. As you list points in your notes, ask yourself about them. Consider how well the ideas fit together and how well the evidence supports the points as compared to what you already know.

Reserve Judgment. Do not make up your mind until you have heard the entire message. Although you may think you know the direction in which the speaker is headed, he may introduce new information at the end of the message that will require you to reconsider. By reserving judgment, you also give yourself a chance to reflect on all the data of your own concerning the message.

Discover Common Ground. Ask yourself what things you know about the speaker that you share with him or her. While you are searching for things in common with a public speaker, consider the way he presents himself. Be careful to look beyond dress, to language usage, posture, gestures and movements; and any other mannerisms that may give you more insight into background, personality, and character. Certainly we all know the danger of forming opinions based on first impressions, but the empathic listener keeps that in mind while searching for any signs that will help him get closer to the speaker's feelings. One good suggestion is to put yourself in the speaker's shoes. And when you have begun to develop empathic listening, balance it with discriminative (critical) listening.[13]

Remain Silent. Do not be afraid to remain silent. If you find yourself in the middle of a conversation that you do not feel genuinely a part of, or when you really are not motivated to join, do not try to fake interest by offering thoughtless comments. You are an interesting person in your own right, and defensive or inadequate feelings about not taking part in certain conversations will not help you in your efforts to develop empathy, understanding, and clarity.

Credibility

Let us close this chapter by stressing that the real need is for credibility. Communication skills that are not backed up by solid products and responsible service bear the sounds of hollowness. But when backed up, it is communication that takes the message to the customer and public. For example, a good public relations man can do much to explain a billing system in understandable language, providing that it is explainable. We build a business by carrying a message which proves true. Robert Mason tells a story to illustrate the relationship between the goods and services and communication skills. It is a simple story of trickery to generate a positive image. But it also tells a folksy story of creative marketing and of a public who want to believe in the companies with whom it deals:[14]

> In the early part of this century a young door-to-door peddler of stockings and undergarments, who worked a few towns in upstate New York, tried an experiment. He got up very early one morning and drove to a town he'd never worked before. He was a good salesman and managed to sell several dozen pairs of ladies' cotton stockings that day. The next morning he started out even earlier, drove to the same town, went back to each of the women he'd sold stockings to the day before and said, "I'm very sorry, madam, I overcharged you one cent a pair on the stockings I sold you yesterday. I discovered the mistake when I got home last night. I just want to return the difference."
>
> Within a couple of weeks his business in that town multiplied several times. It was a carefully controlled experiment. He didn't try that ploy in any other town he worked. He sold the same merchandise at the same prices in the other towns. The experiment was successful, and he came to be known as "Honest Phil." He moved his family to the town of his experiment, opened a retail dry goods store, and prospered. The total cost of his successful public relations program—if it can be called such—was about 35 cents.

People are concerned about integrity. The "Honest Phils" of anecdotal yesteryears will not suffice for today. Governmental regulation and restriction over modern business will increase to the degree that the public loses confidence in the business sector. Over half of the people, for example polled by a Lou Harris survey, wanted more regulation of the oil industry at the peak of the energy crisis. Nearly the same percent (48 percent) felt the drug companies should have more regulation, and auto, insurance and telephone companies a lesser degree. Another Harris Poll reveals how uninformed the average person is about profits: 77 percent are either unsure or believe the average company nets over 30 percent on sales after taxes. Only a few realize that the average profit is actually under 10 percent.[15]

In order to develop a credible image systematically, a company must first inventory community attitudes and needs and next address these needs with competence, quality products, service and goodwill. Without skillful communication of information about the products and services—however high the quality—the public will lack knowledge and appreciation.

Within a company, job satisfaction of employees is directly related to subordinates' faith in superiors. The dimensions of credibility appear to be belief in the (1) competence and qualifications of one's superior, particularly in his ability to transmit information; (2) belief in the good intentions and trustworthiness of one's superior and (3) belief in the energetic activity of one's superior.[16] All of these dimensions of credibility which contribute to a good working climate depend upon accurate, sensitive, and supportive communications.

Sometimes we wonder if honesty is the best policy. We are tempted to pad expense accounts, to exaggerate and to shade the truth. W. Michael Blumenthal, who has held posts as chief executive officer for Bendix Corporation and Burroughs and served as Secretary of the Treasury answers the questions: Do nice guys finish last? in a rhetorically sensitive address to the Detroit Phi Beta Kappa:

> Of course, there are people who may gain some temporary advantage by cheating or cutting corners or by shoving the nice guys to the side of the road. And the rebellious, the perverse, the irresponsible impulses of human nature are such that we can even take pleasure, occasionally, in the spectacle of the scoundrel, especially if it turns out that he is really a brave and virtuous fellow in the end. What Cervantes in-

carnated in Sancho Panza, what Shakespeare incarnated as Falstaff, or even, on a different level, Nietzshe's "human-all-too-human," serve as eternal correctives to the tendency of character to become rigid, inflexible and humorless—to take itself more seriously than it should.

But these are not the models to which we turn in times like these, because we know in our hearts that enduring success, the success with which we can live, the success with which our country can live, cannot be built on flattery, cynicism or dirty tricks. It can only be built on character—which is to say, once again, on courage and on truth.

Character in this sense of the word is so uncommon, so far from being trite and banal., that one sometimes despairs of finding it again where it preeminently belongs—in the Presidency, in Congress, in the established institutions of our country. When one looks back over the disasters of the past fifteen years, over the blindness and blunders which mired us down in South Vietnam, and over the mishandling of the economy, the lack of foresight, the contempt for the consumer, the apparent selling of advantages for money and political favors, the actual criminality in the highest places, one sometimes wonders where the people of character have fled.

Well, I have good news for you. They have not fled at all. People of character remain our country's greatest natural resources, and my real purpose in coming here today is to urge you to join them as soon as you can.

Nor do I think you will have much trouble finding them in the homes, fields and factories, the churches, universities, trade unions and political parties of this country. We live nowadays in what Talcott Parsons, the sociologist, saw as a system of systems, a world of interrelated organizations, large and small. But more and more of us live and work, increasingly, in large organizations and these, more likely than not, will provide the stage on which you will play your role.

Your scholastic achievements suggest that you will be leaders. But *what* you do, as I have tried to impress upon you, is less important—especially at this juncture of our history—than *how* you comport yourself.

Never in our history have we had a greater need for people whose attachment to fairness, to ethics, to honesty and truth is absolute; for people who can marshall the courage to speak out, to say no to wrongs, to swim against the stream—even to resign an attractive job if that is the only way.

When that happens, if it ever happens, I know some corporate executives, a large number of them in fact, who will be very happy to receive your applications. They need your intelligence, your competence, your energy; but it is your character that they will need most of all.

Good character, good sense and goodwill. How necessary they are to any individual. These are the characteristics we want from our employees. These are the qualities we want in our employers.

One of the most moving experiences a parent can have is to be called to the police station and learn his child has been apprehended for shoplifting. The parent may not feel secure in his own home after that. When she/he checks his pocketbook there is that lingering suspicion: Did Janie help herself to a few dollars? It is terrible to live in a climate of mistrust.

Similarly, how disillusioning it is to live in a community in which public officials have been found using public monies for their own ends or to live in a nation which suffers because its highest officials were caught in a coverup. Respect and trust are not luxuries in any family, community or nation.

Recap

The image within the company is largely the image of top management held in the mind's eye of its employees. The complexity and giant size of modern business makes top managers invisible men. One problem, though not the major problem, is that their decisions fail to be communicated down the organizational ladder. Downward communication, however, in comparison to upward communication, is quite good. The major problem most often is getting accurate information up the ladder, keeping it free from self-serving distortion or simple loss somewhere in the many levels through which it must travel.

A systematic upward communication program can be designed. It cannot be a substitute for personal communication between intermediate management and the man in production, but it may do much to convince that worker that top management does care—that his concerns do matter—that his ideas are sought.

Interpersonal competencies are important to any successful work organization. This awareness has motivated numerous training efforts. These training approaches available fall in three broad categories which represent different assumptions: (1) self-disclosure which assumes openness, authenticity, and the transparent self makes for better working relationships, (2) interpersonal investment strategy which assumes that a secure personal base and a supportive network are in the self-interest of every organization, and (3) interpersonal congruence which assumes that sensitivity to others' work related attitudes enhances both manager and subordinates' satisfaction.

It should be stressed that interpersonal competencies can be learned. Those employees who by predisposition or by training place high value upon close interpersonal relationships and collaboration overall are most satisfied with their coworkers, and particularly so if their coworkers also hold these values.

Finally, it is our position that honesty is not just the best policy. Rather it is the best policy for business and organizational life and interpersonal relations alike because trust is so fundamental to societal cooperation and to emotional well-being.

When all levels within a company can be convinced that those at the top are genuinely interested in them, that image within will be contagiously carried to the community outside. That image within is healthy to the degree that members of an organization respect each other because of competence and character.

NOTES

1. Everette M. Rogers and Rekha Agarwala Rogers, *Communication in Organizations* (New York: The Free Press, 1975), p. 7.
2. Gerald M. Goldhaber, "The ICA Communication Audit: Rationale and Development," Paper presented at the Academy of Management Convention in Kansas City, August, 1976.

3. *Business Week,* May 4, 1974, p. 44.
4. Bruce Harriman, "Up and Down the Communication Ladder," *Harvard Business Review,* Vol. 52 (September-October 1974), pp. 143-151.
5. See Charlotte L. Stuart, "Architecture in Nazi Germany: A Rhetorical Perspective," *Western Speech,* Vol. 37, Fall 1973, pp. 253-263.
6. Harold D. Lasswell, "The Signature of Power," *Society: Transaction Social Science and Modern Society,* Vol. 14 (November/December, 1976), p. 82.
7. Proxemics and Kinesics, Slide-cassettes, Columbus, Ohio, Center for Advanced Study of Human Communication, 1974.
8. Carol A. Roach, "Actions and Images May Find You Wordless," *Journal of Communication Management,* Vol. 4, 1981, pp. 12-14.
9. Kenneth N. Wesley, Ralph A. Alexander, James P. Greenwalt and Michael A. Couch, "Attitudinal Congruence and Similarity as Related to Interpersonal Evaluations in Manager-Subordinate Dyads," *American Academy of Management,* 21, 1980, pp. 320-330.
10. Nicholas Dimarco, "Life Style, Work Group Structure, Compatibility, and Job Satisfaction," *American Academy of Management,* 16 June 1975, pp. 313-322.
11. Virginia Satir, *People-Making.* Palo Alto, California: Science and Behavior Books, Inc. 1972.
12. C.U. Shantz and K.E. Wilson, "Training Communication Skills in Young Children," *Child Development,* Vol. 43, 1972, pp. 693-698.
13. Larry Barker, *Listening Behavior,* Chapter 5, Englewood Cliffs, N.J.: Prentice-Hall, 1971.
14. Robert S. Mason, "What's a P.R. Director For Anyway?" *Harvard Business Review,* Vol. 52 (September-October, 1974), p. 126.
15. John L. Curry, "The Deteriorating Image of Business Public Opinion Points to a Pressing Need," *Bell Telephone Magazine,* Vol. 54 (January-February, 1975), pp. 10-13.
16. Raymond D. Falcione, "The Relationship of Supervisor Credibility to Subordinate Satisfaction," *Personnel Journal,* Vol. 52 (September, 1973), pp. 800-03.

A Look Into Your Future

Study Guide

I. *Primary Objective:* To gain experience composing and presenting a short speech from manuscript. *Secondary Objective:* To think about integrity.

II. Model: Bill Meade's "In Business In Good Concience"

III. Analysis: Each of us wants to be well thought of by our supervisors and the management of the place in which we are employed. Often, we are selected for a position with an organization because we convey the image that our sympathies and loyalties will be with the business. We want to fit in and to do so in good conscience. Study the following speech presented by a man in middle level management in which he reflects upon his determination to fit in and yet to be able to face himself in good conscience. After reading this speech, write one which you might present after working for ten years with a company. Let your audience be a service club or church group. Read the speech from manuscript. Occasionally a presentation or parts of a presentation will be most effectively presented if read. Particularly, when it is important that what we say is word-for-word accurate. So practice reading. Typing with dark ribbon and double space may facilitate your reading. Practice it until you can look up for several phrases in each paragraph.

IN BUSINESS IN GOOD CONSCIENCE

Bill Meade, Manager of Marketing Division,
Yusuf A. Alghanim and Sons, W. L. L., Kuwait

My present employer is a four billion dollar corporation. I am a marketing manager of a nine million dollar segment of that conglomerate and have two people working for me.

I have been in the business world since 1963 when I returned from the Peace Corps. During those ten years I have seen a steady increase in responsibility and income. During those ten years I have been told in the interest of the business to do things which conflict with my standard of being fair and honest at all times:

1. I have been told to quote to the United States Government higher prices because we are the only source. When I knew we didn't do the same to commercial accounts.

2. I have been told to charge two accounts different prices for the same product.

3. I have been told to raise prices in excess of price guidelines.

4. I have been asked to be an informer.

5. I have been told to tell my assistant he should stay fifteen to thirty minutes beyond quitting time because it looks better. How did I respond?

1. I complained about overcharging the United States Government. I was told it was about time we got back our tax money and think of the additional paperwork. That didn't satisfy me until I remembered the dentists that treated me during Peace Corps training that charged the United States Government four times the going rate.

2. I learned that different prices to different customers was legal. It still didn't seem right but since then I have seen competitive threats bring some order to our pricing.

3. I refused to violate the price guidelines because it was illegal. I did not threaten to blow the whistle I just refused to do something I considered unethical. My stand was honored. We lowered prices and reprinted price list.

4. I refused to be an informer because I respect the confidence people place in me. In the same vein, I refuse to engage in office politics because the falsehoods, intrigue, inneundos conflict with my standard of honesty and truthfulness.

5. I told my superior I saw no need for my assistant to stay late. He came in early. He worked through his lunch hour. He put in more than a fair day's work. However, I did discuss the matter with my assistant. I told him while I knew he was a hard worker, management only noticed he left on time. I counselled him that I understood he was anxious to get home to his family but placing his family as his highest priority would probably hurt his growth in the company.

I don't want the above list to lead you to believe there is a constant conflict between my values and business values. On the contrary, it has taken ten years to record those incidents. Conflicts are the exception rather than the rule. I enjoy my chosen field tremendously, I find my work challenging, rewarding and worthwhile.

I am pleased that in general I have been able to operate successfully in the business world. I have been pleased and encouraged by management's willingness to listen to my concern when I believe my job is in conflict with my standards.

Has my adherance to my values hurt my career? I am not sure. I don't believe I have reached my peak. However, I have noticed that individuals who never speak out or take a stand have progressed a little more rapidly than I. It could be I am less competent or it could be I am experiencing the honesty-dishonesty dilemma which pervades every type of organization in our American culture. That is, concern with honesty and human values becomes the sign that an individual is not mature enough to be entrusted with the responsibilities of making realistic political and economic decisions.

Bill Meade graduated from the Wharton School of Business, served in the Peace Corps in Tunisia, worked for a small manufacturing firm in Ohio, served as Manager of Marketing in Kuwait, and upon his return to the States went into business consulting located in North Carolina.

Whistleblowers vs. Informers

Study Guide

Consider the following opinions. Indicate your agreement or disagreement with each quotation.

Agree
or
Disagree

"The men the American people admire most extravagantly are the most daring liars, the men they detest most violently are those who try to tell the truth."
— H.L. Mencken, famous journalist

Agree
or
Disagree

"If I were asked to name the deadliest subversive force within capitalism — the single greatest source of its waning morality — I should without hesitation name advertising. How else should one identify a force that debases language, drains thought, and undoes dignity?
— Robert Heilbroner — author *New York Review of Books,* June 1981

Agree
or
Disagree

" 'Whistle-blowing' after all, is simply another word for 'informing.' And perhaps it is not quite irrelevant that the only societies in Western history that encouraged tyrannies — Tiberius and Nero in Rome, the Inquisition in the Spain of Philip II, the French Terror, and Stalin...For under 'whistle-blowing,' under the regime of the 'informer' no mutual trust, no interdependencies, and no ethics are possible."
— Peter Drucker, business consultant, *The Public Interest,* Spring, 1981

Agree
or
Disagree

"When an employee is concerned about the public's welfare or worker's health, but the boss is cutting corners to boost the profit margin, whistles will be blown. Likewise, government officials who are favoring old friends or paying off campaign contributions to the detriment of the public should be hearing whistles in their dreams."
— Michael Jackson, codirecter of the Center for Science in the Public Interest
in *Business and Society Review,* Fall 1981

Whistle-blowing is called for in cases in which an employee is told to cooperate or not to worry
1. in knowingly false reporting to the government in matters of auditing.

Agree
or
Disagree

2. when work with a product or process will result in dangerous or unsafe levels beyond acceptable health standards
3. violating consumer protection laws, anti-trust decrees, waste disposal, poison to the public, etc.
4. age, sexual or racial discrimination, or harassment.
— paraphrased from Alan Westin, professor of public law at Columbia University and author, *Whistle-Blowing!,* McGraw-Hill, 1981

**Agree
or
Disagree** States should pass Whistle Blowing Protection Laws such as passed by Michigan. Michigan's Act provides that where an employee contacts public authorities (not the media) over alleged illegal conduct by the employer and is then discharged or punished for doing so, the employee can bring suit in the courts. If the employer can not prove that its action was based on valid personnel reasons, the employee can be awarded damages or reinstated and the employer fined.

**Agree
or
Disagree** "Employees who make cost-cutting suggestions are rewarded; why not reward employees who focus attention on corporate problems that could turn into disaster later? The worst that can happen is that a reckless employee will make irresponsible charges; but unlike an individual who is a victim of an 'informer,' a corporation has major resources to fight back."

— Robert Ellis Smith, publisher of *Privacy Journal*
in *Business and Society Review,* Fall 1981

**Agree
or
Disagree** "You might say that corporations have begun to distribute whistles to employees. ....An internal self-policing system has obvious direct benefits for health and safety."

— Monte Throdahl, Senior Vice President of Monsanto
Business and Society Review, Fall 1981

3

Communicating with the Community

Chapter Outline

    General Considerations
    Formats
    The Speech of Praise
    Telling Your Company's Story
    Graceful Speech
    Introductions
    Facing the Camera
    Recap

Project Three-1:	*The Speech of Praise for Your Community*
Project Three-2:	*Telling the Organization's Story in the Community*
Project Three-3:	*Graceful Speech*

Chapter Objectives

    Those who complete this chapter should better understand:

1. the importance of audience adaptation;
2. how certain formats can be employed in developing the speech of praise;
3. the role of business in addressing its wider constituencies.

> The 1904 World's Fair was in Saint Louis. It was Labor Day. The American Cereal Company gave away free samples of Quaker Rolled Oats to the delight of snacking children, but something bigger was at hand. Spanish War cannons were unveiled to the fanfare of a band. They were heated in gas-fired ovens, while the crowd was told that the 550-degree heat was converting the moisture to steam in the gains within their plugged muzzles of the cannons. Then they were removed from the ovens and fired. Puffed rice shot from guns rained down. Covered with caramel coating the puffs were boxed and sold to gaping onlookers.
>
> —paraphrased from Arthur F. Marquette,
> *The Story of Quaker Oats*

We want to be proud of the place where we live and work. To be sure, it takes time to cut the grass and to plant flowers. Any place can grow weeds and slums and crime. Pride is the message every business must peddle. To neglect this is an expense that no business can afford. A prideless community is ripe for vandalism, crime, ghettos and weeds. So, how do we go about selling a people on the place where they live? We must do a good job, for our businesses are at stake. Obviously, leaders in business and industry must lead the drives for physical beauty, for parks and golf courses, for reclamation of rivers that have too long been dumping stations. It is business that must encourage lighting and plazas and the policeman walking the streets. It is business that must spearhead drives for the Community Chest and the United Fund. Hygiene and health factors, of course, are in our self interest.

Now any good thing takes time and money. And since time and money are two commodities which we each prize, the decision to part with these involves considerable persuasion. It's not that humankind is unsufferably selfish, it's just that we want to invest wisely—and we have a long history of our dollars being spent by bureaucrats. Therefore, it behooves every institution in the community to join forces to talk up the town.

John Irwin and Herman Brockhaus: "The Teletalk Project: A Study of the Effectiveness of Two Public Relations Speeches." *Speech Monographs,* 30, (1963), 359-68.

Basic Question(s): Can a public relations' speech by representatives of a business organization improve the public's attitudes toward the organization? Specifically, which of three speech formats (lecture, slides, or demonstration may result in greater interest, information gain and favorable attitude toward several telephone companies in Wisconsin?

Subjects and Procedures: Some 500 adult women of all ages who were members of eighteen women's organizations listened to one of two speeches. One was on technical advances with no appeal for support of the telephone companies; the other favored career women directly appealed for the company. A young man, a mature woman, and a mature man working for the company's public relations presented the speeches in rotated order. Pretests revealed a positive attitude toward the telephone company. In groups of twenty-four, the women listened to the speeches during one of their regular meetings. During the presentations, the twenty-four listeners indicated their interest by moving a lever between high and low levels on a instrument especially constructed for this purpose.

Results: Both speeches elicited more positive attitude toward the telephone company. The speech on technical matters was rated more interesting but the one on careers generated more goodwill for the company, possibly because that speech made an appeal for support or because the speech showed how the telephone company helped women who wanted careers in business. Neither the lecture, slide presentation or the demonstrations aroused a greater interest or more improved attitude than the other form of presentation.

Implication: This carefully controlled study demonstrated that public relations' speeches did enhance an already positive image of a company. A speaker's bureau, therefore, may prove to be one of the more effective kinds of public relations a business can have. Lecture, slide presentations and demonstrations appear equally on attractive medium.

Figure 3.1. Can P.R. speakers help their company?

General Considerations

The message must be affirmative and it must be personal. This chapter is designed to develop skills in telling that story. So let's now look at a basic format for a short presentation intended to create a positive community image.

Consideration 1. Adapt to the audience and occasion. A presentation that is designed to please every audience is one that likely means very little to any audience. This is true for almost all community gatherings—be they patriotic, religious, social or educational. Consequently, adaptation is a matter of discovering what interests a particular group of people. If the occasion is a Tee-Off banquet at the Firestone World Series of Golf, the speaker should find stories about the community that dip into the sport's history in that region and, more particularly, of the personnel involved in that particular tournament.

Consideration 2. The message should be "warm." Warmth grows out of struggle and sweat. Often it is closely linked with tears, and, sometimes, with colossal blunders.

Consideration 3. The story is the basic form of support. A story in itself doesn't prove a point so much as it helps one visualize and empathize. It is when we visualize that we vicariously experience, particularly when that story is factual rather than hypothetical. Almost anything that involves people has a story behind it, or lurking nearby. The story does not have to begin "Once upon a time" but it usually begins with some reference to when and where it took place and with *your* connection with the story. That is, did it happen to you, one of your friends, was it told to you by someone involved in it, or did you come across it in the newspaper or some other way? Following this orientation, the story usually proceeds in a chronological order, describing the people involved and their relationships. Interest grows out of conflict, struggle and absurdity. Imagery is elicited out of figures of speech, color, movement and references to the senses. Few executives, no matter how successful and sophisticated, can easily stir and stimulate an audience without the aid of a story.

Consideration 4. Make the message personal. Your listeners are interested in you—in your ideas and in your feelings about this community. So *do* use the word "I" and do share some of your experiences and dreams for this place.

Consideration 5. People read your muscles. If you want to generate enthusiasm, you must be psyched up and pepped up. If you want to generate commitment, your intensity must be visible in your face, gestures and voice. Do not think you must be an actor or a preacher, but rather a businessman, who lives here and wants to make this place one of the nicest spots on earth.

Formats

The Reasons Why Format. One of the authors once, for an after dinner speech, drew from a hat the topic "Three Reasons Why I Love My Wife," and to the amusement of all he stammered a bit trying to find the appropriate words for that seemingly easy assignment. We mention this "three reasons" format as one design for a short Great Town Speech which, for example, might be given at the dedication of a new park. The skeleton of such a presentation might look like this: "There are three reasons why I like this community":

  1. We are a people who love to eat and drink;

2. We are a people who love beauty and who are beautiful lovers;
3. We are a people who care about our children.

The businessman who would elect such a format, of course, would need to have at least one story to illustrate each of these reasons. The format is simple, but effective. The ostensible purpose of such a presentation would be to celebrate the occasion, but the real purpose is much more profound. The persons who join in such a celebration, whether it be after the completion or at the initiation of such a community project, are publicly committing themselves to the community. They are joining hands by word and deed. Sometimes this occasion includes lifting a spade full of earth, cutting a ribbon or toasting one another. The net effect is getting a sense of community *identity*.

One Reason I Think We Have a Great Town. This could be a simpler type of format; for example, "I think this is a great town because of its senior citizens." Two or three stories about the achievements or kind deeds rendered by this class of citizens completes the one reason format. The formula is direct: One Reason + Three Illustrations = Point. The point, as we stated before, is not proved so much as it is affirmed. The person who makes such a speech, of course, is stroking the senior citizens. But more importantly, he is acknowledging them as fellow citizens and affirming his willingness to hear their concerns, as well as indicating his willingness to profit from their toil and sweat which built the community.

The Fantastic Time Format. Yet another simple format is what might be called the "Fantastic Time." It consists of a simple statement such as: "It's been a fantastic year," which is followed by a list of several events. Each event can be humanized by a short account of some person who was instrumental in seeing that event through. "It's been a fantastic time" can be completed with any length of time from fifty years or one week. The important thing is that the stories illustrate some warmly human concern.

Let's Dream for Our Town Format. Pride comes from becoming part of great dreams. And it is a city's business community which must articulate and communicate those dreams. We live in an age in which more than eighty percent of the people of our country live on two percent of the land. Such crowding means trouble, and dictates that those who have a stake in that crowded space must lead the way in planning. Recently, the Goals for the Greater Akron Area (GGAA), which, incidentally, is a city near the authors' homes, brought together some fifty-five residents for a three- and one-half-day conference. The chairpersons were a housewife and M. G. O'Neil, President of the General Tire and Rubber Company. In that weekend conference, the group spun some seventy-seven dreams, foremost among which were dreams for the economy. The GGAA's report of these dreams also called for a positive community attitude and image: "We must tap the ingredients for greatness-character, pride, uniqueness, a strong work force and other community resources." And then it listed the ingredients to attract industry and commerce: such amenities as sewer, water, transportation, housing, schools, parks, and cultural activities.

The report stressed the dreams for a "strong public-private partnership to strengthen the area economy" through such varied approaches as land banks, bonds to stimulate new industrial growth, tax relief, and cooperative promotion campaigns. In calling forth such a dream, the GGAA defined and identified with the future. They became a rhetorical force helping the community realize that "business and labor must recognize the mutual benefits of a strong competitive economy, and cooperate fully, to create a climate conducive to meeting our ideal goals." Increasingly, O'Neil discovered that his involvement led to his spokesmanship for those dreams. It was he who was asked to address the United Fund-Red Cross Campaign. It was he who was called upon to speak to the Chamber of Commerce in cities in adjoining states. In his address for the United Fund he said:

> Most of you will recall that the United Fund in Summit County was born twenty-two years ago when certain leaders in the community saw the great need for combining Red Feather and other agencies along with the Red Cross into one fund-raising drive. It is fair for me to say the advantages to the community of this wise undertaking have proven distinctly favorable! . . . and profitable.
>
> Now the leaders see another need . . . and that's the need I'd like to use the remainder of my time to talk about. What I'm really doing is taking time to talk publicly for the first time about the new job I've undertaken for this area where you and I live.[1]

His address continued to outline the need for pride:

> Pride in the community is a powerful thing. The wider it is demonstrated, the easier it is to achieve results. It is a motivator—the force that moves mountains.[2]

The Speech of Praise

The "Let's Dream for Our Town," thus, is more than lofty rhetoric. It is a way of gaining public commitment to mutually beneficial goals. What are the basic components in such a presentation?

The Times. Every effective address is a unique event. The times, the speaker, occasion and audience are brought together, for better or worse. Most often there are motivating stimuli on the part of both speaker and listener for making an arrangement to bring each together. Likely the reputation of a man or woman is the stimulus which prompts the invitation. Upon other occasions, it is the position which dictates who will preside or address a body; for example, it is expected that the president of a company will address the annual stockholders' meeting.

In a very real sense an invitation to speak poses a challenge. The challenge laid down dares a man to be as good as his reputation, and yet not to be a carbon copy. He must be more than expected. Somehow, he must fit the image held and yet reveal more of himself—new ideas, or old ideas put in a novel way. Not to do so is similar to Babe Ruth or Hank Aaron striking out!

The creative interaction of the social environment and a rhetorical event may be well illustrated by an acceptance speech of a "gold key" award presented by the Avenue of Americas Association. This Association is one of a number of "neighborhood" groups of businessmen based upon the geographical location, such as the Fifth Avenue Association, a Lower Manhattan group, a Times Square Association. In 1972 Sheldon Fisher, President of McGraw-Hill, Inc., and its Chief Executive Officer, was named as recipient of the Association's annual "gold key," along with Miguel Aleman, former President of Mexico.

The events which prompted the award were obvious. The McGraw-Hill Corporation had recently made a decision to stay in New York City at a time when the press had given front page coverage to another firm which chose to move its corporate headquarters from the city.

Mr. Fisher's topic for his acceptance speech thus grew out of a decision to stay in town. Moreover, McGraw-Hill had just completed an "ascertainment" study of conditions in several other communities to aid them in a petition which they had filed with the Federal Communications Commission to acquire five television stations. The "ascertainment" study of local problems in other cities had convinced Mr. Fisher and his top executives who assisted him with the study that other communities also had problems, some of them as serious as did New York

City, and that these cities could not match New York City in advantages.

These were the circumstances which prompted the "gold key" award and motivated the message which Mr. Fisher prepared for its acceptance. Yet when the evening came it was scheduled at the tail end of a long evening. Ambassador Aleman's speech which came first required simultaneous translation and an already restless audience grew even more uneasy and noisy.[3] Mr. Shelton Fisher thus was forced to ask for attention. He began: "I cannot compete with nine hundred of you. If you will give me ten minutes to listen to me, I will stay behind to listen to anything you have to say, even if it takes all night." The request was effective. And after the speech was over, he was greeted with a tremendous ovation. In the next few days, requests for copies of the speech came in. *The New York Times,* which had formerly consigned the earlier "good news" that McGraw-Hill had decided to stay in town to page 58, asked permission to reprint the speech in a promotional brochure it issued some time later.

Yet another amusing sidelight was recounted. Abraham Beame, the controller later to become Mayor, was engaged in a running battle with Standard and Poor's Corporation over the unsatisfactory rating this firm accorded New York bonds. (Standard and Poor's is a McGraw-Hill subsidiary.) After the speech by Mr. Fisher, Mr. Beame approached him and said: "I wish you'd send a copy of that talk to your own people downtown."[4] Again some two years afterward, Mr. Beame recalled that evening and speech in a conversation with Mr. Fisher.

An effective address is a unique rhetorical event melding together the times, a speaker (or speakers), an occasion and audience. Bear this in mind as you read Shelton Fisher's acceptance speech for the gold key award.

Identification. Notice, too, as you read, the sense of identity revealed in the address. Shelton Fisher clearly and modestly revealed who he was and how he identified with his audience. A speech is only a now event when it is personal. Mr. Fisher identified with his audience and he demonstrated that identity by his frequent use of "I" terms. In this short address of approximately six hundred words, he used such terms as "I, my, we, our, and us" over sixty times, and "you" terms only thirteen times. The personalness, moreover, is revealed in the content of the message. His whole address was a personal narrative about why he and his McGraw-Hill staff liked New York well enough to stay there. He talked about his colleagues and about the streets and people of New York.

But let us examine the speech as a whole.

Remarks of Shelton Fisher
The Avenue of the Americas Association
Western Hemisphere Day Dinner
New York Hilton Hotel
October 11, 1972

Thank you very much for this special recognition.

I am accepting it tonight on behalf of my company, and I intend to share this award with my colleagues in our new headquarters just four blocks south of here on the Avenue.

Sharing this award with the McGraw-Hill staff is not a grand gesture, for they are the real reason we are located in your midst instead of some other city, or the suburbs, or even some more remote rural retreat. And thus, they deserve the credit given the company and its officers for contributing to the stability of New York City. I know that's the real reason why I am one of your honorees tonight.

You might like to know why our decision to stay in New York with 3,000 people (featured on page 58 or one of our local papers) was in contradiction of a trend of some corporations to leave the city with, for example, a headquarters of 250 people (featured on page one of one of our local papers).

In the early Sixties it became apparent that we had outgrown our building on West 42nd Street. We had already spilled over into eight other buildings. What to do? Should we consolidate in New York City? Or should we move out?

We considered both alternatives — and in doing so, discovered some interesting things about ourselves. One, especially, led to our decision to stay. We early realized that a company like ours — a company which has no manufacturing facilities but relies for its fortunes on the creativity of many people — such a company simply does not have a real option to leave this city.

If we had moved away, our human loss might well have been crippling. Much of our talent, particularly the younger ones, would have balked at being closer to the solitude of some remote spot than to other editors, artists, writers and sales, promotional, creative people of their own kind.

Commentary

Opener

Mr. Fisher, in his first simple sentence thanks those who made the award. Following this greeting, he demonstrates goodwill toward his colleagues by stressing that *they* are the ones who deserve the award because they were the real reason that McGraw-Hill decided to locate its new headquarters in the neighborhood of the Avenue of the Americas.

In a modest way, Mr. Fisher quickly established his competence to speak: reference to their new headquarters building and the problem in the early Sixties of whether to consolidate in New York served as tangible evidence earning his right to speak about that decision; by reference to his position as a publisher in a city of publishers; and by reference to a more recent search of other cities for a suitable location for McGraw-Hill's new TV stations.

The subject of the speech — "keeping business in New York" was obviously of interest to those who belonged to the association.

The bad press served as a stimulus to justify the choice of topic.

In things spiritual, as well as in things material, there is considerable truth in the maxim that "only a diamond can cut diamond." Talents develop and grow when exposed to other talents. In New York, and in particular in this, our new neighborhood, we are rubbing shoulders with all sorts of talent, and some of the best in the world. Why should we want to escape that fraternity? Think of our neighbors... *Time-Life, The New York Times, Newsweek* and *Esquire* and other major magazines are only steps away. This is the center of *book publishing* activity. And all along our Avenue are the *television* networks — and TV is McGraw-Hill's *newest* endeavor.

In short, the comfort, productivity, and growth of our employees depend more on their proximity to their fellow professionals than to their proximity to green pastures.

Moreover, we publish for all ages and all strata of American society. It takes a plentiful supply from all ethnic groups and creeds to do that. Only here could we be sure of finding enough of *this* talent.

In a word, our people — rather than the economic or sociological factors — were our first and determining consideration.

To be absolutely certain of our decision, however, we took a long look at the advantages and disadvantages of the city versus the suburbs. Our conclusion: There's not a great deal wrong with the suburbs; there *is* a great deal right with the city. People talk of New York's problems—perhaps they overstate them because *everything* in New York is bigger and better illuminated, including the problems. And while people talk of the advantages of the suburbs— it's just possible they overstate those, too.

As for crime, New York does not have a monopoly on it, as lurid as our published record is. F.B.I. figures *do* show that crime rose by three percent in cities of over a million population. But the crime rate was up 10 percent in rural areas, 11 percent in the suburbs, and 12 percent in small towns. You can lose your wallet in Westchester, too, and drugs today are no respecter of geography. If you think so, talk to the Police Chief, as I have, in Bakersfield, California.

Transportation is something of a standoff. It's bad here, but at least a vast system is in place and new rolling stock is coming. Washington is digging its first subway, and Denver doesn't have *any* public transportation. On the other hand, driving to work in the smaller cities and suburbs—while it favors some employees—is absolutely impossible for others, particularly those who can't afford two cars.

As we continued examining the relative merits of the city and countryside, an interesting thing happened. We realized that you don't really appreciate something you have until you consider the possibility of giving it up.

For example, we reawoke to the fact that New York is the commercial and financial center of the country, the hub of its communications and the heart of our cultural activity. With our involvement in all these fields, we just could not be anywhere else.

In addition, even as we discovered that life can be difficult in New York, we discovered that this wasn't necessarily a disadvantage. Some folks tried to tell us that life was too competitive here, that you had to scramble too hard to overcome transportation and other problems, that you have to be tough to be a New Yorker. And we asked ourselves: What's wrong with building your *business* with people who are competitive, who are used to scrambling, and are accustomed to overcoming problems? Do you build success with *non*competitors?

Moreover, as we looked closer at New York, we discovered that it isn't just a "big city." New York is a small world, with all the cosmopolitan advantages that implies. Nor is our new neighborhood just a neighborhood—Rockefeller Center is a city within a city. Within its limits are shops, restaurants, services, and facilities that even some of our *large cities* cannot boast.

Commentary

Development

The Development of the speech was a narrative description of New York City's comparative advantages to the suburbs, e.g., creative people. The "only diamonds can cut diamonds" metaphor captures his feeling about this interaction with those neighbors: *Time-Life, The New York Times, Esquire,* book publishers, and television networks.

Fisher encapsules his feeling in the short phrases—"There is a great deal right with the city" and *"everything* in New York is bigger and better illuminated, including the problem" serves as a cue to his comparative evaluation of New York's problems with other cities and the suburbs, e.g., crime, drugs and transportation. Here statistics reported by the F.B.I. are used to support his argument that other places also have increasing problems of crime. And reference to a conversation with a police chief in a California city is called up to argue that other places also have drug problems. To illustrate that New York's system of transportation could be worse, Washington, D.C., which is digging its first subway and Denver which has no subway provide concrete contrasts.

He lists the difficulties which New York has, but which others have more of. Then Mr. Fisher shifts again to the offensive — suggesting that one doesn't value what he has until one may have to give it up. He moves dynamically from problems to the advantages of having to scramble and compete in this exciting "small world" of New York City. This climactic language speaks — contagious enthusiasm.

Finally we believe New York has been through the valley. It inherited a bad press, but has retained many great people and that means great business enterprises. Some time, on a clear day or night — (and they are getting more numerous) — go to the top of your favorite building, look out and try to imagine all force of human energy drying up and blowing you away.

I have done that and felt the full force of its impact — economic social and personal. This city is forever... and I hope my company will be.

Thank you, Mr. Salomone, for New York and for McGraw-Hill.

Commentary

In the closure of this address, Mr. Fisher waxes eloquent. His style is still direct and plain. He does not quote literary people, but rather paints with broad strokes a picture of where New York has been "through the valley" and of what she can not become: "go to the top of your favorite building, look out and try to imagine all this force of human energy drying up and blowing away." The highlights of his message are symbolically woven together.

His closing paragraph is poetic and personal: "I have done that and felt the full force of this impact — economic, social and personal. This city is forever..." The acceptance speech is complete with a final word of gratitude. Aristotle put it well when he said of epidictic rhetoric, "To praise a man is akin to urging a course of action." By praising New York, Mr. Fisher urged those 900 business neighbors in the vicinity of Rockefeller Plaza, to affirm anew their determination to keep their headquarters in the city.

Telling Your Company's Story

Modern business is greatly concerned about its public image. Public utilities want to have their consituents understand the costs of service. Private industry wants the public to understand their efforts to correct and prevent environmental damage. Business wants potential investors to have faith in the future and for consumers to understand that profits are not unreasonable. The Eaton Corporation, for example, published an ad which pictured a spade being pushed into the earth. A red, white and blue bow was tied to the spade to celebrate the ground breaking. The script described Eaton's expansion and the 135 billion dollars which American Companies spent for that purpose in 1975.

The Chesapeake and Potomac Telephone Companies serves some 126 communities in a territory between Wheeling and Baltimore. In the face of steadily declining public confidence toward the business community in general, C & P launched a program to build confidence at the community level. They developed community relations teams. Members of the teams come from employees in customer service, network services, operator services, and staff departments. In some cases, personnel from other lines such as AT&T Long Lines and Western Electric, were also represented.

How to read an annual report

By Jane Bryant Quinn

International Paper asked Jane Bryant Quinn, business commentator for the <u>CBS-TV Morning News</u>, columnist for <u>Newsweek</u>, and author of <u>Everyone's Money Book</u>, to tell how anyone can understand and profit from a company's annual report.

To some business people I know, curling up with a good annual report is almost more exciting than getting lost in John le Carré's latest spy thriller.

But to you it might be another story. "Who needs that?" I can hear you ask. *You* do—if you're going to gamble any of your future *working* for a company, *investing* in it, or *selling* to it.

Why should you bother?

Say you've got a job interview at Galactic Industries. Well, what does the company do? Does its future look good? Or will the next recession leave your part of the business on the beach?

Or say you're thinking of investing your own hard-earned money in its stock. Sales are up. But are its profits getting better or worse?

Or say you're going to supply it with a lot of parts. Should you extend Galactic plenty of credit or keep it on a short leash?

How to get one

You'll find answers in its annual report. Where do you find *that*? Your library should have the annual reports of nearby companies plus leading national ones. It also has listings of companies' financial officers and their addresses so you can write for annual reports.

So now Galactic Industries' latest annual report is sitting in front of you ready to be cracked. How do you crack it?

Where do we start? *Not* at the front. At the *back!* We don't want to be surprised at the end of *this* story.

Start at the back

First, turn back to the report of the *certified public accountant.* This third-party auditor will tell you right off the bat if Galactic's report conforms with "generally accepted accounting principles."

Watch out for the words "subject to." They mean the financial report is clean *only* if you take the company's word about a particular piece of business, and the accountant isn't sure you should. Doubts like this are usually settled behind closed doors. When a "subject to" makes it into the annual report, it could mean trouble.

What else should you know before you check the numbers?

Stay in the back of the book and go to

in its pocket. Are earnings up? Maybe that's bad. They may be up because of a special windfall that won't happen again next year. The footnotes know.

For what happened and why

Now turn to the *letter from the chairman.* Usually addressed "to our stockholders," it's up front, and *should* be in more ways than one. The chairman's tone reflects the personality, the well-being of his company.

In his letter he should tell you how his company fared this year. But more important, he should tell you *why.* Keep an eye out for sentences that start with "Except for..." and "Despite the..." They're clues to problems.

Insights into the future

On the positive side, a chairman's letter should give you insights into the company's future and its *stance* on economic or political trends that may affect it.

While you're up front, look for what's new in each line of business. Is management getting the company in good shape to weather the tough and competitive 1980's?

"Reading an annual report can be (almost) as exciting as a spy thriller—if you know how to find the clues. I'll show you how to find the most important ones here."

the *footnotes.* Yep! The whole profits story is sometimes in the footnotes.

Are earnings down? If it's only because of a change in accounting, maybe that's good! The company owes less tax and has more money

Now—and no sooner—should you dig into the numbers!

One source is the *balance sheet.* It is a snapshot of how the company stands at a single point in time. On the left are *assets* – everything the company owns. Things that can quickly be turned into cash are *current assets.* On the right are *liabilities*—everything the company owes. *Current liabilities* are the debts due in one year, which are paid out of current assets.

The difference between current assets and current liabilities is *net working capital,* a key figure to watch from one annual (and quarterly) report to another. If working capital shrinks, it could mean trouble. One possibility: the company may not be able to keep dividends growing rapidly.

Look for growth here

Stockholders' equity is the difference between total assets and liabilities. It is the presumed dollar value of what stockholders own. You want it to grow.

Another important number to watch is *long-term debt.* High and rising debt, relative to equity, may be no problem for a growing business. But it shows weakness in a company that's leveling out. (More on that later.)

The second basic source of numbers is the *income statement.* It shows how much money Galactic made or lost over the year.

Most people look at one figure first. It's in the income statement at the bottom: *net earnings per share.* Watch out. It can fool you. Galactic's management could boost earnings by selling off a plant. Or by cutting the budget for research and advertising. (See the footnotes!) So don't be smug about net earnings until you've found out how they happened—and how they might happen next year.

Check net sales first

The number you *should* look at first in the income statement is *net sales.* Ask yourself: Are sales going *up at a faster rate* than the last time around? When sales increases start to slow, the company may be in trouble. Also ask: Have sales gone up faster than inflation? If not, the company's *real* sales may be behind. And ask yourself once more: Have sales gone down because the company is selling off a losing business?

If so, profits may be soaring.

(I never promised you that figuring out an annual report was going to be easy!)

Get out your calculator

Another important thing to study today is the company's debt. Get out your pocket calculator, and turn to the balance sheet. Divide long-term liabilities by stockholders' equity. That's the *debt-to-equity ratio.*

A high ratio means that the company borrows a lot of money to spark its growth. That's okay—*if* sales grow, too, and *if* there's enough cash on hand to meet the payments. A company doing well

"For inside information, an annual report is second only to meeting with the brass behind closed doors. Come on in!"

on borrowed money can earn big profits for its stockholders. But if sales fall, watch out. The whole enterprise may slowly sink. Some companies can handle high ratios, others can't.

You have to compare

That brings up the most important thing of all: *One* annual report, *one* chairman's letter, *one* ratio won't tell you much. You have to compare. Is the company's debt-to-equity ratio better or worse than it

used to be? Better or worse than the industry norms? Better or worse, after this recession, than it was after the last recession? In company-watching, *comparisons are all.* They tell you if management is staying on top of things.

Financial analysts work out many other ratios to tell them how the company is doing. You can learn more about them from books on the subject. Ask your librarian.

But one thing you will *never* learn from an annual report is how much to pay for a company's stock. Galactic may be running well. But if investors expected it to run better, the stock might fall. Or, Galactic could be slumping badly. But if investors see a better day tomorrow, the stock could rise.

Two important suggestions

Those are some basics for weighing a company's health from its annual report. But if you want to know *all* you can about a company, you need to do a little more homework. First, see what the business press has been saying about it over recent years. Again, ask your librarian.

Finally, you should keep up with what's going on in business, economics and politics here and around the world. All can—and will—affect you and the companies you're interested in.

Each year, companies give you more and more information in their annual reports. Profiting from that information is up to you. I hope you profit from *mine.*

Jane Bryant Quinn

Each team used films,talks, exhibits, telephone office tours, community leader interviews, company sponsored membership and telephone educational tools such as the Teletrainers. However, the team was more than public relations. One of its first chores was to inventory the community communication needs and to assess problems in meeting these needs.

The team also investigates the adequacy and appropriateness of public information, and tries to determine if employees have enough information to make them effective spokesmen for the company. In one instance,the community relations team purchased 465 garden and craft tools and made them available through lending libraries to "Adopt-A-Lot" participants to help inner city residents who wanted to neighborhood garden.[5] (Also see fig. 3.1)

Every speech is a unique event wedding the times, the audience and the speaker. It is a personal interaction. It is a now event. Therefore, it behooves a speaker to remember that he has an identity, not just a personal but an organizational identity, and that he conveys a message that may enhance or hurt his organization. The business leaders of a community often realize and act above and beyond the ordinary citizen. They are the ones who must be the builders and preservers of the community. They have a natural and necessary enlightened self-interest in communicating with the community.

The company story most certainly is told. Hopefully it is a positive one. (Study the models at the close of this chapter.)

Graceful Speech

Speeches of tribute are ritualistic instruments of socialization, or in plainer language "being civilized." To honor one another is to affirm and reinforce honorable behavior. And it is to identify oneself and one's organization with that worthy individual and organization. Such speeches should be brief, as short as 30 seconds (particularly if there are several other awards being presented on that occasion) and at most 10 minutes. Most presentations or toasts can be well done in one to two minutes. Speak from the heart. Do not use notes.

Tips for making a Presentation or Toast
1. Refer briefly to the occasion.
2. Refer to the achievement of the recipient(s).
3. Express your own good will on behalf of the audience.
4. Present the gift, certificate or toast. If it is a toast, lift the glass in tribute as you speak, and then lead the group in taking a sip. It is customary for all to rise during a toast.

Accepting a gift and accepting a tribute may be as short as a "Thank you" but in a few words may also gracefully acknowledge your debt to the group and organization making the presentation, and thus modestly turns the spotlight back to them.[6]

Toasts may be simple wishes for future success and happiness or more poetic or humorous tease such as is domonstrated by the examples which follow:

- Tonight I propose a toast
  To one person so modest she will
  Think we are toasting someone else.
  Ms. Jay, may there be many more
  Like you. Please accept our thanks
  for serving as our chairperson. May
  this next year be a lot less stressful.

- Let us have wine and women, mirth and laughter.
  Sermons and soda water the day after.

- Here's to those who love us
  And here's to those who don't.
  A smile for those who are willing to
  And a tear for those who won't.

- Here's to the wine,
  Here's to the glass,
  Here's to a lady
  With a lot of class.

- You only live once, and if you live
  right as the man we honor tonight,
  once is all you need. Cheers.

- May we never flatter our superiors
  Or insult our inferiors

- May we all live in pleasure
  and die out of debt

- Here's to our very own computer technologist
  who still uses all his fingers and toes for the
  simpler problems of arithmetic.

Introductions

If you were preparing an introduction what would you say? Remember that the purposes of an introduction are twofold: first to help the audience feel warmly receptive to the speaker and secondly to help the speaker feel comfortable with his audience. When introducing, one should be careful not to praise and list so many of a speaker's accomplishments that he feels that he must apologize or make light of his achievements. An introduction should present the speaker's name loud and clear. If he is well known, once may suffice. If he is not well-known to the audience, his name should be mentioned two or three times.

Background material often is available about the speaker. From that material prepare your remarks in fifty words or less to accomplish the two goals of a good introduction. If the speaker you are to introduce can not provide you with a written "bio," do some informal probing. Notice the artifacts (trophies, photographs, certificates in his/her office). Chatting even a few minutes before you present the speaker often elicits human interest items you might find relevant to your introductory remarks.

One must avoid several pitfalls when introducing a speaker:

- Stealing the spotlight by speaking on the same topic or by being so clever that the speaker seems dull.
- Exaggerating the speaker's qualifications, so much so that he is embarrassed.
- Forecasting his/her success. Do not set a speaker up by telling the audience what a great speaker you're about to hear.
- Overused introductory languages such as "We have with us a person who needs no introduction..." "We are gathered here..." "It is indeed a pleasure..." "Without further ado, I give you..."
- Telling too much. An introduction should not be a cradle to platform account. Rather it should focus on the topic of the hour and the reason for this speaker for this audience.

The Jaycee Lessons in Effective Speaking which the authors have taught suggest the following question serve as a formula for introduction preparation. Answering this succinctly will set the stage nicely:

Why this subject for this audience at this time by this speaker?

One of the most popular speakers to business audiences suggests a sure-fire way to get an appropriate introduction: **"Write it yourself and hand it to the person who asks, 'What shall I say about you?'."** When you then rise to speak and acknowledge the kind words of introduction you can say in all honesty, "I appreciate those fine words of introduction; you read them well, just the way I wrote them."

Facing the Camera

Organizational representatives had better get some training for appearing on television. It is unwise to wait until a crisis, be it a chemical spill or a nuclear disaster, when the media will force your appearance to seek professional advice or to wing it. Here are some tips. They will only help if you arrange for practice and feedback in a nonthreatening situation.

1. Prepare. Know your facts and how they were gathered, when and where. But don't overload your listeners with statistics. Short examples are easier to remember and more interesting. Never try to bluff or fabricate. It is much better to say I don't know than to be trapped in an exaggeration or an unfounded claim. Good interviewers can smell out lies and fabrication. Rehearse. Rehearse. Rehearse. Practice answering questions put forth by your coworkers. Before you speak for your organization, go through the proper organizational red tape to get whatever authorization necessary to do so.

2. Deliver your message with conviction. Use simple words and emphasis. Avoid rigidity in voice and gesture. Don't preach or play tough on the one hand and don't pussyfoot and gesture limply on the other.

3. Package it small. Prepare to say what you have to, that which is essential, in 60 seconds. Don't feel you must provide an elaborate preparatory statement. There will be a time later, if at all, to elaborate.

4. Don't get angry. Even if an interviewer tries to picture you and your company in a bad light. Don't reply in anger. Rather focus on the positive. Avoid sarcasm and never try to clown. Assume a serious yet friendly demeanor.

5. Don't hang back. If several are being interviewed or are there to participate in a discussion, don't wait to be last or have to be coaxed to join in. Of course, talking over another is rude and makes it impossible for others to hear clearly, but you do need to assert yourself. The reason you are there is to present your opinions. So stay alert.

6. Remember the central message you wish to present. Do not be sidetracked. Return to your theme. Say it in another way.

7. Dress conservatively. Solid colors, pastels are better than whites. Leave the flashy jewelry and the glitter at home, unless of course you are in show biz.

8. Don't speak to the camera. Rather talk to the interviewer unless your host invites you to speak to the audience out there. In that case, talk directly to the lens.

9. Prepare visual aids. Keep them simple and uncluttered. Use color and symbols rather than detailed graphs. Do not use more than one or two aids for a short presentation.

10. Prepare a press release to accompany your presentation.

Recap

In this chapter we have focused upon public relations, in particular on the speech addressed to the community. It is particularly important to adapt, to be warm, to use a narrative (story) approach, to be personal, and genuine. Organizational formats, of course, may vary from the very simple to the complete. The beginning speaker will find his presentation clearer and easier to give if he follows simple patterns.

The last portion of this chapter focuses upon ritualistic speech. Such speeches of introduction, tribute, toasts and acceptance of recognition, indeed, are important instruments contributing to social harmony.

NOTES

1. M. G. O'Neil, "Goals for Now and the Future," Mimeographed copy of an address to the United Fund and Red Cross Campaign, September 13, 1973.
2. *Ibid.*
3. Theodore S. Weber, Jr., Senior Vice President of McGraw-Hill, Inc., in a letter to the authors, July 22, 1974. The authors are indebted to Mr. Weber for the background commentary upon this address.
4. *Ibid.*
5. Frank Ovaitt, "Facing The Communities We Serve," *Bell Telephone Magazine,* January—February, 1975, Vol. 54 pp. 22-27.
6. *Members Guide to Speak-Up.* Tulsa: U.S. Jaycees, 1967, pp. 7 and 8.

Project Three-1

The Speech of Praise for Your Community

Study Guide

The "Great Town" presentation is one of the easiest places to start one's training as a spokesperson for business and professional organizations. To speak in behalf of one's own community raises our awareness to those many positive struggles and simple victories that are not far from where we live. To speak in behalf of one's community not only opens one's eyes to the positive efforts all about us, but it tends to motivate us to want to give more of ourselves to constructive enterprises. Business and industries intimately interact with the quality of life in the communities in which they are based. In addition to Mr. Fisher's speech about the "Big Apple," two "small great town" speeches prepared by students in business and professional speaking classes may serve as models. Study them and then construct a Great Town speech of your own. (They are found on the following pages.)

There is some controversy over whether it is advisable to write out one's speeches in full. Those who argue that speeches should be only outlined believe that outlining only maintains spontaneity. The mind must remain active searching for the right word, adapting to the moment and making contact with the audience. Persons who write out manuscripts tend to use them. They often are more focused upon the manuscript than the audience. In some cases they read poorly. In others they try to memorize them word for word and present them canned. The antimanuscripts arguments are persuasive.

What then are the reasons for taking the effort to put one's words into manuscript? There are equally sound reasons for putting one's speech into manuscript. A manuscript provides a record as well as a fluent instrument to aid one's delivery. Some speeches or parts of speeches may be presented to a different audience. A manuscript may also serve as a press release. Organization of one's message may be more carefully examined and language more carefully selected. A speaker should be able both in reading a manuscript speech and in delivering a speech extemporaneously from a detailed or a key word outline.

Our recommendation is that a speaker prepare a manuscript when there is sufficient advance time and that the manuscript should be revised for clarity and impact. For most situations, we recommend that the speaker should speak from a keyword outline. For your Great Town speech try following the sequence:

- Make a rough list of ideas and examples you want to put into your speech
- Do a manuscript
- Revise and polish your manuscript
- Make a key word outline for use in the delivery

1. Write your rough list of ideas and examples here. Use only a few words.

2. Study the two models which follow.

Not Even a Night Spot
But a Nice Spot

Spending nineteen years or an entire lifetime in one place has its disadvantages but these seem to be outweighed by the fact that I can call this place my home. My home is not something everyone would like; there is no congestion. There is not even a wild night spot. But Copley, Ohio, is a place that does not need those things since Copley is only about ten miles west of Akron and twenty miles south of Cleveland. We are a small township of 8,600 people which makes for good school sizes. Most of the schools in Copley are relatively new; the high school is only five years old and is the nicest in the district. People in Copley are very education minded and always are passing levies to better our system. Copley schools rank high on the accrediting scales of Northeastern Ohio. The schools are not the only good feature of Copley though. In fact the area itself is even more important to me. There are hundreds of playing fields and grounds along with all sorts of parks. Copley also has many streams running through it, that are good for having lots of fun. One thing we do not have is a lot of are factories to pollute the waters or air. Copley refuses to in-corporate because it does not want to grow too quickly or get too many factories. Of course we are expanding but we are still preserving the township we now have.

To most people who have heard of Copley, they think of it as hayseed country, an area of continuous farms. Although there are numerous farms in the area, there are also very developed allotments just packed with houses. But most homes in Copley are neither farmlike nor citylike, they sit on a number of acres and the houses are rather far apart. This does not keep the neighbors distant though. I have grown up with my neighbors and they treat me with much warmth and respect. One of our oldest residents was never lucky enough to have grandchildren of her own, so everyone that knows her has adopted her as Grandma or Mom. It took me years to figure out that she really was not my grandmother. These people who live in Copley are very friendly and helpful. If someone is in need, then someone else is not too far away to help.

More often than not those who do the helping are not even paid. Specifically I am talking about Copley's Volunteer Rescue Squad, which the whole town is proud of. Most communities do not compare with our system. This department is funded by our taxpayers who have never voted NO on the annual ballot. They also contribute a lot of money towards new equipment such as the telemeter. One day last summer after a collection was taken for the Squad, my friend's grandfather collapsed. We immediately called the Squad and they were there in less than three minutes. An am-bulance could have taken three times as long and the Rescue Squad does not cost a cent. Besides the patient get four paramedics instead of the normal one. Because of the tremendous work these volunteers are doing, Copley is constantly donating more and more. Recently the fire department expanded to five trucks and two rescue vehicles. People are also willing to donate hundreds of hours in training and duty to insure our safety. I feel so much safer with the volunteers around than if a funded department was established.

Copley Township is my home and I am proud to tell people I am from there. Its people are friendly and concerned and, its area gives chances for many different types of life. I enjoy the variety of life styles that Copley offers because there is always another area to go explore. Besides Copley really is not located out in the sticks, there are places to go and things to do. I think just about anybody would feel at home and fit in here.

Deborah Lowry

They Don't Make Many Towns Like That Anymore

Twenty-one years is a long time to stay in one place, especially when the average person moves every five years according to national statistics. I'v lived in Petersburg all but six months of my life, and I wouldn't mind spending the next twenty-one years there too, because I don't think they make too many towns like Petersburg anymore.

Petersburg is a small town twenty miles south of Youngstown and just this side of the Pennsylvania border. I wish I could take you there to see it. It's not very big— only eight hundred people, but they are some of the warmest people I know. One example of their caring is what recently happened in connection with the drugstore.

The drugstore is the only one in town, serving not only Petersburg, but two or three other communities as well. The town lies in a farming area, so the farmers have come to rely on the drugstore for veterinary supplies. Mothers go there for prescriptions and a sick room supplies, and sooner or later, nearly everyone in town ends up there to ask advice or to simply pass the time of day and exchange local gossip. A few months ago, the store was burned almost completely on the inside when thieves attempted to break in from the basement. The store has been robbed on several occasions, and this attempt, like the others was by adolescents to obtain narcotics for street sale and use.

Within a week after the fire, the townspeople had set up a trust fund for the drugstore, and a short time later, ten thousand dollars was in it. The man who owns the hardware across the street donated part of his warehouse facilities for the druggist to use as a store to help him get back on his feet. A nearby pharmacy assisted in getting the drugs and supplies needed to get the druggist back in business. The burned building is being torn down now, and within six months the druggist hopes to have a new store. Townspeople are tearing down the old building, townspeople are helping to pay for and put up a new one, and townspeople will patronize the new drugstore when it's done.

The drugstore isn't the only important place in town. Down the street, the Presbyterian church has just lost its minister. He moved to Dayton to serve a church there, but no one in Petersburg wanted to see him go. The last Sunday he preached, the church was packed. Chairs were set up in the basement, and people stood the entire time, some nearly in the rain, to hear his sermon that day. After the service, the minister didn't even stay to shake hands. He took his coat and immediately went home. He said later, that it seemed easier on everybody not to say good-bye.

The town cares about its students, too. Being a farming community, we are not rich, and money is often hard to come by for college. Realizing this, the Volunteer Fire Department of Petersburg gives out a one-hundred dollar' scholarship each year, and the local Ruritans give a three-hundred dollar scholarship. The church takes up special collection twice a year, dividing the receipts among the college students of the congregation.

People like these make me glad I've stayed in one place so long and make me think about spending the rest of my life there, because they don't make too many other towns like Petersburg, Ohio, anymore.

                                                                    Phyllis Sutherin

3. Developing your stories. Select stories that you can describe in detail, that you can visualize the settings, hear the dialogue and can recall the sequence of events. Practice story development by completing the following sentences.

1. Where did it begin?_____

2. When did it start? _____

   and what time of year was it?_____

3. Where were you when it started? _____

4. Who was involved at the beginning?_____

5. What was the setting?

   Inside? _____ Outside?_____

   What colors were visible? _____

   What smells? _____

6. Now what conflict occurred, if any?_____

   _____

7. What sequence, events, accidents, problems, frustrations, conversations, thrills, adventures

   took place? _____

8. What feelings do you have about this story? _____

   _____

9. Finally what were the outcomes? What happened to whom with what results? _____

   _____

Crafting your manuscript may involve extensive rewording, additional examples and/or striking out here and there. If possible, type or have your final draft typed. Be sure to make an extra copy. Use typing paper.

Title: _____ Your name _____

Write in one sentence what you want your audience to understand, to feel or to believe after you have finished speaking.

_____

_____

_____

Opening Statement _____

_____

_____

Development. Remember the strength of the story to support each point or use at least two stories to support your theme.

First point _____

      Story #1

      Story #2

Second point _____

      Story #1

      Story #2

Closing Paragraph _____

_____

_____

_____

Telling the Organization's Story in the Community

Free enterprise at its best believes in paying its dues to the community in which it is headquartered. It is also well aware that the human resources and many of its natural and financial resources come from the land and products of those many communities wherein its plants are located.

Study the address to the Akron Bar Association by Charles J. Pilliod Jr., Chairman of the Board and Chief Executive Officer of the Goodyear Tire and Rubber Company, February 1980.

Answer the study questions below.

1. What is Mr. Pilliod's thesis? What belief, conviction, emotional support or action does he desire from his audience?

2. What impressive statistics does he use to help his listeners realize how vital Goodyear is to Akron?

3. Read the closing section of this address aloud. Notice the use of the word "will." Can you convey a spirit of determination and optimism in your voice and body?

A Look at Akron in a Competitive World

An address before the Akron Bar Association

Charles J. Pilliod Jr.
Chairman of the Board and Chief Executive Officer
The Goodyear Tire & Rubber Company
February 7, 1980

I was very pleased when Dick Chenoweth asked me to speak on the U.S. competitive situation as viewed from Goodyear headquarters and to offer an opinion on the future of Akron. Strange as it may seem, from Goodyear's viewpoint, the two are inter-related. But, I'll save my comments on Akron until the last.

In considering Akron's future and the forces bearing upon it, I'm going to echo a theme made famous by one of your colleagues, possibly known personally by some of the verteran members of the Akron Bar Association.

I refer to that famous lawyer Wendell Willkie who reminded us so often 40 years ago that we live in one world. That was never more true than today when every country, from a business standpoint, is just across Akron's doorstep.

There was a time, however, when that was not so. And, unfortunately, there are some — many in high places of authority — who still find that one world concept hard to accept and tend to base our national and business policies, in part at least, on conditions as they existed in the past.

Until a few decades ago we were a nation envied throughout the world; a nation with an abundance of low cost raw materials ready at hand; a highly motivated, productive work force; a more than adequate supply of capital; leadership in technology; a growing population providing an ever-expanding market; and the opportunity for volume production with the resulting low cost.

We were self-sufficient in every sense, and we parlayed that position, dominating world markets and creating the greatest standard of living the world has ever known.

But in so doing, our appetite for raw materials gradually exceeded our own known supply and over a period of time we have lost some degree of that self-sufficiency. Our most noticeable lack of raw materials, of course, is petroleum, but there are others, such as copper, vanadium, rubber, etc.

Technology no longer USA exclusive

Many of the other advantages we long held have now disappeared as well. Raw materials are now a world market commodity available in all major markets at competitive prices to all. Technology is no longer a U.S.A. exclusive; U.S. labor has long ceased to be a model of productivity; capital, if not available in local markets around the world, can be obtained from any number of international institutions at competitive interest rates; and as there are fewer and fewer real trade barriers between nations, for all practical purposes, U.S. industry is just one of many striving to market its products in a common international arena.

If you have any doubts of the international scope of business today just look around you. If you represent a cross section of the U.S. citizenry, and I believe you do, 25 percent of you will be driving imported cars, probably from Japan, Europe or even Brazil. That same percentage will be returning home this evening to view television on imported sets, your dinners will be prepared on an imported stove. Possibly you will sit down to work on your U.S. income tax utilizing a pocket computer made in Japan or play electronic games on units made in Taiwan. Fifty percent of the heat in your home will be provided by imported fuel, and even the alarm clock that awakens you in the morning to start the new day will have been made in Switzerland or Japan.

World economy is competitive

U.S. products are also visible in foreign markets so insofar as business of all nations is concerned, Wendell Willkie was correct — it's one world. The only thing I'd add to that is that it's also a very competitive one.

And, accepting the fact that the world economy is a competitive one, we must ask ourselves how we, as a nation, are faring. Where do we stand in relation to our major trading partners? Are we ahead, or behind and what plans are being formulated to insure our leadership for the future? The answers to those questions could tell us what we can expect in the way of a solution to our inflation and unemployment problems as well as true improvement in our standard of living.

We already have the answer, in part — we have a growing negative balance of trade, indicating we are selling less abroad than we are buying, inflation is increasing at an alarming rate and unemployment is up, so the answer is obvious... "Not so well."

We started from a higher base than our competition. But, we are losing ground rapidly to such dynamic nations as Germany and Japan which are outperforming us on nearly every level.

It's an over-used crutch

And we cannot fall back on the excuse that it is all due to our dependence on imported oil. That's an over-used crutch for politicians at election time that should not be acceptable as an excuse for lack of economic progress.

As an example, Germany, Japan and even Switzerland, which are experiencing greater true growth, more improvement in standards of living, less unemployment and a slower rate of inflation than the United States are required to import 100 percent of their petroleum requirements, as compared to our 50 percent. In addition, they are not blessed with the same degree of alternative sources of potential energy that we enjoy.

A further indication of our competitive rating that might surprise you: we have not increased the number of U.S.-made cars sold in this country since 1965. In 1965 approximately 8.5

million of the passenger cars sold in the United States were produced in the United States. In 1979, 14 years later, we had yet to surpass that figure; although we had begun to approach it with about 8.3 million U.S.A. produced cars sold in the domestic market. In other words, the natural growth in passenger car demand over the last 14 years has been supplied not by U.S. production, but by foreign imports, produced with foreign labor.

Even if we were to exclude Canadian imports, which are produced in part with U.S. components, the results change very little. As of last year, 22 percent of the cars sold in the domestic market originated in countries other than the U.S. and Canada vs. 6 percent in 1965.

Imports equal to 11.5 million tires

Akron is the rubber capital of the world and that figure might be more meaningful to you if I said 1979 auto imports represented over 11.5 million tires — or, on a normal U.S.A. plant schedule, more than 45,000 units per day. That would require a larger plant than any you have seen in this area, and at today's cost represents an investment of over $350 million, manning or employment exceeding 2,300 hourly and 470 salaried personnel, with an annual payroll above $40 million.

Other facts could be provided to illustrate the declining competitive posture of U.S. industry in the world market but it can all be summed up in the following: our trade balance over the past 10 years has fallen from a surplus of $607 million in 1968 to a deficit of $28 billion in 1978, the last reported period.

We are living beyond our means — making up the difference with a devalued currency, and growing debt adding to our inflation. We are fast approaching the point when we must recognize the old axiom, "as an individual, a company, or a nation, over any extended period of time, we can only consume what we produce," and adjust our standard of living accordingly. That in effect is what government leaders are telling us when we speak of gas rationing, heat controls, higher taxes, etc.

The reasons behind this are many and no area of our society can escape shouldering a portion of the blame. The government, overreacting to the demans of special interest and pressure groups, has increased costs unduly through over-regulation in all areas including environmental, safety, consumer protection, equal rights, shareholder protection, etc. The list is endless and while each taken on its own is deserving of government interest, the accelerated rate of regulation and costly controls being applied have increased costs far above that experienced by any of our foreign competition and have added to our cost disadvantage. It also is true that these regulations have contributed little in the way of material value and thus have added to inflation at home.

Business — labor cooperation needed

In the area of productivity, U.S. management and labor have failed to put their act together on a basis competitive to our foreign counterparts in the more productive nations such as Japan and those in Europe. Because of the high cost of capital, many foreign plants, in our field in particular, are operated on a 7-day-a-week basis with 40 hour rotating shifts. This provides for greater capital utilization and overall lower labor cost per unit of output.

Also, we find a greater recognition of the need for efficiency moves on the part of foreign labor even at some sacrifice as they understand, in the long run, high productivity is their best guarantee of job security and increased income.

Business also must shoulder a portion of the responsibility for its failure to ensure the modernization and capital required to provide labor with the tools for improved production efficiency. It also has failed to ensure a level of research and development effort sufficient to maintain technological leadership.

Possibly our greatest concerns, however, are with the Administration's failure to properly address the energy problem and its policy of mixing foreign politics and trade relations with friendly nations long supportive of U.S. goals. An outstanding example of this is the uneven application of the human rights doctrine.

Doctrine has been misapplied

We all support human rights and that is not the issue. But the lop-sided application of that doctrine has brought a deterioration of trade with some of our most important trading partners, adversely affected our balance of payments, and created problems that could plague us for generations.

It's not possible to estimate the total loss of business for American companies — and jobs for American workers — resulting from various restraints based on the human rights issue. But, a few examples of the countries affected are well worth mentioning.

There was little the U.S. could do in promoting a civil rights program in socialist-oriented countries where human rights, as we know them, have never existed. So the burden of U.S. government restriction fell upon friendly nations whose levels of respect for human rights, while evident, had not yet attained a level enjoyed in the United States. In the process, we turned on many countries long noted for their friendship and support of U.S. trade, forcing them to take their business elsewhere.

While some countries may accept this as a temporary measure and renew their trading ties with us at a later date, it does establish us as an unreliable supplier and it may take generations to repair. A good example of the harm of this policy is Brazil, the largest and most progressive nation in Latin America, which has been forced to seek other sources of supply both in product and capital. Investments from European countries have been sought and are now well established. As a result, U.S. trade with Brazil has continued to decline and despite the best of efforts may never be fully recovered.

Last year a study of our foreign trade policies indicated that they actually bordered on an anti-trade policy. As a part of the human rights program, we had applied trade restrictions to the three largest countries in South America — Chile, Argentine and Brazil. We had a boycott against the two leading industrial nations in Africa — Rhodesia and South Africa. We had an Arab boycott in the fastest growing area of the Middle East and trade restrictions resulting from human rights issues against the two largest in Southeast Asia — The Philippines and Indonesia.

Common sense is the answer

At this point we must ask ourselves, can all this be corrected and the U.S. competitive position be restored. The answer is yes! All it requires is the application of good common sense in the establishment of our policies and actions in the major segments of society — government, business and labor.

First of all, we must address the energy problem with the objective of encouraging the rapid development of all potential sources. This should include full use of our available coal, nuclear power, synthetic fuels and, of course, expansion of the production of the conventional fuels, oil and gas.

It is a known fact that with normal methods we obtain only 25 percent of the available oil in a well and an additional 25 percent can be obtained through tertiary recovery methods. It's more expensive but the price in world markets today should encourage it given the proper incentive. Natural gas is still available if we look for it. Maybe not in large quantity but it's there. We have a number of wells operating and I see by this morning's paper Cuyahoga Falls is about to make application for OPEC membership as well.

The point is we should not confuse our objectives between developing our energy sources and tax issues. We all understand the need for energy expansion but I'm afraid of greater importance in the eyes of our politicians is the opportunity to get their hands on further taxes to spend in non-productive areas.

Consumers pay the added cost

A tax is a tax by any name and who among us does not realize that you as the consumer will pay it as added cost to your fuel.

If we are afraid the oil companies will reinvest in other areas, set your tax structure in such a way that they are encouraged to invest only in the energy field. That should not be difficult and it will work to the advantage of the nation. They are experienced in the field and can do the job much more efficiently than the government or newcomers.

The recent signing of the Foreign Trade Agreement providing for more equal treatment in the tariff field is a step in the right directions. The Carter Administration has also shown a tendency to relax trade restrictions on human rights issues where it applies to friendly nations. The improvement of human rights should be encouraged but I would hope we will see a return to the doctrine applied in the past which was based on the United States supporting democracy where-ever it appeared in the world but acting as custodian solely of its own.

There also is a great deal of encouragement in the effort of business and labor to work closer together in ensuring the competitive status of U.S. production. Certainly the attitude of more and more for less and less must be abandoned in favor of a joint program promoting higher productivity which will result in greater job security and increased material benefits for all.

There is a strong awakening on the part of U.S. business that their competition is international and they are gearing up to meet it. A good example of this is the automobile industry and its accelerated drive to re-equip their manufacturing facilities in order to provide the more fuel efficient cars of the future. I have little doubt that they will succeed and given time for their efforts to come into being we will see a marked turn around in imports.

The same is true of the tire industry, which, whether you appreciate it or not, is going through the same trauma as the automobile industry. We too are called upon to make massive investment, in order to re-equip our facilities to produce smaller, as well as, radial designs. In the process, some older, less efficient plants have fallen by the wayside as you so well know. Also some of the smaller firms such as Mansfield and Gates have dropped from the tire business completely.

We're gearing up to meet competition

I believe the worst is past, however, and we are rapidly gearing up to meet the demand and competition from any source.

In the area of government regulation, all politicians are voicing support of reduction, but this is an election year. It will be interesting to see if they follow through once the votes have been cast.

There is no alternative, however. Inflation and unemployment are the priority issues in the minds of the public today. Neither can be properly addressed without giving full consideration to our worldwide competitive posture. Old Wendell was right. It's one world and we can't get off. So, let's recognize it and get competitive.

In Goodyear, as we are multinational, no major move is made without due consideration to the worldwide effect. We do, of course, favor local manufacture for local consumption but investments involving supply to third nations are carefully scrutinized in order to determine the most efficient base. The selection of equipment is only made after investigating all known worldwide sources to determine the latest in technology and price. It is only in that way that we will maintain world leadership.

Performance measurements also are conducted on a worldwide scale not only in manufacturing units but in the service areas as well. We run cross-checks on product unit cost, labor productivity, capital utilization, etc., on a regular basis in all operations regardless of nationality. As a good example, we check mold cost between our two plants—one in Stow and the other in Luxembourg—when placing an order for molds to a third country. Happily, Stow has fared well but it is a close comparison and we cannot let up on our efforts for continued improvements in efficiency or Stow will soon be left behind.

Our development center in Luxembourg also competes with our development operation in the U.S. Luxembourg has had an edge in facilities but we expect to rectify that with the Tech Center now being established in Akron which will be the most advanced in the world.

Goodyear will grow in Akron

Akron is our headquarters, the place where members of our top management and our corporate staff live and one we would like to see grow and prosper. I believe we can support that statement with the fact that we have continued to invest in this area. Last year our capital expenditure in Akron for expansions and modernizations exceeded $21 million. In addition, we have approved plans such as completion of the Tech Center, the facilities required to manufacture centrifuge units at Aerospace and other miscellaneous projects—in progress which total over $70 million. I would see no reason to stop there and would expect our investments in Akron to continue to grow, particularly in the service areas such as research, development and other support functions for our worldwide operations.

I believe this is all to the good for Akron. A gradual move away from dependence on labor-oriented manufacturing has been taking place over the past decade and has had beneficial results. Employment, I am told, is at an all-time high and certainly we must all admit that service industries are much more stable than manufacturing which is more responsive to the volatile fluctuations of demand.

Akron is extremely well equipped as a location for service industries and the highly educated technical and administrative people they will employ. For a city of this size, we are abundantly blessed with cultural facilities—the E.J. Thomas Performing Arts Hall, the Art Museum, the Ohio Ballet, the nearby Blossom Center and the University of Akron. Our school system is one of the best in the state. Recreational facilities are excellent and varied—gold, tennis, boating, fishing, skiing, hiking; name it and the Akron area has it.

And the neighboring Colisuem has proved a boon to sports fans.

Akron is still the rubber capital of the world, the nerve center of the huge tire and rubber industry. It is also a focal point of the trucking industry and a growing center for service and technology.

Akron has grown with changes

Its character has changed in the past decade, and it has grown with the changes. It will continue to do so as long as the community and its leaders exercise a collective "will" for improvement of the area and the quality of life it offers.

Our community "will" seems extra strong these days. It shows in the determination to improve the downtown area; to preserve the downtown YMCA building; in the plans for a new Art Museum; the communications effort to stimulate pride in Akron and action for its improvement, and the movement for noncompetitive scheduling of public service fundraising.

Since it is the headquarters for so many large multinational companies, national and international developments certainly will impact on this community. But, the manner in which the community reacts to exterior forces will be up to its citizens. The cutting edge that will shape Akron's future is in our own hands. That future looks good.

This community is entering the '80s with a positive sense of direction, a new cohesiveness reflecting better intra-community communications, a new respect for coordinated planning and a new willingness of formerly divergent forces — such as business and labor — to work together toward common goals.

With sound and active leadership, and I believe we have it, that work will succeed.

Graceful Speaking

Study Guide

II. Objective to gain experience in making a public presentation and in acknowledging a presentation.

II. Guidelines. Using the guidelines on a graceful presentation speech and toasting, prepare such a tribute to a classmate. To avoid duplication each class member's name should be put into a hat and another's name should then be drawn.

Immediately after the tribute, the individual accepting it should acknowledge the gift or toast, also in keeping with the guidelines.

4

Using Written Channels and Technical Media

Chapter Outline

Written Media
Supportive Visual Media
On-the-Spot Graphics
Supportive Audio Visual Media
Three Dimensional Media
Recap

Chapter Objectives

Those who complete this chapter should better understand:

1. how to write clear memos;
2. how to organize and prepare their own resume;
3. principles of effective visual-audio media;
4. principles of appearance on television.

"All media work us over completely. They are so pervasive in their personal, political, economic, aesthetic, psychological, moral, ethical and social consequences that they leave no part of us untouched, unaffected, unaltered. The medium is the message."

—Marshall McLuhan[1]

In the preceding quotation, Marshall McLuhan presents his belief in the pervasiveness of channels or media of communication. The media are extensions of ourselves and hence our selection of media and how we use them in turn communicates something about us—they are extensions of ourselves. They speak about us. They can tell others if we are prepared or unprepared; confident or unconfident; neat or untidy; organized or disorganized.

The implication here is that the media are our message. Thus, choices we make about how to send our messages are important ones. We are not only communicating something to others through our message but we also tell something about who we are through our selection of media.

The questions that should confront every organizational communicator is this: Am I choosing the most efficient and effective channel possible to get my message across to my receiver? and Should more than one channel be used to get my receivers to understand my message as I desire them to understand it? These are important questions for all communicators to answer.

You will recall that in chapter two your authors present basic principles/functions of communication. It is important that you realize the significance of these principles if you plan to utilize them effectively when communicating within the organizational setting. For example, if I believe that communication is a symbol-creating, picture making and image-eliciting process whose purpose is to change uncertainty to greater certainty, what are my responsibilities as a communicator within an organization?

One responsibility I have is to be sure the image or picture I have in my mind is comparable, at least, to the image or picture you have in yours. That is, to reduce the amount of misinterpretation people can place on the symbols or words I use to communicate. One way I can aid the communication process is selecting appropriate channels of communication, given the context and what I know about my receivers. I can increase the chances of my messages being received as I desire them to be received by utilizing more than one channel of communication.

What are the types of media or channels available to organizational communicators? They are many and varied. Consider the following:

Memoranda, reports, company manuals, attitude surveys, house organs, newsletters, resumes, job application forms, directives, brochures, maps, posters, charts, cartoons, industrial movies, slide show presentations, video taped training films and graphs.

These are some examples of the media available to us, but what do we actually communicate to others through our use of these media? If McLuhan is right, if the medium is the message, what message are we sending through our selection of these various media? In order to answer this question, let's take a closer look at the media.

With such a vast array of media available it would be impractical to deal with all of these in this one chapter. Therefore, we have decided to present the most common media you may have to utilize as an organizational communicator. For analysis purposes we have divided these media into four basic categories.

1) Written media
2) Supportive visual media
3) Supportive audio-visual media
4) Three dimensional media

Let's now closely examine these four categories and see how and why one might utilize these media in business and industrial settings.

Written Media

This category describes the kinds of media that utilize solely the written channels of communication. Printed materials are sent to receivers in the hope that they will pick them up, read them and understand the intent of the message. In this case the medium is the message. You have only one channel to capture and keep their interests so you have to make the most of it. Examples of these media would be: company reports, house organs, directives, memoranda, and resumes. You can see from these examples that these media are designed to use the visual senses only. Although some of these media may be used along with oral presentations, their primary purpose is to communicate in writing. Let's examine two written media you might be expected to utilize in an organization.

The Memoranda. The memoranda or memos are in-house means of communicating from one organizational member to another or a group of people. They are used to announce or arrange meetings; to request action be taken; or to notify individuals of an incident, event or happening. It is important to use this written medium when proof of correspondence is required. In preparing to use this medium you should indicate *who* the message is directed to, *from whom* the message is being sent, *what* the message is about, and *when* it was written. In framing the contents of the memo it is important to remember the following points:

- Be clear and concise (don't use ambiguous words)
- Adapt to the reader's knowledge of the subject (you need not go into detail if the reader is knowledgeable of the event being discussed)
- Keep in mind the reader's position in the organizational hierarchy (adapt the language to the reader)
- Adapt the tone of the memo to the formalness or informalness of the situation or context.

How to write clearly

By Edward T. Thompson

Editor-in-Chief, Reader's Digest

International Paper asked Edward T. Thompson to share some of what he has learned in nineteen years with Reader's Digest, a magazine famous for making complicated subjects understandable to millions of readers.

If you are afraid to write, don't be.

If you think you've got to string together big fancy words and high-flying phrases, forget it.

To write well, unless you aspire to be a professional poet or novelist, you only need to get your ideas across simply and clearly.

It's not easy. But it *is* easier than you might imagine.

There are only three basic requirements:

First, you must *want* to write clearly. And I believe you really do, if you've stayed this far with me.

Second, you must be willing to *work hard*. Thinking means work—and that's what it takes to do anything well.

Third, you must know and follow some *basic guidelines*.

If, while you're writing for clarity, some lovely, dramatic or inspired phrases or sentences come to you, fine. Put them in.

But then with cold, objective eyes and mind ask yourself: "Do they detract from clarity?" If they do, grit your teeth and cut the frills.

Follow some basic guidelines

I can't give you a complete list of "dos and don'ts" for every writing problem you'll ever face.

But I can give you some fundamental guidelines that cover the most common problems.

1. Outline what you want to say.

I know that sounds grade-schoolish. But you can't write clearly until, *before you start*, you know where you will stop.

Ironically, that's even a problem in writing an outline (i.e., knowing the ending before you begin).

So try this method:

• On 3"x 5" cards, write—one point to a card—all the points you need to make.

• Divide the cards into piles—one pile for each group of points *closely related* to each other. (If you were describing an automobile, you'd put all the points about mileage in one pile, all the points about safety in another, and so on.)

• Arrange your piles of points in a sequence. Which are most important and should be given first or saved for last? Which must you present before others in order to make the others understandable?

• Now, *within* each pile, do the same thing—arrange the *points* in logical, understandable order.

There you have your outline, needing only an introduction and conclusion.

This is a practical way to outline. It's also flexible. You can add, delete or change the location of points easily.

2. Start where your readers are.

How much do they know about the subject? Don't write to a level higher than your readers' knowledge of it.

CAUTION: Forget that old—and wrong—advice about writing to a 12-year-old mentality. That's insulting. But do remember that your prime purpose is to *explain* something, not prove that you're smarter than your readers.

3. Avoid jargon.

Don't use words, expressions, phrases known only to people with specific knowledge or interests.

Example: A scientist, using scientific jargon, wrote, "The biota exhibited a one hundred percent mortality response." He could have written: "All the fish died."

4. Use familiar combinations of words.

A speech writer for President Franklin D. Roosevelt wrote, "We are endeavoring to construct a more inclusive society." F.D.R. changed it to, "We're going to make a country in which no one is left out."

CAUTION: By familiar combinations of words, I do *not* mean incorrect grammar. *That* can be *un*clear. Example: John's father says he can't go out Friday. (Who can't go out? John or his father?)

5. Use "first-degree" words.

These words immediately bring an image to your mind. Other words must be "translated" through the first-degree word before you see

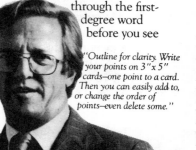

"Outline for clarity. Write your points on 3"x 5" cards—one point to a card. Then you can easily add to, or change the order of points—even delete some."

"Grit your teeth and cut the frills. That's one of the suggestions I offer here to help you write clearly. They cover the most common problems. And they're all easy to follow."

the image. Those are second/third-degree words.

First-degree words	Second/third-degree words
face	visage, countenance
stay	abide, remain, reside
book	volume, tome, publication

First-degree words are usually the most precise words, too.

6. Stick to the point.

Your outline— which was more work in the beginning—now saves you work. Because now you can ask about any sentence you write: "Does it relate to a point in the outline? If it doesn't, should I add it to the outline? If not, I'm getting off the track." Then, full steam ahead—on the main line.

7. Be as brief as possible.

Whatever you write, shortening—*condensing*—almost always makes it tighter, straighter, easier to read and understand.

Condensing, as *Reader's Digest* does it, is in large part artistry. But it involves techniques that anyone can learn and use.

• *Present your points in logical ABC order:* Here again, your outline should save you work because, if you did it right, your points already stand in logical ABC order—A makes B understandable, B makes C understandable and so on. To write in a straight line is to say something clearly in the fewest possible words.

• *Don't waste words telling people what they already know:* Notice how we edited this: "Have you ever

wondered how banks rate you as a credit risk? ~~You know, of course, that it's some combination of facts about your income, your job, and so on. But actually,~~ Many banks have a scoring system...."

• *Cut out excess evidence and unnecessary anecdotes:* Usually, one fact or example (at most, two) will support a point. More just belabor it. And while writing about some-

Writing clearly means avoiding jargon. Why didn't he just say: "All the fish died!"

thing may remind you of a good story, ask yourself: "Does it *really help* to tell the story, or does it slow me down?"

(Many people think *Reader's Digest* articles are filled with anecdotes. Actually, we use them sparingly and usually for one of two reasons: either the subject is so dry it needs some "humanity" to give it life; or the subject is so hard to grasp, it needs anecdotes to help readers understand. If the subject is both lively and easy to grasp, we move right along.)

• *Look for the most common word wasters:* windy phrases.

Windy phrases	Cut to...
at the present time	now
in the event of	if
in the majority of instances	usually

• *Look for passive verbs you can make active:* Invariably, this produces a shorter sentence. "The cherry tree *was* chopped down by George Washington." (Passive verb and nine words.) "George Washington *chopped* down the cherry tree." (Active verb and seven words.)

• *Look for positive/negative sections from which you can cut the negative:* See how we did it here:"The answer ~~does not rest with carelessness or incompetence. It lies largely in~~ having enough people to do the job."

• Finally, to write more clearly by saying it in fewer words: when you've finished, stop.

Edward T. Thompson

Remember, you are primarily dependent upon the written media to get your message across. Put yourself in the "psychological shoes" of your readers.

The Resume. The resume is a written summary description of a person's personal information, education and work experiences. It usually is the first formal contact with an organization. It can be your gateway into an organization. The importance of a well-planned and organized resume is undeniable. With the competitiveness in today's job market the prepared job applicant has the upper hand. The resume can give you the edge you may need in attaining part-time or full-time employment.

What does this medium communicate? The way in which the resume is constructed, the way it is written, the way it is typed, the overall format all speak about you. The medium is more the message than the message itself!

Preparing to write the resume. You should prepare to write your resume with the same diligence you apply to writing a research paper. Consider the following suggestions:

- Gather data (personal records; high school records; dates of positions held/jobs; military service; awards; activities)
- Decide on career objective (what are your long range and short range goals?)
- Read job reference materials (acquaint yourself with current information on companies and job opportunities)

The above suggestions are steps every serious job applicant should go through *before* writing a resume. Job reference materials can be found in the reference sections of most public and university libraries. You might find the following reference books useful.

1. *Dictionary of Occupational Titles*
2. *Occupational Outlook Handbook*
3. *Thomas Register of American Manufacturers* and *Thomas Registry Catalogue*
4. *College Placement Annual*
5. *Moody's Industrial Manual*

Writing the resume. Now that you have compiled the pertinent information it is now time for you to write the contents of your resume. Most resumes contain the following sections:

1. **Name of the Applicant** — your name should be prominent
2. **Address and Telephone** — you should include both permanent and temporary addresses and telephone numbers; be sure to include zip codes and telephone area codes
3. **Personal Data** — this may include your birthdate and place, height, weight, health, marital status, number of children, willingness to relocate. (Please note: many personal data items are optional.)
4. **Career Objective** — what are your short range career goals and where do you hope to be in the future?
5. **Education** — the last degree received is usually sufficient. If you decide it suits your general objectives to include high school education you may do so. You should indicate dates degree conferred; major area of specialization; special recognition; awards; scholarships. You may want to indicate your grade point average if it serves your objective.
6. **Occupational Experience** — identify full-time employment positions; specify dates; indicate specific duties performed; outstanding performance evidence; any other achievements.

7. **Additional Occupational Experience**—you may want to list part time employment if you feel it serves your objective. For example, if you lack full-time employment experience or if you worked while attending college.

8. **References**—you should either indicate several people an employer can contact (give their names, addresses, and telephone numbers) or indicate that you will send references upon request (the last suggestion assures the privacy of your references).

Consider the following pointers when writing your resume:

- Organization of the data should be based on your specific material or lack of material. (For example, if your occupational experience is strong you may want to put it before the Education section. If you lack specific work experience you may want to indicate extra curricular activities that are significant).

- It is always best when arranging information to place your most recent accomplishments *first* then proceed chronologically backwards.

- Watch for time lags. Be sure you can explain any skips in the chronology of your material.

- Don't overlook any military experience. Be sure to equate your military job description with its civilian counterpart.

- Use only one page for all the pertinent information. Unless you have extensive work experience you should keep your resume to one page.

- Use standard sized paper 8 ½ inch by 11 inch. You may want to get noticed by using unusually sized paper but you may find that you are a candidate for the "circular file" because your resume does not fit the folders businesses use to file things they plan to keep.

- Use white or off white color paper. Don't use unusual colors; remember, the medium is the message. Off-white paper will subtly get their attention without being too obvious.

- Always type your resume.

- Watch general format of the material. The overall appearance should be striking. It should look organized.

Look at the sample job resume to see how some of these suggestions are utilized.

Cover Letter. It is important to remember that the resume is developed for a *general* audience. It is a one page summary of your life, your experiences both educational and work. Your resume should be accompanied by a cover letter. It is the cover letter that provides the prospective employer with reasons why you would be qualified for the position. This is the medium that sells yourself as a qualified candidate for the job.[2]

Sample Resume

John Michael Vale

7156 Oak Drive
Poland, Ohio 44514

Telephone:
(216) 757-6359

(this is optional)
Marital Status:
Married
No children

Date and Place of Birth:
July 25, 1960
Youngstown, Ohio

Career Objective

To obtain a position with direct customer contact leading to a more responsible position in sales management.

Occupational Experience

Sales Consultant, Photo Corporation of America, Inc. July 1982-
As a sales consultant and team manager in the largest photography sales corporation in the world, this position mandates extensive knowledge in all facets of sales and sales management. In addition to being accountable for managing a team of sales consultants, this position includes extensive public relations work, on-the-job training responsibilities, sales and cash audits and bookkeeping.

Warehouseman, Atlantic and Pacific Tea Company August 1978-June 1982
Primary responsibilities included almost all functions related to the efficient operations of a five hundred employee warehouse center. More specifically, responsibilities and accountabilities included billings, shipping, receiving, distribution, and the operation of heavy machine equipment. I held this job while I attended college.

Additional Occupational Experiences
While in high school and during the summer vacations, I performed the following jobs: Director of Recreational Activities, busboy, and work in a fast food chain in both cooking and counter service areas.

Education

Bachelor in Business Administration, Kent State University, Kent, Ohio 44240. Granted June 1982. Major area of specialization was Marketing (B+ average), Minor in communication (A average). Emphasis in salesmanship, advertising and organizational communication.

Professional and Personal Interests

Active in Toastmaster's Club. Play tennis and golf. Stamp collecting hobby.

References

Will be furnished upon request.

Sample Cover Letter to Accompany Resume

7156 Oak Drive
Poland, Ohio 44514
March 15, 198___

Ms. Diana Parsons
Personnel Director
Kodak Corporation
State Street
Rochester, New York 11587

Dear Ms. Parsons:

   I am writing this letter to express my interest in a postion with your company as a sales management trainee. In reading about your company at the Kent State University Career Planning and Placement Center, I was pleased to find that your training programs lead to significant management positions for those who successfully complete the training.

   As you can see from my enclosed resume, I have worked the past few years in the photographic sales area while studying for my degree. In the Spring I will be receiving a Bachelor's degree in Business Administration from Kent State University. I feel that my work experience combined with my academic achievements provide me with the background necessary for a sales management position.

   Also, I want to point out that I have had some sales management experience in my current position as Team Manager of a small group of photography salespersons. I have experienced both the rewards and the responsibilities that go with a management position. I enjoy the challenges of management. We are proud that our team has led our region in sales for the past three months.

   I hope we will get a chance to talk in depth about this position when you come to the Kent Campus this Spring for interviews. I will contact you in two weeks to learn if an appointment suitable to your schedule can be arranged.

Sincerely,

John Michael Vale

Supportive Visual Media

For purposes of our study supportive visual media will include those written materials/visuals whose purpose is to support the oral message. These materials by themselves would provide the receiver with little or confusing information. They need to be explained and/or be accompanied by words. Examples of these media are: charts, graphs, chalk and flannel boards, maps, still pictures, overhead transparencies, slides, opaque projected materials. These will aid the organizational communicator in getting his/her message received and understood.

How to write a business letter

Some thoughts from Malcolm Forbes

President and Editor-in-Chief of Forbes Magazine

International Paper asked Malcolm Forbes to share some things he's learned about writing a good business letter. One rule, "Be crystal clear."

A good business letter can get you a job interview.

Get you off the hook.

Or get you money.

It's totally asinine to blow your chances of getting *whatever* you want—with a business letter that turns people off instead of turning them on.

The best place to learn to write is in school. If you're still there, pick your teachers' brains.

If not, big deal. I learned to ride a motorcycle at 50 and fly balloons at 52. It's never too late to learn.

Over 10,000 business letters come across my desk every year. They seem to fall into three categories: stultifying if not stupid, mundane (most of them), and first rate (rare). Here's the approach I've found that separates the winners from the losers (most of it's just good common sense)—it starts *before* you write your letter:

Know what you want

If you don't, write it down—in one sentence. "I want to get an interview within the next two weeks." That simple.

List the major points you want to get across—it'll keep you on course.

If you're *answering* a letter, check the points that need answering and keep the letter in front of you while you write. This way you won't forget anything—*that* would cause another round of letters.

And for goodness' sake, answer promptly if you're going to answer at all. Don't sit on a letter—*that* invites the person on the other end to sit on whatever you want from *him*.

Plunge right in

Call him by name—not "Dear Sir, Madam, or Ms." "Dear Mr. Chrisanthopoulos"—and be sure to spell it right. That'll get him (thus, you) off to a good start.

(Usually, you can get his name just by phoning his company—or from a business directory in your nearest library.)

Tell what your letter is about in the first paragraph. One or two sentences. Don't keep your reader guessing or he might file your letter away—even before he finishes it.

In the round file.

If you're answering a letter, refer to the date

"Be natural. Imagine him sitting in front of you—what would you say to him?"

it was written. So the reader won't waste time hunting for it.

People who read business letters are as human as thee and me. Reading a letter shouldn't be a chore—*reward* the reader for the time he gives you.

Write so he'll enjoy it

Write the entire letter from his point of view—what's in it for *him*? Beat him to the draw—surprise him by answering the questions and objections he might have.

Be positive—he'll be more receptive to what you have to say.

Be nice. Contrary to the cliché, genuinely nice guys most often finish first or very near it. I admit it's not easy when you've got a gripe. To be agreeable while disagreeing—that's an art.

Be natural—write the way you talk. Imagine him sitting in front of you—what would you *say* to him?

Business jargon too often is cold, stiff, unnatural.

Suppose I came up to you and said, "I acknowledge receipt of your letter and I beg to thank you." You'd think, "Huh? You're putting me on."

The acid test—read your letter *out loud* when you're done. You might get a shock—but you'll know for sure if it sounds natural.

Don't be cute or flippant. The reader won't take you seriously. This doesn't mean you've got to be dull. You prefer your letter to knock 'em dead rather than bore 'em to death.

Three points to remember:

Have a sense of humor. That's refreshing *anywhere*—a nice surprise in a business letter.

Be specific. If I tell you there's a new fuel that could save gasoline, you might not believe me. But suppose I tell you this:

"Gasohol"–10% alcohol, 90% gasoline–works as well as straight gasoline. Since you can make alcohol from grain or corn stalks, wood or wood waste, coal– even garbage, it's worth some real follow-through.

Now you've got something to sink your teeth into.

Lean heavier on nouns and verbs, lighter on adjectives. Use the active voice instead of the passive. Your writing will have more guts.

Which of these is stronger? Active voice: "I kicked out my money manager." Or, passive voice: "My money manager was kicked out by me." (By the way, neither is true. My son, Malcolm Jr., manages most Forbes money–he's a brilliant moneyman.)

"I learned to ride a motorcycle at 50 and fly balloons at 52. It's never too late to learn anything."

Give it the best you've got

When you don't want something enough to make *the* effort, making *an* effort is a waste.

Make your letter look appetizing –or you'll strike out before you even get to bat. Type it–on good-quality 8½" x 11" stationery. Keep it neat. And use paragraphing that makes it easier to read.

Keep your letter short–to one page, if possible. Keep your paragraphs short. After all, who's going to benefit if your letter is quick and easy to read?

You.

For emphasis, underline impor-

tant words. And sometimes indent sentences as well as paragraphs.

Like this. See how well it works? (But save it for something special.)

Make it perfect. No typos, no misspellings, no factual errors. If you're sloppy and let mistakes slip by, the person reading your letter will think you don't know better or don't care. Do you?

Be crystal clear. You won't get what you're after if your reader doesn't get the message.

Use good English. If you're still in school, take all the English and writing courses you can. The way you write and speak can really help –or *hurt*.

If you're not in school (even if you are), get the little 71-page gem by Strunk & White, *Elements of Style*. It's in paperback. It's fun to read and loaded with tips on good English and good writing.

Don't put on airs. Pretense invariably impresses only the pretender.

Don't exaggerate. Even once. Your reader will suspect everything else you write.

Distinguish opinions from facts. Your opinions may be the best in the world. But they're not gospel. You owe it to your reader to let him know which is which. He'll appreciate it and he'll admire you. The dumbest people I know are those who Know It All.

Be honest. It'll get you further in the long run. If you're not, you won't rest easy until you're

found out. (The latter, not speaking from experience.)

Edit ruthlessly. Somebody ~~has~~ said that words are ~~a lot~~ like inflated money–the more ~~of them that~~ you use, the less each one ~~of them~~ is worth. ~~right on.~~ Go through your entire letter ~~just~~ as many times as it takes. ~~Search out and~~ **A**nnihilate all unnecessary words, ~~and~~ sentences–even ~~entire~~ *paragraphs*.

"Don't exaggerate. Even once. Your reader will suspect everything else you write."

Sum it up and get out

The last paragraph should tell the reader exactly what you want *him* to do–or what *you're* going to do. Short and sweet. "May I have an appointment? Next Monday, the 16th, I'll call your secretary to see when it'll be most convenient for you."

Close with something simple like, "Sincerely." And for heaven's sake sign legibly. The biggest ego trip I know is a completely illegible signature.

Good luck.

I hope you get what you're after.

Sincerely,

Malcolm S. Forbes

Remember, using more than one channel increases the chances of our message being received as we desire it to be received. Let's explore the supportive visual media by examining the kinds of visual aids available to the communicator and how and when these media should be used. We'll be examining the following: chalk and flannel boards; charts and graphs; still pictures and posters; use of overhead transparencies and opaque projected materials; and slides.

Chalk and Flannel Boards. An often overlooked visual aid is the chalk or blackboard. This medium is one of the most accessible aids available to speakers. The communicator might want to use this medium under the following conditions:

- when expenses need to be kept to a minimum
- when producing visual aids is a problem
- when an informal presentation is desired
- when the speaker wishes to involve the audience in the presentation or if the audience is expected to become involved
- when one wants to gradually reveal the developmental portion of the speech

It is important to remember that the blackboard can be a hindrance to the speaker and his/her receivers. You must remember not to turn your back to your audience nor to stand in front of the message you placed on the board. Both can be extremely detrimental to message reception. For an inexpensive visual aid device, however, the blackboard is still a good visual to utilize.

The flannel or the magnetic boards are other good visual devices. These media give a more formal and planned appearance. The advantage of using these media is the fact that you can add or subtract information as you present your oral message to the audience. Although they serve the similar functions as the chalk or blackboards they do give a more professional appearance. The cost of course is higher than the chalk board. You need to follow the same precautions when using these media so you do not become a barrier in the communication process by blocking the channel!

Charts and Graphs. Charts and graphs are used by speakers to help visualize statistical data. They are used to present in visual form materials that may be difficult to understand if only presented through the oral channel. The following are the types of charts and graphs that may be used by the organizational communicator.

Organizational or flow charts. These charts depict relationships between superiors and subordinates within an organization. It visualizes the overall structure and functions within the organizational hierarchy. A flow chart may also be used to describe the overall flow of a process, for example, the steps in producing a piece of pottery.

Tree charts. These charts are used to indicate branches or divisions of an organization or they may be used in describing the various components of a specific subject under study. Most of you probably associate this type of chart with your geneology or your family tree.

Bar graphs. Bar graphs are a series of bars presented on a chart that represent numerical or proportional relationships between data. Bar graphs usually represent items during various periods of time, over several years' span. Although they are traditionally depicted as vertical bars you might also present the data horizontally.

Pictographs. Like the bar graphs the pictographs show relationships or comparisons between items. They may also show losses or gains. Instead of using bars you would use a stereotypical diagram easily recognized by most people to represent the category under consideration. Common pictorial symbols are dogs, people, automobiles, food products, etc.

Line graph. The line graph is an excellent visual to use when you are trying to demonstrate trends or variations of a specific item over a period of time. You can also depict several variables by using different color lines or showing a solid line to demonstrate one factor and dots or dashes to represent other factors.

Visual Aids Can Arouse Interest

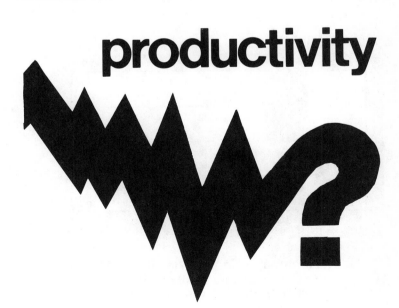

Be Creative in the Use of Graphs

91.6% NOW!

Be Sure to Make Your Aids Large and Uncluttered

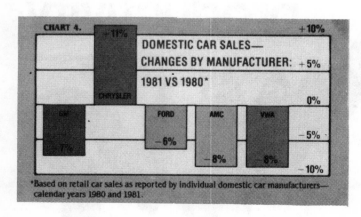

CHART 4.

DOMESTIC CAR SALES—
CHANGES BY MANUFACTURER:
1981 VS 1980*

+10%
+5%
0%
−5%
−10%

CHRYSLER +11%
GM −7%
FORD −6%
AMC −8%
VWA −8%

*Based on retail car sales as reported by individual domestic car manufacturers—
calendar years 1980 and 1981.

**The Information in Your Visual Should
Be Grasped More Easily Visually
Than by Spoken Words Only.**

Circle graph. Most of you are probably familiar with this type of graph. It is commonly called the pie graph or the divided circle. This is an excellent and easy graph for the audience to read and understand. It can be used when you wish to demonstrate segments of a whole. This type of graph is typically used to illustrate tax dollar expenditures where each section of the circle or piece of the pie represents a specific expenditure. Caution needs to be taken. You should not have so many divisions represented that the pieces become so miniscule that they can not be seen by members of your audience. You also need to be sure that your labels are printed large enough for every audience member to see.

Manual and Flip Charts. Manual and flip charts are unmounted or mounted charts used to present information to a small audience. These media are particularly useful for small presentations because of their flexibility. It also gives a very planned and professional appearance. The disadvantage of using manual or flip charts is the inability to add or subtract information from them easily. One student prepared these four aids on a flip chart to help present her speech on career planning.

Before deciding whether or not you are going to use charts and/or graphs to supplement your oral presentation you should examine the material below regarding when charts and graphs should be used and some precautions you need to keep in mind if you decide to use them in your presentation.

You should use charts and graphs:

- when a professional appearance is desired
- when you want to save time putting materials on chalk boards (nothing is more boring than to wait for a speaker to put information on the board)
- when you don't know the spatial arrangements for the presentation (chart and graphs can be moved so everyone can see them, a chalk board does not have that mobility)
- when you don't want to depend on machinery to work (you don't need to worry if the room has too much lighting, if there are electrical outlets, etc.)
- when you need to present the message several times
- when you have the time to prepare charts or graphs

Precautions need to be taken when using these media, however. Consider the following:

- charts and graphs require time to prepare
- they can not be used for a very large audience because the distance is too far from the speaker and the receivers
- use of too many charts may hinder and not help your message since you will have to juggle these charts and graphs and try to integrate them in your speech
- you can not add or subtract information as you are presenting your materials to the audience

Still Pictures and Posters. When used selectively still pictures and posters can be good attention getting devices. It is important, however, to remember not to use too many in supplementing your oral presentation. Instead of complementing your oral presentation they may become distractions. They are also terrific tools because they are inexpensive and require little time in preparing. One distinct advantage of using still pictures and posters is that they cannot be used for larger audiences. That is why it is always important to know the size of the room and the number of people you will be addressing before you decide to use these media.

Do not hesitate to use aids that are unusual. One might begin a speech on superior-subordinate relations by showing this picture and taking a vote on which caption is most appropriate:
"The Boss Doesn't Approve"
or
"Who *Me*??????????

Overhead Transparencies. Transparencies are acetate sheets that are placed onto overhead projectors to transmit a picture or a diagram, etc. onto a screen or a wall. The image is enlarged and thus is suitable for presentations to a large audience. Transparencies can be made or they can be bought. You may want to use these media

- when you want to control the developmental sequence of your ideas
- when you want to demonstrate the relationship of a whole with its parts. This can be done through overlays in which you can gradually add parts until you see them in relation to the whole; you can also subtract parts
- when adaptation to your audiences' feedback is desired or expected

- when you want to maintain contact with your audience (with the overhead projector you face the audience as you use the projector unlike other projecting machines)

Jay Spitulnik (1979), an engineering assurance educator, talks about the importance of using transparencies when time is a factor. He found that transparencies were good to provide highlights of engineering assurance procedures to the trainees in his organization. It was an important visual aid he used to emphasize certain portions of his messages. It also provided his trainees with definitions and spellings of difficult terms used during the training presentation. Mr. Spitulnik is an organizational communicator who recognizes the importance of using as many channels of communication as are available to get the message across to the receivers. He communicates his concern for his subordinates — he wants them to understand his message.

Opaque Projected Materials. The distinct advantage of utilizing this medium is the fact that almost anything can be projected through this projector — if it fits! This machine can project most printed materials but the color is restricted to black and white images. For example, most books, cartoons, diagrams, small charts, graphs, maps, etc. can be projected. It is an excellent tool to use under the following circumstances:

- when you have a limited amount of time to prepare visuals for your presentation
- when you wish to share already printed materials — such as graphs or charts that are too small to just hold up to your audience
- when you have a large audience receiving your message

You should be careful, however, before you use this medium. Note the following precautions:

- be sure there is an electrical outlet in the area where you are to address your audience
- be sure the machine does not block the audience's view
- be sure to speak above the noise made by the machine
- be sure the room is adapted for projected images, that is, are there drapes or blinds to close off the light from the windows

Slide Projector. Slides can be extremely proficient when a continuous and standardized presentation is desired. Like the other projected materials they are good to use when directing a message to a large audience but they are also adaptable for a smaller audience.

There are several precautions one needs to heed before investing time and money into this medium. You need to ask yourself if the time and money you will have to invest is worthwhile. Can you coordinate your oral presentation with the slides available to you? Are they really going to aid in understanding your message or just confuse things? After you have addressed these issues, you should feel confident that the slides will be an asset to your presentation.

On-the-Spot Graphics

Graphics should not be limited to the art department, nor should they be restricted to advance preparation. The process of group communication can be enhanced by on-the-spot graphics.

Equipment. The equipment needed is simple:

- walls on which newsprint pads or wrapping paper may be taped.
- it is preferable to use large sheets 28 inches wide.
- masking tape is ideal because it is easily removed. Be sure to test the surface with the tape to make sure no damage will be done.
- several colored, wide-tipped markers which are not permanent (El Marko, Papermate, etc.)

Techniques. The techniques also are simple. Variations in form, color, lettering and recording of group ideas and decisions lend insight to the process. Several variations should be in the repetoire of a leader such as:

- Use of diagrams to illustrate roles of participants. Circles, squares, triangles, rectangles.
- Use of lists. When recording ideas, one should be faithful to what is said and urge the contributor to shorten his remarks rather than to change it for him/her.
- Use emphasis by printing in large block letters, shading in or outlining with color, indentation, underlining, arrows, stick figures, mini-pictures for cues, etc. Your imagination is the only limit.

Hints. Write, or better still, print distinctly and large. Write in a straight line, leave plenty of space. Margins may be used to add notes. Don't over emphasize techniques. Don't worry about your artistic ability. You already know enough to do group graphics.

Benefits. On-the-spot graphics offer special benefits to group processes. They help focus attention and prevent memory lapses. They involve participants. They center the problem solving process on the problem and away from persons. Joint ownership thus is encouraged and co-operation is displayed graphically.

Possibilities for Graphing. The equipment, techniques and hints for on-the-spot graphics, to be sure, must fit the momentary needs of the situation. Likely a leader will be offended if another in the group always insisted on grabbing the magic marker and takes over the graphing job. But groups can be introduced to on-the-spot graphics by volunteering for the task in advance when special problems arise.

A leader, because of his role as initiator and structurer of ideas, is in the best position to acquaint a group to on-the-spot graphics. Others may then take turns assisting in this role.

What lends itself to group graphics? The most natural first suggestion is Agenda Posting. An agenda may be posted in advance and submitted for prioritizing or modification, or it may be built from items contributed on-the-spot by the group.

- Listing is a second natural for group processes: brainstorming, "to do" lists, criteria, parties who should be contacted. The possibilities are many.
- Memory Notes serve a valuable function for a group. Seeing the ebb and flow of group topics, like a flow chart a debater or lawyer might keep, enables a group to monitor its progress.
- Diagramming of a situation, a systems in, put through and put out, facilitates a group's perspective. Sometimes a real map or a calendar may enable a group to visualize who are involved, responsible and the time frames which are set. The colored

markers may be used to make notations on the map or calendar.

- A matrix or grid may be used in a number of ways to indicate relationships or responsibilities such as which employees are assigned certain functions and who should be consulted before acting, etc. A matrix also might be used to compare options A, B, C with respect to manpower, cost, time and work.
- Sometimes symbols or figures may be used, such as a thermometer, building, or the human body. Most importantly, on-the-spot graphing should be flexible and fun.

Supportive Audio Visual Media

This category describes the media that are used in business and industrial settings to complement the oral report or presentation. For example, tape recordings, movies, and video tape recordings. Let's take a closer look at these media and how they might be used by organizational communicators.

Tape recordings. Tape recordings utilize the aural senses alone so they are used infrequently in business and industry as a communicating tool. They are as the name implies useful for recording communication transactions that occur within the organization. How can they be useful as media of communication in an oral presentation? They can be useful when used along with the oral presentation or report. For example, you can play back portions of an address delivered by the Chairman of the Board at the Annual Stockholders meeting. Thus, instead of you quoting or paraphrasing what you heard, you let the audience hear it for themselves. It will add the dimension of accuracy to your report.

It is important to be sure that the tape you use is audible to all listeners. You should also be sure the tape has a limited number of distortions or physical noise in the background. It is best not to use any tape recordings if you must use ineffective ones.

Movies. Movies are typically not used in business and industrial settings as an oral reporting device. Movies can, however, be extremely effective devices when one has enough time and money to invest in them. They can be useful when the following conditions are present:

- when one wants or needs to dramatize events or ideas to the receivers for a desired effect
- when a continuous message is desirable
- when one wants to report specific action or motion ("how to do it" films, for example)
- when one has the equipment, personnel and budget to produce the film and to project it to an audience

Video Tapes. Video tapes can be used quite effectively as training devices. For example, it is difficult to describe in words *only* how a person should do something. It is even more difficult to explain to a person what he/she is doing wrong! Video tapes can clear up these problems. First, through the use of visual demonstration followed by taping the person performing the task and playing the tape back for the trainee to observe how they did! Additionally, the video tapes can be used to supplement the presentation by using the tapes as demonstrating devices. You can present demonstrations of conducting an appraisal interview, working a piece of equipment, administering shots to patients, etc. You can stop the tape, talk about the procedures, and then start the tape again or play back any part which the audience would like to see.

Video tapes should be used:

- when training is involved and immediate feedback is desired
- when demonstrating a task to a large number of people (by projecting the film/tape onto a television screen a larger group of people can receive the message at the same time)
- when flexibility and adaptability to your audiences' needs is desired (you can stop, start, playback, tape and retape any number of times)

Three Dimensional Media

This category describes objects or models that one might use to complement their oral presentations. Bringing in the real thing or almost the real thing is an eye catcher! It is an alternative aid to the one dimensional media discussed thus far in this chapter.

Objects. The communicator would bring in the actual object or part of that object which their presentation addresses. It is obvious that some objects would not be suitable nor practical to present to an audience. Some objects may be too big, others too small for everyone to see. Bringing in the actual object being talked about does aid the audience in understanding your message. You reduce the amount of misinterpretation the audience can place on the words you use to communicate if you utilize more than the oral channel. It will help your audience see what you are talking about. It will get them involved with your message. It will also make your message more concrete.

Models. Bringing in the real things can, as we said, be too difficult either because the size is too large or too small. Models are a solution to the size issue. Models are substitutes for the real thing. They are replications of the object made to scale.

Both objects' and models' biggest disadvantage is their ability. Where do you find a model of the SST? or the human heart?

Recap

In this chapter, we have presented many forms of media available to the organizational communicator: memos, resumes, chalk boards, charts and graphs, still pictures, transparencies, opaque and slide projectors, tapes — both audio and visual, movies and three dimensional objects.

As you can see the media can communicate. And what a wide variety we have available to us. That makes it all the more challenging for the organizational communicator of the 80's.

Remember that the purposes of visual aids are:

1. To make information more understandable and memorable.
2. To enhance the interest of the audience, and
3. To make the presentation easier for you to present.

Notes

1. Marshall McLuhan and Quentin Fiore, *The Message is the massage* (New York: Bantam Books, 1967), p. 26.
2. You might want to examine the text written by Dr. Lawrence Brennan *et al* listed below in the bibliography section. The authors present approximately 280 types of resumes according to occupational titles.
3. Material abstracted in part from O. Lee Reed Jr., ''Eighteenth Century Legal Doctrine Meets Twentieth Century Marketing Techniques: F.T.C. Regulation of Emotional Conditioning Advertising,'' *Georgia Law Review* 11 (Summer 1977), 733-782.

Additional References:

Brennan, Lawrence D. and Stanley Strand, Edward Gruber. *Resumes For Better Jobs.* New York: Simon Schuster, 1973.

Brown, James W. and Richard Lewis, Fred Harcleroad. *AV Instruction: Technology, Media and Methods.* New York: McGraw Hill Book Company, 1973.

de Kieffer, Robert E. and Lee W. Cochran. *Manual of Audio Visual Techniques.* Prentice-Hall Education Series, 1962.

McLuhan, Marshall and Quentin Fiore. *The Medium is the Massage.* New York: Bantam Books, 1967.

Spitulnik, Jay J. *Audio Visual Instruction,* April 1979, *24* #4, 35 + .

Vardaman, George. *Effective Communication of Ideas.* New York: Van Nostrand Reinhold Company, 1970.

Wilcox, Roger P. *Oral Reporting in Business and Industry.* New Jersey: Prentice-Hall, Inc., 1967.

Resume Writing

Preparing to meet the challenges of resume writing requires that the serious job applicant know as much about his/her area of specialization and the company to which he/she is applying as is feasible.

Activity:

Prepare a profile on your area of specialization (accounting, nursing, education, sales, engineering, computer science, etc.) by using the job-reference books outlined in this chapter. Remember most public and university libraries have these books in the Reference section. If you are undecided as to what you want to do, use this as an opportunity to discover information about any field that sounds interesting. Consider the following: What opportunities are available in today's job market in your field? What types of jobs can you apply for in the field? What are the names of some companies you might want to work for in the future? Find out something about them. Prepare your resume.

Class Activity:

Now that you have researched your occupational and company materials prepare to share this information with a group of your classmates.

Discussion:

1. What jobs are available in today's market? Is it better or worse than you thought it would be?

2. What prospects are there in the future for these fields?

3. Of all the profiles of companies presented by your group members, which companies seem most attractive to work for? Why?

4. Knowing what you now know about your field and companies in this field, how might you go about writing your resume?

5. Given the information about your field and the profile of the companies how might you go about actively getting a job?

Project Four-2

Visual Aids Contest

Supportive visual materials can increase the level of understanding of your oral presentation. Keeping in mind the pros and cons of using the various types of supportive visual aids, prepare *one* visual you plan to use for a major oral presentation.

Class Activity:

Divide the class into two groups (A and B). Group B will go out in the hallway while members of Group A set up their visual aids throughout the room. Group B will then come back into the room and examine the visual aids that are of interest to them. Group A members should stand next to their visuals in order to explain what they mean for the receivers who mill about from one aid to the next.

The process should be repeated having members of Group B sharing their visual materials with members of Group A.

Class Discussion:

You can vote for those visuals you felt were the best from each group. Or you can just discuss the characteristics of a good visual aid giving examples from the visuals you examined today.

Project Four-3

Outlining the Slide Presentation

Study the outline by Don Manning. Notice that the outline serves as a reminder for the speaker. Sentences are not complete. Notations are made for when each slide should come on the screen.

1. What is the underlying rationale for the arrangement of Mr. Manning's presentation?

2. What important information about himself did Mr. Manning use to establish his own credibility? And about his company?

3. What tone was conveyed by reading the outline of this message? Why do you feel this way?

Donald S. Manning is a senior vice president of Parker Hannifin Corporation. He also serves as Vice-Chairman of the Board of Directors of that company.

Communications in an Industrial Company

I. **Introduction**
   A. It's nice to be back in the classroom, even up front — I tried for a full-time job at Cornell, 10 years out, and Dean asked me what I had published lately — I got the picture.
      1. I might still be in school, but my wife refused to support me any longer.
   B. I just took a post graduate course in communications myself, 12 days in the interior of Mainland China in the industrial area *Ruhrgrbeat*, as the Germans call it in negotiations on a joint venture.
      1. You think it's tough to communicate with your professor — you ought to try it with the Chinese who haven't seen Americans in 30 years, much less talk with them.
      2. As usual I learned something, i.e., make things very clear and brief when you say this is your last offer. If they think it's not your last offer, they have a lot of staying power.
   C. If you put "whereas" in a contract you better be prepared to explain why you need it. Our lawyers got rid of half the words (early on they changed word from *owner* to *supplier* of technology) and that set the tone.
   D.·· Dr. Gorden gave me a wide charter for this talk, but to relate it to communications and the way it is in our business in 1980. I'll try.

II. **Tell you what you are going to hear**
   A. A brief commercial on PH where I've spent 30 years since H.B.S. in the form of two short films
   B. Secondly, I'll talk about communications in business
      1. How it's used
      2. Its importance
      3. What jobs are like in communications of an industrial company
   C. Third, the value of communication skills in the general field of business and how those skills help get things done — for you.

III. **Mike will help me with the commercial**
   A. Part of the first film done in 1934 when the industry was in its infancy for this kind of communications and Parker was a very small company of less than 100 people.
   B. The film develops a certain feeling for the company — establishing concepts about its quality, engineering, people, its proprietor.
   C. It is meant to show a certain pride in accomplishment over the years.

IV. The second film explains fluid power, hydraulics & pneumatics.
   A. We are a supplier of parts, very sophisticated parts, or components and some very basic industrial items.
   B. This movie developed in 1980 uses today's technology to explain our business in 4

minutes, that we used to take 20 or 30.
C. Especially for stockholders, security analysts and brokers (who help sell our stock) and stockholders in general.
   1. The importance of selling stock is that it is a major way we raise capital besides earnings (that is another story).

Movie — Mike

V. **How communications are used in an industrial company business — PH**
   A. *To Customers* — I will not spend time on all the media that is used for *consumer products* because you are very knowledgeable from the cradle but will discuss industrial techniques.

Slide 1   1. Catalogs to explain how to apply our products, more complex than how to erect a swing set — our life blood of communications and tell our customer how to apply our technology.

Slide 2   a) Don't do in chinese yet, but we do them in many foreign languages — Chinese don't do at all now!

Slide 3   2. Magazines — advertising is modest compared to consumer, but we reach audiences who use our products.

Slide 4   3. Industrial shows are a valuable tool for displaying our products to potential customers.

   B. *Employees* — you have seen movie but we use several other methods.

Slide 5   1. *Parker World* — we are experimenting with our first worldwide house organ.
          a) Difficult to say something interesting to that wide audience.
          b) Tough little black woman is doing a good job . . . 3 years out of Georgia.
       2. *Biddle meeting*
          a) Every manager must go on the floor twice a year to talk to all of his people.
       3. *Quality Circles*
          a) We're going to try to beat Japanese at their game of sitting in small groups weekly

Slide 6   4. Employee Benefits
          a) Tell our employees about our benefits, hospital insurance, vacations — work 6 days, no vacation — ours are better.

   C. *Public Sector*

Slide 7   1. Sign — Cleveland airport for recognition
       2. Community projects

Slide 8   a) United Fund, hospital boards
          b) Support education, PH Foundation
          c) Help Voinovich beat Kucinish
       3. Producers of jobs is one of our main contributions
          a) Work hard to produce good jobs for as many people as we can

   D. *Stockholders*

Slide 9   1. Annual report, quarterly reports — its to tell them we are making them money or plan to! Pick up.

VI. **What are the job opportunities in business?**
  A. There are good jobs in communications to tell the business story. Not well done yet. We've shown you what we do.
  B. Long way from Rockefeller and Vanderbilt ideas of what business was all about.
  C. If you think business contributes to our society and have the skills, there will be many opportunities.

VII. **The Value of Communication Skills in the General Field of Business**
  A. The highest call of all "to persuade others to your point of view" that is (leadership). The rich may inherit the earth, but in the meantime communications experts are going to do O.K.
    1. That is politics—world leaders—they know how to communicate—some good, some bad
    2. Helpful in all social situations from getting a date on Saturday night to getting a job
    3. Very important in business. There are always alternative ways of doing things and if you want it done "your way" you have to persuade others. That is communications. That is the way it's done at PH which is a very decentralized company.
      a) That is making decisions and "getting things done" in business.
  B. The most important communications is oral
    1. Face-to-face ability to articulate, i.e., boss $200/hr. I make a list, essential points, ask for decision, *appropriation*, policy change in acquisition area, strike decision, go-no-go, firing a key subordinate—concise—prepared.
  C. Writing is also important
    1. Make it short—1 page if possible
    2. Put conclusion (why) and recommendation to accept your decision less than one page and up front.
    3. Support information is to be leafed through. It is expected from your integrity it will be there to support.

Conclude with a few thoughts on:

VIII. **Business as a career**
  A. Being able to communicate is a tremendous asset
    1. To become preseident if that is your goal
    2. To convince the value of your creativity, ideas, contributions
  B. Attitude towards work and others is very important
    1. Stewardess—sunny attitude toward their job is all important
    2. Need to enjoy people—lots of teamwork involved
  C. Business is where the action is
    1. Competitive—fun—make decisions that turn out well—where it's at.
    2. Exciting—travel—make money.
    3. Contribute—jobs—livelihood—the roots of success of the U.S.A. or any other country. *Production* to be divided by all the consumers—it's simple.

IX. **Three principles for top success**—nobody is a 10 in everything, but rate yourself on these on a scale of 1-10 against your peers.
- A. Work hard
  - 1. Do a little extra
  - 2. Do what needs to be done and don't complain
- B. Must be smart
  - 1. Intelligent
  - 2. Street wise
  - 3. Good judgement
  - 4. Do unto others—a good rule with people
- C. Must be fortunate
  - 1. Right place at the right time
  - 2. Knowing the right people
  - 3. Becoming a protege
  - 4. Loyalty

X. **Conclusion: Any Questions?**

Donald S. Manning is a senior vice-president of Parker Hannifin Corporation. He also serves as Vice-Chairman of the Board of Directors. He delivered the following presentation November 19, 1980 at Kent State University.

How to write with style

By Kurt Vonnegut

International Paper asked Kurt Vonnegut, author of such novels as "Slaughterhouse-Five," "Jailbird" and "Cat's Cradle," to tell you how to put your style and personality into everything you write.

Newspaper reporters and technical writers are trained to reveal almost nothing about themselves in their writings. This makes them freaks in the world of writers, since almost all of the other ink-stained wretches in that world reveal a lot about themselves to readers. We call these revelations, accidental and intentional, elements of style.

These revelations tell us as readers what sort of person it is with whom we are spending time. Does the writer sound ignorant or informed, stupid or bright, crooked or honest, humorless or playful – ? And on and on.

Why should you examine your writing style with the idea of improving it? Do so as a mark of respect for your readers, whatever you're writing. If you scribble your thoughts any which way, your readers will surely feel that you care nothing about them. They will mark you down as an egomaniac or a chowderhead – or, worse, they will stop reading you.

The most damning revelation you can make about yourself is that you do not know what is interesting and what is not. Don't you yourself like or dislike writers mainly for what they choose to show you or make you think about? Did you ever admire an empty-headed writer for his or her mastery of the language? No.

So your own winning style must begin with ideas in your head.

1. Find a subject you care about

Find a subject you care about and which you in your heart feel others should care about. It is this genuine caring, and not your games with language, which will be the most compelling and seductive element in your style.

I am not urging you to write a novel, by the way – although I would not be sorry if you wrote one, provided you genuinely cared about something. A petition to the mayor about a pothole in front of your house or a love letter to the girl next door will do.

2. Do not ramble, though

I won't ramble on about that.

3. Keep it simple

As for your use of language: Remember that two great masters of language, William Shakespeare and James Joyce, wrote sentences which were almost childlike when their subjects were most profound. "To be or not to be?" asks Shakespeare's Hamlet. The longest word is three letters long. Joyce, when he was frisky, could put together a sentence as intricate and as glittering as a necklace for Cleopatra, but my favorite sentence in his short story "Eveline" is this one: "She was tired." At that point in the story, no other words could break the heart of a reader as those three words do.

Simplicity of language is not only reputable, but perhaps even sacred. The *Bible* opens with a sentence well within the writing skills of a lively fourteen-year-old: "In the beginning God created the heaven and the earth."

4. Have the guts to cut

It may be that you, too, are capable of making necklaces for Cleopatra, so to speak. But your eloquence should be the servant of the ideas in your head. Your rule might be this: If a sentence, no matter how excellent, does not illuminate your subject in some new and useful way, scratch it out.

5. Sound like yourself

The writing style which is most natural for you is bound to echo the speech you heard when a child. English was the novelist Joseph Conrad's third language, and much that seems piquant in his use of English was no doubt colored by his first language, which was Polish. And lucky indeed is the writer who has grown up in Ireland, for the English spoken there is so amusing and musical. I myself grew up in Indianapolis, where common speech sounds like a band saw cutting galvanized tin,

"Keep it simple. Shakespeare did, with Hamlet's famous soliloquy."

"Be merciless on yourself. If a sentence does not illuminate your subject in some new and useful way, scratch it out."

and employs a vocabulary as unornamental as a monkey wrench.

In some of the more remote hollows of Appalachia, children still grow up hearing songs and locutions of Elizabethan times. Yes, and many Americans grow up hearing a language other than English, or an English dialect a majority of Americans cannot understand.

All these varieties of speech are beautiful, just as the varieties of butterflies are beautiful. No matter what your first language, you should treasure it all your life. If it happens not to be standard English, and if it shows itself when you write standard English, the result is usually delightful, like a very pretty girl with one eye that is green and one that is blue.

I myself find that I trust my own writing most, and others seem to trust it most, too, when I sound most like a person from Indianapolis, which is what I am. What alternatives do I have? The one most vehemently recommended by teachers has no doubt been pressed on you, as well: to write like cultivated Englishmen of a century or more ago.

6. Say what you mean to say

I used to be exasperated by such teachers, but am no more. I understand now that all those antique essays and stories with which I was to compare my own work were not magnificent for their datedness or foreignness, but for saying precisely what their authors

meant them to say. My teachers wished me to write accurately, always selecting the most effective words, and relating the words to one another unambiguously, rigidly, like parts of a machine. The teachers did not want to turn me into an Englishman after all. They hoped that I would become understandable – and therefore understood. And there went my dream of doing with words what Pablo Picasso did with paint or what any number of jazz idols did with music. If I broke all the rules of punctuation, had words mean whatever I wanted them to mean, and strung them together higgledy-piggledy, I would simply not be understood. So you, too, had better avoid Picasso-style or jazz-style writing, if you have something worth saying and wish to be understood.

Readers want our pages to look very much like pages they have seen before. Why? This is because they themselves have a tough job to do, and they need all the help they can get from us.

7. Pity the readers

They have to identify thousands of little marks on paper, and make sense of them immediately. They have to *read,* an art so difficult that most people don't really master it even after having studied it all through grade school and high school – twelve long years.

So this discussion must finally acknowledge that our stylistic options as writers are neither numerous nor glamorous, since our readers are bound to be such imperfect artists. Our audience requires us to be sympathetic and patient teachers, ever willing to simplify and clarify – whereas we would rather soar high above the crowd, singing like nightingales.

That is the bad news. The good news is that we Americans are governed under a unique Constitution, which allows us to write whatever we please without fear of punishment. So the most meaningful aspect of our styles, which is what we choose to write about, is utterly unlimited.

8. For really detailed advice

For a discussion of literary style in a narrower sense, in a more technical sense, I commend to your attention *The Elements of Style,* by William Strunk, Jr., and E.B. White (Macmillan, 1979).

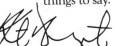

"Pick a subject you care so deeply about that you'd speak on a soapbox about it."

E.B. White is, of course, one of the most admirable literary stylists this country has so far produced.

You should realize, too, that no one would care how well or badly Mr. White expressed himself, if he did not have perfectly enchanting things to say.

SMOG Clearance Formulas

In the special feature articles throughout this book, you will find examples of the best writing a corporation can buy. The International Paper Company employed famous personalities to write to the public about **Communicating**.

1. The advice they give is worth a million. How might we learn from their advice? Study them.
    Look, for example, at Jane Bryant Quinn's tips (page ____) on "How to Read an Annual Report." Then select an annual report of a company in which you'd like to work. Examine it step by step.

    *   Does the third party auditor give the annual report a clean bill or does the account suggest doubt?
    *   What is the tone of the letter from the company chairman? Are there clues to trouble in sentences beginning with "Except for..." and "Despite the..."
    *   Do the math. Figure debt-to-equity ration. Compare it with industry norms and past corporate financial statements.

2. Next apply the following SMOG Formulas. First apply them to the Annual Reports and next to the writing of the essays in the Special Features throughout the book. Could the writers of the Annual Report profit from these models of good writing in the Special Features. Once you have applied these formulas to an Annual Report and the Special Features, apply them to a paper you have written. Finally, list the conclusions you have reached from this assignment. Details for administering the SMOG Formulas and their interpretations follow:

Readability

One way to measure readability is to count the number of words per sentence. A sentence is a unit of thought which is grammatically independent of another sentence or clause providing its end is **not** punctuated by a comma. It may be punctuated by a colon, semi-colon, exclamation point, question mark, or period. Incomplete sentences or sentence fragments should be counted as sentences also.

Here is how you may interpret your results:

Description of Style	Typical Magazine	Average Sentence Length
Very Easy	Comics	8
Easy	Pulp Fiction	11
Fairly Easy	Slick Fiction	14
Standard	Digests, *Time,* mass non-fiction	17
Fairly Difficult	*Harper's, Atlantic*	21
Difficult	Academic, Scholarly	25
Very Difficult	Scientific, Professional	29

Limitations of this Instrument:

Short sentences can be filled with difficult words just as long sentences can be filled with simple, monosyllabic words. Either combination can be hard to read, to listen to and to understand.

Another way to measure readability is to count in each sentence the number of syllables above one per word. This is called the easy listening formula (ELF). For example, take these two sentences: (1) He was a magnanimous supervisor; and (2) He was a generous boss. The first sentence has an ELF score of 6 and the second sentence has an ELF score of 2.

Here is how you may interpret your results:

Writing Source	Average ELF score for each sentence
New York Times	17.4
CBS TV News	9.8

No highly rated television news writer had an ELF score above 12. Television network news writers averaged 10.4. In general, newspapers averaged 15.0.

Limitations of the instrument:

ELF measures clarity. A sentence that scores 20 may be perfectly clear and may be the best way to deliver a fact. A series of parallelisms, delivered rhythmically may be perfectly comprehensible, yet it lengthens the sentence and increases the ELF score. Despite these limitations the ELF is much easier to use than Flesch's Reading Ease Formula and takes into consideration the same two variables as Flesch does: average sentence length and average number of syllables per 100 words.

Human Interest

Human interest is measured by the average number of personal words and the average number of personal sentences.

Personal Words are:

(a) All first, second, and third-person pronouns except the neuter pronouns *it, its, itself,* and the pronouns *they, them, their, theirs, themselves,* if referring to things rather than people. For example, count the word *them* in the sentence "When I saw her parents, I hardly recognized them," but not in the sentence "I looked for the books but couldn't find them." However, always count *he, him, his* and *she, her, hers* even where these words refer to animals or inanimate objects.

(b) All words that have masculine or feminine natural gender, e.g. John Jones, Mary, father, sister, iceman, actress. Do not count common gender words like teacher, doctor, employee, assistant, spouse, chairperson, even though the gender may be clear from the context. Count a phrase like President Jimmy Carter as on "personal word" only. (Only the word Jimmy has a natural masculine gender.) Mrs. Gorden contains one "personal word" with natural gender, namely Mrs.; Ms. Gay Gorden contains two, namely Ms. and Gay.

(c) The group words *people* (with the plural verb) and *folks.*

Personal Sentences are:

(a) Spoken sentences (direct quotes). But do not count quoted phrases such as, the senator accused Moore of being "a hypocrite". Count all sentences included in long quotations, as part b (below).

(b) Questions, commands, requests, and other sentences directly addressed to the reader as: "Does this sound possible?" or "Imagine the implications." Do not count sentences that only vaguely address the reader, like: "*This is typical* of our national character."

(c) Exclamations.

(d) Grammatically incomplete sentences as "Handsome, though." If a sentence fits under two of these classifications count if *only once*.

There are two ways to compute *Human Interest Score*: mathematically or visually.

Mathematically:

multiply the no. of personal words per 100 words by 3.635 _____

multiply the no. of personal sentences per 100 sentences by .314 _____

add the products of the previous two lines for *Human Interest Score* _____

Visually:

Use the chart below:

How do you interpret the *Human Interest Score?*

Human Interest Score will put the writing on a scale between 0 (no human interest) and 100 (full of human interest).

Human Interest Score	Description of Style	Typical Magazine	Percent of Personal Words	Percent of Personal Sentences
60 to 100	Dramatic	Fiction	17	58
40 to 60	Highly Interesting	*New Yorker*	10	43
20 to 40	Interesting	Digests, *Time*	7	15
10 to 20	Mildly Interesting	Trade	4	5
0 to 10	Dull	Scientific, Professional	2	0

Realism

Realism or the lack of abstraction may be measured in this way:

1. Count the number of finite verbs per 200 words. Count all verbs of any tense which are the first, second, or third person and which have subjects, either expressed or

understood. Do not count nonfinite verb forms or verbals. In verb forms with auxiliary words, count the auxiliary rather than the main verb. Do not count any form of the verb "to be" (is, was, are, were, will be, have been, etc.) when used only as a copula to link the subject with a predicate complement.

2. Count the number of deinite articles and their nouns per 200 words. Count both the article *the* and the noun it modifies, but only if that noun is a single word not otherwise modified, either by an intervening adjective or by a clause or phrase following the noun. Do not count *the* when modifying adjectives or noun-adjectives, as in *the best, the Irish.*

3. Count the number of nouns of abstraction per 200 words. Count all nouns ending in the suffixes *-ness, -ment, -ship, -dom, -nce, -ion,* and *-y,* including the plurals of such nouns. Count nouns ending in -y even when it is the end of a longer suffix like *-ity* or *-ology* but not when it is used as a diminutive (tiny).

4. Add the numbers found in Steps 1 and 2 and add 36 to this sum.

5. Multiply the number found in Step 3 by 2.

6. From the total found in Step 4, subtract the result of Step 5. The result of this subtraction is the abstraction score.

How are the scores to be interpreted?

0-18   Very Abstract
19-30 Abstract
31-42 Fairly Abstract
43-54 Standard
55-66 Fairly Concrete
67-78 Concrete
79-90 Very Concrete

What scores do different sources get?

True Confessions 68
Reader's Digest 51
Atlantic Monthly 41
A college philosophy text 31

Read about these formulas in the following:

Rudolf Flesch, *How to Write, Speak, and Think More Effectively* (New York: Harper and Row, 1960), pp. 303-307.

Irving Fang, "A Computer-Based Analysis of T.V. Newswriting Style for Listening Comprehension," Unpublished Ph.D., University of California (Los Angeles), 1966, pp. 136-7.

Paul J. Gillie, "A Simplified Formula for Measuring Abstraction in Writing," *Journal of Applied Psychology,* XLI, no. 4 1957, pp. 315-320. This formula was validated against the Flesch abstraction formula. It cannot be any more valid than Flesch's. But it is easier to apply.

5

Designing and Delivering the Major Address

Chapter Outline

Audience Audit
Behavioral Goals
Organization
Supports, Interest and Credibility
Delivery
Recap

Project Five-1: *Thesis and Behavioral Objectives*
Project Five-2: *Outlining*

Chapter Objectives

Those who complete this chapter should better understand:

1. the target audience and the fundamental components in an audit;
2. the importance of establishing and effectively stating one's goals in a speech in terms of feelings, beliefs or actions desired from the target audience;
3. design formats for organizing and outlining a presentation in terms of subject and audience expectations;
4. how to select supports that will generate interest and believability;
5. that delivery skills can be learned and enjoyed.

"In a question-and-answer session, you should think first and avoid pouncing on a question," says Susan Perkins, who has been questioned by groups from Savannah to Seattle since she was crowned Miss America of 1978.

Perkins, who now works as a representative for several companies, always tries to pause long enough to form a rough outline in her mind and determine if her ideas make sense and follow a logical plan.

"Answer the difficult and hostile questions candidly," she recommends. "Keep your voice in the same tone, speak slowly, and don't get embarrassed. Try to determine why the question was asked and what the questioner wants to know."

—Ford's Insider

"...the speech writer must be prepared to contend with eleventh-hour assignments, subject matter experts who come down with infectious hepatitis, and chief executives who can't be reached because they're half way around the world."

— Robert Borson, speech writer for
top executives for the Bank of America,
Journal of Communication Management, 1982/1, 12.

A newly elected President of Goodyear recently put his philosophy into a capsule: "The only way to get a job done is through people—the right people with the right information flowing in both directions."[1] This holds true, in his opinion, all the way down the line of supervision and it applies whether it be in manufacturing, sales or public relations. We will not take the time in the introduction of this chapter to list again the many times an executive and his subordinates will be expected to make major presentations either in house reports, pep talks or policy announcements or addresses to conferences, national, state and local audiences.

Some companies have speech writers and many have public relations departments with speakers' bureaus. As helpful as ghost writers, speakers' bureaus, a pack of journalists and ad men may be, they cannot, in our opinion do the job for the company that *you* must do to design and deliver your own message. In short, no canned address packaged by someone else for you will fit your tongue and personality. This chapter, therefore, is concerned with the basics of designing and delivering a major report and address. We believe that even the greats prepare much, if not all, of their addresses. And these presentations must be good or they may be your swan song—like George Washington's farewell address which announced his retirement to Mount Vernon.

The steps from design through delivery are:

Step 1. Audience Audit,

Step 2. Setting Behavioral Goals,

Step 3. Organizational Design,

Step 4. Selecting Supports for Listener Alertness and Credibility,

Step 5. Delivering the Message.

Audience Audit

A message is a live event. It has a sender and a target audience. Either the sender or the audience want something from the other and, hopefully, they can provide something for each other which is mutually gratifying. The executive may want to convince the city fathers to create an industrial park. The city politicians may want greater tax revenues. Thus, the central concern of the speaker is two-fold: my interest and their interest. The underlying intention of a presentation is to make my interest your interest, just as it is the intention of a salesman to make the customer want to purchase his product. How this is accomplished, of course, is an ethical question. We authors want it to be understood that the skills described in this chapter may be used to distort and manipulate, just as an ax may be used to maim or kill, but it is our contention that these skills should not be used to manipulate or persuade an audience against its own perceived best interest. Moreover, we believe that to lie or mislead even for a good cause ultimately results in setting man against man and generates an unhealthy skepticism and distrust even among friends.

The purpose of an audience audit is to help the communicator be better able to understand the target audience and, consequently, to design and deliver his message in a manner which will be understood and given a fair consideration. There are three fundamental components in an audit of a target audience: (a) their interest level, (b) their relationship to the speaker, and (c) their measure of identification with the speaker.

Interest Level. The interest level of an audience may range from concerned, to moderately interested, to apathetic, to hostile. The message, and particularly the introduction, must adapt to that level of interest present in the audience. If the audience has paid ten dollars to come to hear a presentation, obviously the speaker will not have to spend much time stirring up reasons why his listeners should care about his topic. Also on the other hand, when faced by an angry mob, a speaker does not have to arouse interest; rather, he'd better seek to channel that interest toward constructive ends. The captive audience, represented by persons required to go, is perhaps the more difficult audience. In such cases, a speaker must arouse interest.

Possibly the most important step in any audit for any spokesman for business is asking the two questions: What does this audience know about me and my message? And what questions probably are in their minds? The questions in the minds of the audience, for example, might include: Why should I be interested in his ideas? What's he really trying to sell?

Relationship. The relationship between the speaker and the audience may be that of (a) superior to subordinate, or the reverse of that, (b) politically or socially obligated, or (c) obligation free. Relationships within a structure influence how a message will be received.

The speaker's psychological preparation cannot help but influence the design and delivery of his message. He must acknowledge his own feelings toward his audience. That is, does he *feel* "in," or is he to some measure in an "out-group"? How he assesses his role, of course, is a matter of his thinking about what they "think of me." One must guard against fantasy—second guessing how an audience feels. There are enough indicators to make this judgment an intelligent one by noting whether one is a member of the group which that audience represents, is in the decision-making circle, on the fringes or, possibly, in a competing group.

The speaker must candidly assess how he would like to be thought of by that audience. Does he want to be respected, included socially, included in their decision making? The construction of a message, whether directly or subtly, ought to provide answers to the relationship desired by the speaker.

Identification. An audit can provide yet another cue for the message designer. That is, what measure of identification is there between the sender and receiver? In practical terms, a speaker should instinctively seek to establish commonalities with his audience while at the same time more subtly pointing up his unique differences. If sender and receiver are perfectly alike, there would be little need for any communication. But, if they are completely different, the possibility for communicating would be so slim that all the time would be taken by simply learning each other's language. The audit, thus, may cover "likes" socioeconomically, intellectually, values and lifestyle. When the audit reveals that the dress, for example, between speaker and audience ordinarily is miles apart, it is the presenter's task to modify his appearance or explain why he chose not to.

Behavior Goals

In a sense, all speech wants to control a listener's attention and requests his understanding. Yet in another sense, some speech is more to entertain, some more to inform, some more to impress and some more to convince. These general ends are not so important as are the explicit behavioral ends desired by the communicator. Three examples of how a speaker's goals might be more specifically stated are as follows:

One—I want my audience to laugh at my stories of how our company came into being, so much so, that they will tell their friends these stories. Yet a further outcome from this speech should be a legend which will be propagated by the employees in the Chamber of Commerce.

Two—After hearing my presentation, the Research and Development Department will allocate $25,000 toward a more economical and safer process of . . .

Three—After my address to the City Club, at least twenty-five persons will give a pint of blood in this current Red Cross drive.

A behavioral goal includes *what* measureable thing you want to happen, *who* you want to perform it, and *when*. The design questions relative to a behavioral objective evolve about whether these objectives should be announced and, if so, at what point in the presentation. And, how can these behavioral goals be made attractive and memorable?

Answering each of these questions must depend upon the topic and audience. They are a matter of strategy and style. Nevertheless, it is safe to suggest that the behavioral goals to be remembered must be repeated, and to be attractive must be easily repeatable. This is to suggest that President Kennedy's "Ask Not What Your Country Can Do For You But What You Can Do For Your Country" served as a statement which was picked up by the press and young and old who would do such things as join the Peace Corps.

One of the authors was the guest speaker at a community banquet at which the annual "Citizen of the Year" award was to be presented. He knew that his presentation was expected to be largely ceremonial and inspirational. The six community clubs which had joined together in making this award wanted to hear that they were doing a nice thing, that they were each in this symbolic way recognized as civic organizations and that their community would be more unified because of this celebration.

The address, therefore, was an affirmation of those good times and experiences which have been and can be had by working together for community causes. The behavioral goal arrived at by this speaker was: the clubs should continue to sponsor this award and should join together in other similar activities. The speaker for the evening would not know if these goals were to be achieved unless he would be invited back another year or upon other occasions to celebrate like events. To symbolize this message he chose a phrase which tied together an historic event and the occasion. A new comet had recently been sighted and, therefore, the theme which echoed in his address was "Our Community Can Be in Step With the Stars."

Organization

The disorganization or organization of a message has both an intellectual and psychological impact upon the audience and the speaker himself. An audience usually can recognize a disorganized presentation, but in doing so, its estimation of the speaker will be lowered. Disorganization communicates an untidy mind. People have a basic hunger for order. Without structure, relationships are unstable and unsure. It behooves the presenter of any message, and particularly a message from the business community, to be clearly, logically and attractively organized. Furthermore, strong organization may assist the speaker in his own thinking, as well as in his delivery.

A message, like a house, may be designed in a number of ways. Most importantly, like a house it should suit, if not express, the personality of the owner, and should complement the land and the community. And as with houses, there are a number of stock designs. Their economy enables quicker and often more assuredly tasteful design than do all custom built homes or speeches. And since the stock design for a speech, unlike the prefab home, is only a broad framework, there is ample opportunity, in fact necessity, to tailor each speech to the personality of the presenter and the liking of the community. Therefore, with this preface in mind, let's look at a list of design formats:

1. *Time Sequence* (Past, Present, Future, or any chronological order);
2. *Space Sequence* (Geographical divisions, such as East, West, South and North, or regions):
3. *Parties Involved* (proponents, opponents, indifferent, etc.);
4. *Journalistic* (Who, What, When, Where and Whys);
5. *Reflective Thinking* (Locating a problem, defining, assessing cause, setting up criteria for a solution, considering how well alternative solutions satisfy the criteria);

Know Your Subject

6. *Medical Diagnostic-Prescriptive* (Ill, Blame, Cure and Cost);
7. *Military* (Attacking the enemies);
8. *Q-A* (Answering the questions in the mind of the target audience);
9. *Residues* (A process of analysis and elimination of possible solutions until the best is left);
10. *Motivational* (Attention, Need, Satisfaction, Visualization, Action);[2]

Know Your Subject

11. *Narrative* (The story of how I became interested and involved in this cause, field, etc.);
12. *Negotiation* (What we want, what they want, and what we might trade off);
13. *Justificatory* (Reasons why we had to do it, or how the devil made me do it);
14. *The Journey* (The account of getting around detours and road-blocks, and choices of roads to a destination);
15. *Problem-Solution* (**Or** a series of parallel problem-solutions);

Know Your Subject

16. *Extended Analogy* (Comparisons between a known experience and the experience advocated).

These stock designs reveal to the target audience the designer's conceptualization of himself, of them and of their relationship. For example, a speaker who selects an attack-the problem design sometimes puts himself into a posture of a lone warrior against a giant establishment (reforming the tax structure is such a posture). Or at other times, it positions the speaker on the side of the establishment waging war upon the foes of that institution (such as the federal government's war on crime). In either case, the audience asks: who does the speaker think he is, what kind of power does he have, and how does he view us, as friends or foes? The "Attacking Metaphor" implies destruction of the enemy. Therefore, one speaking for business might wisely use the attacking design for a speech against inflation, but not in a speech attacking the Department of Labor, unless one truly desires its destruction.

The medical metaphor, on the other hand, positions the speaker in the role of the wise doctor able to both diagnose the disease and to prescribe the remedy. The target audience is compelled to wonder if the doctor views them as ill, and if so, why the speaker thinks he is so wise as to know their illness and to prescribe their cure. Very few doctors solicit the advice of the patient, and consequently the audience may feel excluded from genuine involvement in working out their own solution. The medical analogy's strength is its familiarity. All of us can follow such a four-step sequence: (a) seeing the symptoms, (b) naming the illness, (c) analyzing the probable cause, and (d) prescribing a cure. And this is the strength of most stock designs: they readily call to the surface in the mind of the audience a *structure*. And this structure consequently provides the enabling climate for thought about the message. Time and/or spatial sequence probably are the most familiar. All of us move from minute to minute, week to week and year to year. Thus there is order in a presentation that begins with the origins of a problem and traces its growth. Similarly, we live and travel through space. It is natural, then, for us to think in terms of the spatial parts of informational and instructional communication. And it is adventurous, yet easily understandable, to think in terms of reaching a destination across distance.

The "Journey" does not pit the speaker against an establishment, but rather suggests that the speaker and audience can travel together. Together they can find ways around detours and one day come singing down the yllow brick road into a new and better land.

Now there are many other ways a message may be partitioned. One of the attractive and challenging designs is the scientific. To those living in a scientific age, testing an hypothesis serves as an understandable problem-solving approach. In such a case, the speaker proposes a theoretical postulate and follows this with a plan for testing this theory. The plan may involve a group decision to pilot test the idea. Such an approach, perhaps, is the most convincing format for business proposals, because this suggests a cautious conservative, reach-test mentality.

Closing this list of stock designs is the extended analogy. People find analogical thinking both insightful and stimulating. One speech that lingers in the memory of one of the authors after some twenty years compared getting a PH.D. to courtship and marriage. The speech suggested several phases for comparison, such as the similarity of going steady, to beginning a master's program; proposing, to selecting a chairman for one's thesis committee; engagement, to candidacy for the doctorate; and the wedding to taking comprehensive examinations.

Analogies come in varied species and sizes. They are a form of play, and a mark of intelligence. Aristotle in his *Poetics* said "The greatest thing by far is to be master of metaphor. It is one thing that cannot be learned from others. It is a mark of genius."[3] We do not believe that the use of metaphor (or analogy) cannot be learned. The ladder of success, for example, has a number of rungs. Any businessman can take this ladder and out of his own experience title those rungs and find vivid illustrations for them. And probably a good many spokesmen for business can compare the manufacturing process of their own firm to the concerns which a community must give to health care.

An analogy simply is giving something a name which belongs to something else, and in so doing often it makes the persuasive comparison or insightful leap. It may stretch the imagination by either making the familiar strange, or the strange familiar. It was Alexander Graham Bell who derived the idea for the telephone from the tiny hammer, staples, and anvil bones of the inner ear. An internal communication consultant, for example, might illustrate how a business could improve its communication system by comparing it to a beehive queendom or to a computer. Suffice it to suggest that the extended analogy is yet another framework for the major address.

Outlining. What should be accomplished in a major speech? The presentation is a means to an end. The process of designing thus is a matter of making an idea attractive enough to get a fair hearing. To achieve this, the speaker searches for ways to establish his own credibility and create a listening experience which will cause identification with his concern. To achieve this rhetorical experience, the speaker should carefully consider how he will meet certain cognitive and psychological expectations of his audience. An outline which is designed to meet the reasonable and emotional expectations of an audience focuses on the receiver rather than the subject alone. With this attitude in mind, then let us present a checklist of expectations in an audience-centered outline.

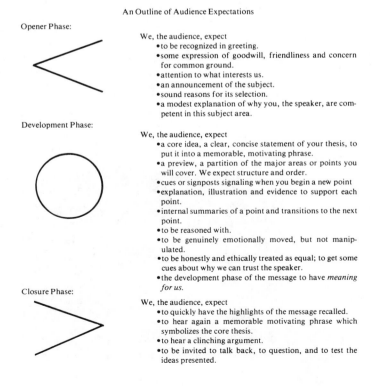

An Outline of Audience Expectations

Opener Phase:

We, the audience, expect
- to be recognized in greeting.
- some expression of goodwill, friendliness and concern for common ground.
- attention to what interests us.
- an announcement of the subject.
- sound reasons for its selection.
- a modest explanation of why you, the speaker, are competent in this subject area.

Development Phase:

We, the audience, expect
- a core idea, a clear, concise statement of your thesis, to put it into a memorable, motivating phrase.
- a preview, a partition of the major areas or points you will cover. We expect structure and order.
- cues or signposts signaling when you begin a new point
- explanation, illustration and evidence to support each point.
- internal summaries of a point and transitions to the next point.
- to be reasoned with.
- to be genuinely emotionally moved, but not manipulated.
- to be honestly and ethically treated as equal; to get some cues about why we can trust the speaker.
- the development phase of the message to have *meaning for us.*

Closure Phase:

We, the audience, expect
- to quickly have the highlights of the message recalled.
- to hear again a memorable motivating phrase which symbolizes the core thesis.
- to hear a clinching argument.
- to be invited to talk back, to question, and to test the ideas presented.

How to use a library

By James A. Michener

International Paper asked Pulitzer Prize-winning novelist James A. Michener, author of "Tales of the South Pacific," "Hawaii," "Centennial" and "Chesapeake," to tell how you can benefit from the most helpful service in your community.

You're driving your car home from work or school. And something goes wrong. The engine stalls out at lights, holds back as you go to pass.

It needs a tune-up—and soon. Where do you go? The library.

You can take out an auto repair manual that tells step-by-step how to tune up your make and model.

Or your tennis game has fallen off. You've lost your touch at the net. Where do you go?

The library—for a few books on improving your tennis form.

"The library!" you say. "That's where my teacher sends me to do —ugh—homework."

Unfortunately, I've found that's exactly the way many people feel. If you're among them, you're denying yourself the easiest way to improve yourself, enjoy yourself and even cope with life.

It's hard for me to imagine what I would be doing today if I had not fallen in love, at the ripe old age of seven, with the Melinda Cox Library in my hometown of Doylestown, Pennsylvania. At our house, we just could not afford books. The books in that free library would change my life dramatically.

Who knows what your library can open up for you?

My first suggestion for making the most of your library is to do what I did: read and read and read. For pleasure—and for understanding.

How to kick the TV habit

If it's TV that keeps you from cultivating this delicious habit, I can offer a sure remedy. Take home from the library a stack of books that might look interesting.

Pile them on the TV set. Next time you are tempted to turn on a program you really don't want to see, reach for a book instead.

Over the years, some people collect a mental list of books they mean to read. If you don't have such a list, here is a suggestion. Take from the library some of the books you might have enjoyed dramatized on TV, like Remarque's "All Quiet on the Western Front," Clavell's "Shōgun," Tolkien's "The Hobbit," or Victor Hugo's "Les Misérables."

If you like what you read, you can follow up with other satisfying books by the same authors.

Some people in their reading limit themselves to current talked-about best sellers. Oh, what they miss! The library is full of yesterday's best sellers; and they still make compelling reading today. Some that I've enjoyed: A.B. Guthrie's "The Big Sky," Carl Van Doren's "Benjamin Franklin," Mari Sandoz's "Old Jules," and Norman Mailer's "The Naked and the Dead."

How do you find these or any other books you're looking for? It's easy—with the card catalog.

Learn to use the card catalog

Every time I go to the library— and I go more than once a week—I invariably make a beeline to the card catalog before anything else. It's the nucleus of any public library.

The card catalog lists every book in the library by:

1. author; 2. title; 3. subject.

Let's pick an interesting subject to look up. I have always been fascinated by astronomy.

You'll be surprised at the wealth of material you will find under "astronomy" to draw upon. And the absorbing books you didn't know existed on it.

CAUTION: Always have a pencil and paper when you use the card catalog. Once you jot down the numbers of the books you are interested in, you are ready to find them on the shelves.

Learn to use the stacks

Libraries call the shelves "the stacks." In many smaller libraries which you'll be using, the stacks will be open for you to browse.

To me there is a special thrill in tracking down the books I want in the stacks! For invariably, I find books about which I knew nothing, and

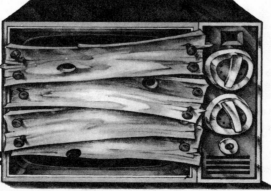

"You don't have to go this far to cut back on the TV habit and enjoy reading more. See my suggestions here."

these often turn out to be the very ones I need. You will find the same thing happening to you when you start to browse in the stacks. "A learned mind is the end product of browsing."

"Every time I go to the library, I make a beeline to the card catalog. Learn to use it. It's easy."

CAUTION: If you take a book from the stacks to your work desk, do not try to return it to its proper place. That's work for the experts. If you replace it incorrectly, the next seeker won't be able to find it.

Learn to know the reference librarian

Some of the brightest and best informed men and women in America are the librarians who specialize in providing reference help.

Introduce yourself. State your problem. And be amazed at how much help you will receive.

CAUTION: Don't waste the time of this expert by asking silly questions you ought to solve yourself. Save the reference librarian for the really big ones.

Learn to use *The Reader's Guide to Periodical Literature*

This green-bound index is one of the most useful items in any library. It indexes all the articles in the major magazines, including newspaper magazine supplements.

Thus it provides a guide to the very latest expert information on any subject that interests you.

So if you want to do a really first-class job, find out which magazines your library subscribes to, then consult *The Reader's Guide* and track down recent articles on your subject. When you use this wonderful tool effectively, you show the mark of a real scholar.

Four personal hints

Since you can take most books home, but not magazines, take full notes when using the latter.

Many libraries today provide a reprographic machine that can quickly copy pages you need from magazines and books. Ask about it.

If you are working on a project of some size which will require repeated library visits, keep a small notebook in which you record the identification numbers of the books you will be using frequently. This will save you valuable time, because you won't have to consult the card catalog or search aimlessly through the stacks each time you visit for material you seek.

Some of the very best books in any library are the reference books, which may not be taken home. Learn what topics they cover and how best to use them, for these books are wonderful repositories of human knowledge.

Your business and legal advisor

Your library can give you help on *any* subject. It can even be your business and legal advisor.

How many times have you scratched your head over how to get a tax rebate on your summer job? You'll find answers in tax guides at the library. Thinking of buying or renting a house? You'll find guides to that. Want to defend yourself in traffic court? Find out how in legal books at the library.

Library projects can be fun—and rewarding

Here are a few ideas:

1. What are your roots? Trace your ancestors. Many libraries specialize in genealogy.

2. Did George Washington sleep nearby? Or Billy the Kid? Your library's collection of local history books can put you on the trail.

3. Cook a Polynesian feast. Or an ancient Roman banquet. Read how in the library's cookbooks.

4. Take up photography. Check the library for consumer reviews of cameras before you buy. Take out books on lighting, composition, or darkroom techniques.

Or—you name it!

If you haven't detected by now my enthusiasm for libraries, let me offer two personal notes.

I'm particularly pleased that in recent years two beautiful libraries have been named after me: a small community library in Quakertown,

"I discover all kinds of interesting books just by browsing in the stacks. I encourage you to browse."

Pennsylvania, and the huge research library located at the University of Northern Colorado in Greeley.

And I like libraries so much that I married a librarian.

James A. Michener

This chapter demonstrates that a speech can be designed in many different ways. The yearnings for innovation in almost all suggest that the message which reveals some new twist will get our attention. The general expectations of an audience, however, are stable. No matter what the design, the audience expects *structure,* and most of the other items listed in the expectations outline. The basic design may vary but the Explanation-Illustration-Evidence (EIE), which will be discussed in the following section, can satisfy that audience hunger for meaning. It's a sound formula, particularly sound when the illustration is drawn from events which are "close to home."

Supports, Interest and Credibility

For some speakers the selection of supporting material appears to be instinctively right. That which interests them inevitably interests their audience, and that which is convincing to them is likewise convincing to their audience. The purpose of providing information is to lessen their uncertainty and to enable them to make wiser choises and successful predictions for them and their organizations.

A speech is more than an idea and yet more than a good outline. It is a personal sharing of thoughts and feelings with another being who for a short time attends to one another. A speech is not an essay on its hind legs written to be delivered to mankind in general. What is it that for a few minutes compels an audience to listen with empathy, discrimination or appreciation? Listenability is attributable to many factors both internal to the listener (his physical state, i.e., hunger, fatigue, sexual excitation) and to the generation of psychic tension (his fears, arousal of pleasure seeking drives, or ego concerns.) The listenability or interest level depends most of all upon its relevance. Do the ideas, examples, illustrations, testimonies, statistics, analogies, and explanation carry meaningfulness to the listener? In plain words, does it hit close to home? This is why a speech at its best is not an essay readable time and time again.

 **Prepared**   **Goodwill**

 **Resourceful**   **No Nonsense**

The sensitive speaker selects the supports which spring from his experience and those which he observes spring from the lives of those about him. Speech materials seem to engulf him. They grow out of the years of working with tough problems, with loveable and difficult people, with facts and figures, new products and old standbys, from heated conversations with colleagues and unusual vacations, from stories and poems memorized as a child, from movies and headlines in today's paper. The interest level depends upon the variety of supports and upon its fluctuation between the concrete and abstract. That is to suggest that a presentation composed of one long story after another would tire an audience to fatigue by its detail just as a presentation composed of high level abstraction would bore them to slow death. Consider a graphic representation of material which may be used to support a point. See the diagram below.

1	2	= 3
3	4	= 7
		= 10

Mathematical Analogy to Supporting a Premise

Illustration or Analogies	Specific Instances or Fictitious Examples	Generate Feelings and Empathy
Statistical Data Explanation	Testimonies Quotations from Literature	Generate Belief and Logical Thought

Premise
Generalizations
Based upon the
Concrete Data

Dignified

A premise or point is made not merely by its statement, but by its support. The supports selected generate the feeling or belief desired only if they are relevant and believable to the listener. Let's think of the totality of the address and the eye of the beholder. First he expects the opening, then the development and finally the closure. That development must look good to him. He must see the core idea and surrounding it, the explanation, illustration and evidence (testimony, statistical research). The eye of the listener thus sees the speech in this way:

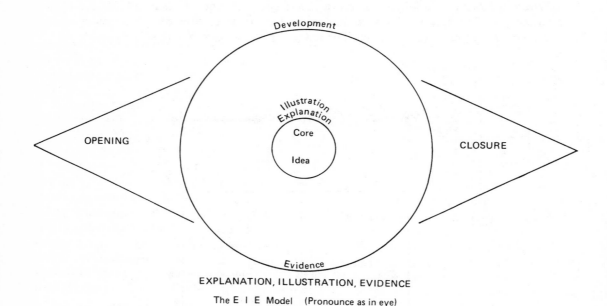

EXPLANATION, ILLUSTRATION, EVIDENCE
The E I E Model   (Pronounce as in eye)

The EIE models what the witness of a presentation must see in order to feel and/or believe. The target audience requests of the speaker: "Explain to me what you mean; illustrate, show me what you believe or feel by a live experience; and present the evidence, lay out the facts, expert opinions and data which causes your beliefs and feelings."

Explanation. In every career people give orders, follow instructions and find it very necessary to be able to explain what they are doing or think should be done. A physician with some forty years' experience put it this way, "The chief communication skill I must use is being able to give patients an explanation." Whether in a one-to-one or a one-to-many situations, explanation is essential to developing a message. The key to presentation of supports is the ability to tie them to the subordinate premises, and the more important linkage to the central thesis of the message. For example, suppose that the central thesis of a message was: "Put your money in a saving and loan institution." The speaker might first seek to establish a subordinate premise: "Don't worry about the future is bad advice." Through explanation these two are tied together. He might say:

Today, I'm here to explain the benefits which can be yours by investments in Savings and Loans. But I know my message faces a giant propaganda machine that holds great appeal. This message comes at us fifteen to twenty times an hour. What is it? Bluntly it shouts Don't Worry About the Future. Let's see if you've heard that message as I have. Yesterday, for example, I counted the number of times I heard such bad advice in a half hour of television. In the dozen spot-ads I witnessed, these are the words I heard at least once: "Now . . . buy it now! Buy now, pay later! You only go around once! You deserve the best. The money is as close as your phone! If you can't afford it, we can help you."

I suggest that such propaganda leads to irresponsible behavior and often very sad consequences: Debts that are not paid. A young generation which doesn't think about the consequences of a venereal disease epidemic. Shortsighted expediency demands that a government owes me a living. The fable of the grasshopper who fiddled all summer while the ant stored food for winter presents a choice for this audience.

In these above paragraphs, explanation and transition have been used to weave together relationships. Transitions help move from one thought to another. Sometimes these transitions are brief rhetorical questions such as, What is it? or, How does that affect us? Other times transitions are introduced with, "But . . .," "In addition . . .," "Let's consider . . .," etc. The transition is the speaker's tool for proceeding in a conversational fashion with his listeners.

Perhaps the most important transitional device is the *signpost*. The signpost serves as a signal that there is something coming. Sometimes the signpost is a simple "First," "Second," or "Third"; other times it is a "Next . . ." or "Now, let's . . ." or "Let's draw our attention . . .," "Let's focus on . . ." or "In conclusion let me recap . . ."

Explanation develops an argument by describing relationships. It weaves together what has been said in a former paragraph to what is being said at the moment. It may introduce an example and evidence, and then it ascends from the concrete up the ladder of abstractions to consider the wider implications. In an address to the 16th Annual Management Conference at the Graduate School of Business in the University of Chicago, David Rockefeller, University Trustee and President of the Chase Manhattan Bank, talked of youth and the profit motive. Excerpts from that speech are included here to illustrate how explanation is typically utilized in developing an argument. Notice how it is through explanation that the speaker reveals his own opinion and exposes that opinion for the consideration of the listener:

More important still, because we live in an affluent society in which "making a living" is no longer the challenge it used to be, business must demonstrate to young people that it offers other than purely material rewards. One of the participants in the Harvard Business School internship program came away from his exposure to industry with the comment: "It is about time businessmen learned that college students are not all that concerned about the profit motive."

To that my instinctive response—and probably yours too—would be: "It is about time college students learned that without the profit motive, this would be a sick society indeed."

But there is little point to shouting such assertions at deaf ears. What we as businessmen must do is to demonstrate through action that the profit motive, properly employed, constitutes a powerful tool with which to achieve the goals that the best of our young people profess to want. We must show beyond dispute that business can become the engine of progress in such areas as civil rights, poverty, urban decay, and pollution of the environment.

You and I know that business has already made significant contributions in some of these areas. In the field of civil rights alone, great strides have been made. Companies have thrown their resources into the battle to improve housing, education, and employment opportunities for the Negro population. Individual businessmen are giving leadership to community action programs like the National Urban Coalition and its local counterparts.

But despite this, I believe it is clear to all of us that the U.S. Business Community is not yet doing enough to meet the great socioeconomic problems of our time.[4]

Good explanation is interpersonal. The speaker reveals his interdependence with the listener. For examples, look again at how Mr. Rockefeller, in this short section of his presentation, made frequent reference to that relationship:

"My instinctive response—and probably yours too—. . ."

"What we as businessmen must do. . ."

". . . the best of our young people. . ."

"We must show beyond dispute. . ."

". . . you and I know that business. . ."

"But despite this, I believe it is clear to all of us. . . for our time."

Count the personal pronouns. There are at least ten instances when "my, yours, we, our, you, I and us" were used.

Good explanation moves from the general to the specific to the general. In this excerpt, we witness such movement, the reaction of the Harvard Business School intern was used to illustrate the premise "Making a living is no longer the challenge it used to be." Reference to the National Urban Coalition was an effort to substantiate the point that individual businessmen are giving leadership to community action.

The interplay between the tangible and the generalization is fluid and frequent. To remain at either level denies the mental interplay necessary to maintain credibility. Examples *ad infinitum* not only tire a listener but in overkill create the impression of a mind so preoccupied by detail that it cannot see relationships. On the other hand, a speaker who talks only in broad strokes creates the impression of a mind who can see only the forest and not the trees. His message lacks credibility and interest because he appears to be out of touch with the dialogue and the hard give-and-take of reality.

Explanation, in some presentations, may be the only form of support. It is rare when such a speech can maintain the interest and intellectual curiosity of the audience. One such presentation which achieves these ends was presented by Jean Schoonover, President of Dudley-Anderson-Yutzy Public Relations, Inc., to the Life Advertising Association and the Institute of Life Insurance in Chicago, Illionis, February 29, 1974. Its title was "Why Corporate America Fears Women." The whole speech consists of explanation except for (a) a brief reference to the speaker's memories of a childhood in which she wished she had been born a boy and (b) a very brief quotation from an unnamed, young, blond psychoanalyst, who was quoted as saying, "It's quite simple, men fear women for a variety of reasons."

As you read this speech by Ms. Schoonover, note the following characteristics which make her explanation so very listenable: (Project Five-1)

1. The speaker, herself, had earned her right to talk on her chosen subject. She had achieved the presidency of a successful business.
2. The speech was personal. It summarized her own feelings and her company's endeavors with this problem.
3. The topic was of current concern. Uncle Sam had recently declared that business organizations must attend to the matter of equality of the sexes.
4. The topic had natural primal interest, i.e., relationship between the sexes.

5. The style was pungent. The sentences were short and personal, pronouns abounded, signposts alerted the listener to the "ten fears," and the overall length was relatively short.
6. The language was vivid and metaphorical. Ms. Schoonover talked about the business as "the hunt," and about home as "the caves of Scarsdale and Westport."

Not all of these characteristics are clearly demonstrated in the short excerpt below, but several of them are in this following section near the end of her speech:

> My friends, there you have them, ten keys to understanding, ten rules, ten common fears in executive America, in Corporate America, of the new women, held by the "old men."
> The old culture.
> The old work ethic.
> The old Wisdom.
> The old Fears.
> The old Waste.
> Yes, I said waste.
> We see it so often, I'm sure you do, too. In your board rooms, in your executive offices, in your clubs and bars, wherever good men gather: The pain, the real anguish, the joylessness of executive America, of Corporate America, thinking about, grappling with, THE PROBLEM OF THE NEW WOMEN—OF BUSINESS AND THE NEW WOMAN.[5]

Illustrations. An illustration may be a factual account of something that actually happened, or hypothetical invented stories of something that probably could happen. Illustrations present the most effective means for dramatizing a premise. A factual illustration consists of a story (narrative), an event. As in the first line of a news article, it should include the who, what, when, and where, and in the subsequent story, enough description of the interaction that the audience can provide some reasonable explanation of why. Imagery, movement across a period of time and actual or paraphrased dialogue may be liberally utilized.

In a slid presentation and address to a Rotary Club, Roger Deer, as Vice President and General Manager of Lamb Electric, stated:

> Over this period we have been able to maintain a fairly stable work force and the company has grown in spite of some very difficult periods—including the great depression of the '30s and various periods of labor unrest. As a matter of fact, we were about the first industry in the community to be organized by labor back in the '30s. The initial organization effort is remembered by many in the community as the "War on Lake Street," and unfortunately our company is known by many for this event rather than for the products we make. The strike was so heated and the controversy so great that it was said that this water tower looked much like a large sieve from the bullet holes that it contained. I know it must have been a rough period for when I first came to the company there were still file cabinets being used that contained bullet holes. . .[6]

An illustration affects the teller as well as the listener. He verbally relives the experience, and in so doing may be caught up again in the tonal and muscle tension of that event. The target audience, seeing and hearing the nonverbal cues, in addition to the narrative, empathically may enter into the feeling level. To understand why someone believes a premise to be true, one must enter into his feelings. The proverbial statement attributed to Indian lore states, "Do not criticize a man until you have walked three moons in his moccasins."

Specific instances are similar to a factual illustration in that they are real, but they do not include the lengthy narrative. They provide a means to demonstrate to the listener in rapid fashion that this phenomena is not an isolated event. Individual cases convey a feeling that people are involved.

How to make a speech

By George Plimpton

International Paper asked George Plimpton, who writes books about facing the sports pros (like "Paper Lion" and "Shadow Box"), and who's in demand to speak about it, to tell you how to face the fear of making a speech.

One of life's terrors for the uninitiated is to be asked to make a speech.

"Why me?" will probably be your first reaction. "I don't have anything to say." It should be reassuring (though it rarely is) that since you were asked, somebody must think you do. The fact is that each one of us has a store of material which should be of interest to others. There is no reason why it should not be adapted to a speech.

Why know how to speak?

Scary as it is, it's important for anyone to be able to speak in front of others, whether twenty around a conference table or a hall filled with a thousand faces.

Being able to speak can mean better grades in any class. It can mean talking the town council out of increasing your property taxes. It can mean talking top management into buying your plan.

How to pick a topic

You were probably asked to speak in the first place in the hope that you would be able to articulate a topic that you know something about. Still, it helps to find out about your audience first. Who are they? Why are they there? What are they interested in? How much do they already know about your subject? One kind of talk would be appropriate for the Women's Club of Columbus, Ohio, and quite another for the guests at the Vince Lombardi dinner.

How to plan what to say

Here is where you must do your homework.

The more you sweat in advance, the less you'll have to sweat once you appear on stage. Research your topic thoroughly. Check the library for facts, quotes, books and timely magazine and newspaper articles on your subject. Get in touch with experts. Write to them, make phone calls, get interviews to help round out your material.

In short, gather—and learn—far more than you'll ever use. You can't imagine how much confidence that knowledge will inspire.

Now start organizing and writing. Most authorities suggest that a good speech breaks down into three basic parts—an introduction, the body of the speech, and the summation.

Introduction: An audience makes up its mind very quickly. Once the mood of an audience is set, it is difficult to change it, which is why introductions are important. If the speech is to be lighthearted in tone, the speaker can start off by telling a good-natured story about the subject or himself.

But be careful of jokes, especially the shaggy-dog

"What am I doing wrong? Taking refuge behind the lectern, looking scared to death, shuffling pages, and reading my speech. Relax. Come out in the open, gesture, talk to your audience!"

variety. For some reason, the joke that convulses guests in a living room tends to suffer as it emerges through the amplifying system into a public gathering place.

Main body: There are four main intents in the body of the well-made speech. These are 1) to entertain, which is probably the hardest; 2) to instruct, which is the easiest if the speaker has done the research and knows the subject; 3) to persuade, which one does at a sales presentation, a political rally, or a town meeting; and finally, 4) to inspire, which is what the speaker emphasizes at a sales meeting, in a sermon, or at a pep rally. (Hurry-Up Yost, the onetime Michigan football coach, gave such an inspiration-filled half-time talk that he got carried away and at the final exhortation led his team on the run through the wrong locker-room door into the swimming pool.)

Summation: This is where you should "ask for the order." An ending should probably incorporate a sentence or two which sounds like an ending—a short summary of the main points of the speech, perhaps, or the repeat of a phrase that most embodies what the speaker has hoped to convey. It is valuable to think of the last sentence or two as something which might produce applause. Phrases which are perfectly appropriate to signal this are: "In closing..." or "I have one last thing to say..."

Once done—fully written, or the main

points set down on 3″ x 5″ index cards—the next problem is the actual presentation of the speech. Ideally, a speech should not be read. At least it should never appear or sound as if you are reading it. An audience is dismayed to see a speaker peering down at a thick sheaf of papers on the lectern, wetting his thumb to turn to the next page.

How to sound spontaneous

The best speakers are those who make their words sound spontaneous even if memorized. I've found it's best to learn a speech point by point, not word for word. Careful preparation and a great deal of practicing are required to make it come together smoothly and easily. Mark Twain once said, "It takes three weeks to prepare a good ad-lib speech."

Don't be fooled when you rehearse. It takes longer to deliver a speech than to read it. Most speakers peg along at about 100 words a minute.

Brevity is an asset

A sensible plan, if you have been asked to speak to an exact limit, is to talk your speech into a mirror and stop at your allotted time; then cut the speech accordingly. The more familiar you become with your speech, the more confidently you can deliver it.

As anyone who listens to speeches knows, brevity is an asset. Twenty minutes are ideal. An hour is the limit an audience can listen comfortably.

In mentioning brevity, it is worth mentioning that the shortest inaugural address was George Washington's—just 135 words. The longest was William Henry Harrison's in 1841. He delivered a two-hour 9,000-word speech into the teeth of a freezing northeast wind. He came down with a cold the

following day, and a month later he died of pneumonia.

Check your grammar

Consult a dictionary for proper meanings and pronunciations. Your audience won't know if you're a bad speller, but they will know if you use or pronounce a word improperly. In my first remarks on the dais, I used to thank people for their "fulsome introduction," until I discovered to my dismay that "fulsome" means *offensive* and *insincere.*

"Why should you make a speech? There are four big reasons (left to right): to inspire, to persuade, to entertain, to instruct. I'll tell you how to organize what you say."

On the podium

It helps one's nerves to pick out three or four people in the audience—preferably in different sectors so that the speaker is apparently giving his attention to the entire room—on whom to focus. Pick out people who seem to be having a good time.

How questions help

A question period at the end of a speech is a good notion. One would not ask questions following a tribute to the company treasurer on his re-

tirement, say, but a technical talk or an informative speech can be enlivened with a question period.

The crowd

The larger the crowd, the easier it is to speak, because the response is multiplied and increased. Most people do not believe this. They peek out from behind the curtain and if the auditorium is filled to the rafters they begin to moan softly in the back of their throats.

What about stage fright?

Very few speakers escape the so-called "butterflies." There does not seem to be any cure for them, except to realize that they are beneficial rather than harmful, and never fatal. The tension usually means that the speaker, being keyed up, will do a better job. Edward R. Murrow called stage fright "the sweat of perfection." Mark Twain once comforted a fright-frozen friend about to speak: "Just remember they don't expect much." My own feeling is that with thought, preparation and faith in your ideas, *you* can go out there and expect a pleasant surprise.

And what a sensation it is—to hear applause. Invariably after it dies away, the speaker searches out the program chairman—just to make it known that he's available for next month's meeting.

George Plimpton

Evidence. Statistics go beyond individual cases to averages, percents and significance. The closest thing that the social sciences has to proof lies in a carefully drawn representative sample or data of a total population. The speaker, when using statistical data, must realize that his audience's ability to understand is directly related to its ability to visualize. Therefore, when presenting figures a presentation not only ought to be repeated, but ought to be made graphic. Visual aids may help and comparisons will help. In addition to saying, for example, that fifty thousand persons are killed annually and several hundred thousands are injured on American highways, a speaker may state that the odds are that three out of every five persons in this room will sometime in their lives be involved in an auto accident.

In a speech to the Society of Automotive Engineers, Semon E. Knudsen, as Chairman and CEO of White Motor Company, made creative use of the hypothetical illustration to present statistical data:

> Let me give you a hypothetical illustration of what I mean. On the Alaskan North Slope, in the Prudhoe Bay area, there are proven reserves of about ten billion barrels of oil. That sounds impressive, and many of us have been comforting ourselves with the thought that this great oil find will solve our energy problem if we can only get the oil piped out. But let's take another look.
>
> At the present time, we are consuming—in the United States alone—between six and seven billion barrels of oil a year. And our consumption of oil is increasing at an annual rate of six or seven percent. Now, suppose we had all that Alaskan oil pumped out of the ground, shipped, refined and in storage tanks. And suppose we decided to use it up so as not to deplete our reserves in the lower forty-eight states, and that we quit importing oil so as to improve our balance of payments and strengthen the dollar. If we followed this course of action, all of that Alaskan oil would be gone in eighteen months.
>
> So, even if we get that Alaskan oil out, and even if we find other equally big fields on the North slope, in off-shore areas, and in other parts of the world, the rate of use throughout the world is so high and growing so fast that we must ultimately find other sources of energy to take over much of the energy load being carried now by petroleum.[7]

Knudsen deftly utilized the "suppose" to the statistical data, and the wedding was performed by the ritual of explanation. Again, yet in a less conventional bonding, we see the marriage of Explanation + Illustration + Evidence.

Testimony is the opinion of someone who should know, possibly an authority in a field or at least a person who has witnessed an event. As in court, the validity and admissibility of the testimony depends upon the credibility of the expert witness. Therefore, when using an opinion, some care should be given to establishing the expertise of the witness and/or his ability to observe. One of the authors once listened to a funeral sermon in which the only support used was testimony. The clergyman read brief statements from forty famous persons affirming their belief in immortality. The event was moving and persuasive because of the credibility of the famous men, despite the fact that none of them had yet actually experienced their own deaths nor did they claim to have seen any one person come back to life after his body died.

Credibility. The name of the game is credibility. All supports must withstand the critical judgment of the target audience. What does the intelligent listener ask? What tests of reason and common sense does he use? Credibility is generated (a) when the speaker has a reputation for honesty and competence, (b) when the supports which he uses are consistent with other knowledge, (c) when the supports appear to come from reputable sources, (d) when the supports appear to be adequate in number, up-to-date and representative and (e) when the presenter conveys sincerity, both verbally and nonverbally. There is some evidence that a dynamic speaker is evaluated by an audience as more credible than a less forceful speaker. This criterion probably relates to the fact that intensity of emotion is associated with conviction.

**When speaking with a microphone,
keep it near the chin.**

Brainy

Zany

Mysterious

Involved

Loving

**Don't go to extremes, but appropriate
grooming aids confidence.**

Delivery

The actual presentation of a message, for some is very threatening and traumatic, but for most is exciting and exhilarating. No book can give you confidence nor can it, in and of itself, cure an extreme case of speech fright. But mastering techniques of skillful speech construction does give one confidence. Practice of these techniques under the guidance of a professional instructor can soon enable almost any motivated person to enjoy the public platform. We come to enjoy that which we do well. First, let us examine several general principles of delivery and following this, provide a number of practical tips for the actual speaking experience.

General Principles:
- Adapt to the size of the room and audience. The larger the room the louder the voice, the broader the gesture; the greater the distance from the audience, the more dramatic should be the presentation.
- Adapt to the mood of the occasion. The voice expresses the emotions in the rate and tension. The body communicates mood by its rate of movement, tension, or relaxation of gesture and muscle.
- Delivery is a means and, therefore, should not call attention to itself. Delivery should emphasize meaning and should direct the audience's attention to meaning. In short, the listener should not think about how melodious is the voice or how dynamic the gesture. Rather, he should be caught up in his own thoughts and feelings about the message.
- Nonverbal cues play an important part in delivery of a message. Space speaks. Generally, movement toward someone, approaching, signals interest and intensity of concern for communication. Retreating provides a time for relaxation or variety. Contrast focuses attention. Standing on a chair or platform, kneeling while others stand, turning one's back to the audience, all of these contrasting actions focus attention. Time speaks. A change of rate of delivery provides emphasis. Speaking much longer or shorter than the expected period may irritate. The body speaks. The muscle tension reveals, by rigidity or relaxation, attitudes of confidence, concern, anxiety, or disinterest. We read each other's muscles and unless they appear congruent with the verbal message, our attention is drawn to them and doubt rather than trust is aroused.
- Delivery is a two-way event. It is a moment in time when one person gives his energy to sharing himself with another. It is not soliloquy, monologue or telling. Public speaking, of course, means that one person is speaking to many. But it does not mean that there is one-way communication only. The speaker attends both to the nonverbal and verbal responses to his message, and should allow ample time for talkback, questions and reactions and dialogue. Eye contact confirms that this exchange is in process while the speaker and audience take turns in verbal exchange.

Ten Tips on Delivery. A speaker may break some of the rules because there are so many variables at work. Likely we all can name friends who hold down a good job despite faulty speech, and can also point to prominent national figures whose distinctive voice or mannerisms helped rather than hindered them: a nasal voice, slouch and drawl, a stoic immobile expression. The tips prescribed here, thus, may be considered advice from the experts for most speaking situations. Just remember that a presentation may be successful in spite of breaking one or several of these do's or don'ts, and the more succesful you are the more tolerance an audience has for your deviance from the rules.

Remember

Eye Contact

Eye Contact.

Eye Contact

1. Approach the platform with confidence. Sometimes, if the mood is one of excitement, you may even hurry to the platform to express your eagerness to greet the audience. Select dress which will be appropriate and comfortable.

2. As you reach the speaker's stand, make contact with the chairman, accept his introduction with a handshake or nod, and greet any other person on the platform.

3. Next, look over the crowd; pause to concentrate upon your verbal greeting and the first words of your message. Don't look at your notes again!

4. Take charge. The platform is yours now. But the room belongs to the audience so, if in doubt, check to learn if your voice is easily heard in the back row. If possible, check out the room before your speech.

5. Acknowledge. Take notice of the situation, but do not strain to make a joke of it or somebody.

6. Avoid a long introduction. Build common ground quickly and get to your topic.

7. Use a key word ouline. Except for rare policy speeches do not read a manuscript. Rather work from a 3" x 5" card with key words to aid recall of important ideas, supports and quotations. Do not try to present a speech from memory or to give a long presentation entirely impromptu. Speeches from memory and impromptu talks are destined for failure. The first suffers from a canned over-prepared action. The second suffers from lack of preparation. Practice that presentation from the beginning to end at least twice. Try saying it different ways. If possible, work in a room where you can talk out loud to an imaginary audience.

8. Do not keep your audience in the dark about your intention. Preview the topics you intend to cover.

9. Make your body work for you. Move to demonstrate a transition into a new point but avoid pacing or fidgeting. Use the hands, head, eyes to convey feelings, to describe and illustrate. Movement causes the eye to follow. Keep gestures up, make them definite, and do not hurry them. Maintain good posture. Suit your movement to the size of the room.

10. Stop at the end of a point. Make your transition and begin the next. Repeat or rephrase once, but do not over explain.

Recap

Designing and delivering a major address requires diligent preparation and practice, but that's as it should be because the speaker is in charge of many people's time. His thirty-minute presentation, when totaled up for three hundred people, amounts to one hundred and fifty hours. Success comes from earning his right to that time. He earns that right by living with the problems he talked about. He earns that right by research and careful reflection. And he earns that right by careful writing and speaking—practice, practice, practice.

NOTES

1. Joseph E. Kuebler, "They're People Movers," Business Report, *The Akron Beacon Journal,* April 7, 1974, p. B-14.
2. Allan H. Munroe, *Principles and Types of Speech,* Fourth Edition (New York: Scott, Foresman and Co., 1955), p. viii.
3. Aristotle, *Poetics,* p. 1459.
4. David Rockefeller, "The Generation Gap and Its Meaning for Business," *The University of Chicago Magazine* (July/August 1968), pp. 2-8. Reprinted with permisssion from the *University of Chicago Magazine.*
5. Jean Way Schoonover, "Why Corporate America Fears Women," mimeographed.
6. Roger Deer, "The Lamb Electric Story," Rotary Club Address, February 5, 1974. (Mimeographed).
7. Semon E. Knudsen, "The Interchange of Technical Information," Presented at Portland, Oregon, August 22, 1973, *Vital Speeches,* Vol. 39, p. 40.

Project Five-1

Thesis and Behavioral Objectives

Study Guide

I. *Objective*: To focus upon the thesis sentence and the behavior desired by the speaker. When Project Five-1 is completed the student should be able to differentiate between a general end, a thesis statement, an impelling proposition and a behavioral objective of a message.

II. *Model:*Read

Jean Way Schoonover, Remarks at The School of Business, Pennsylvania State University. As you read, number the lines of the speech.

III. *Analysis:*

1. With which of these general ends is Ms. Schoonover most concerned?
   a. To entertain.
   b. To inform.
   c. To impress.
   d. To convince.
   e. To activate.

   Answer: This address is hard hitting. It attempts to form a belief that women should play a vital role in American corporate business. It does not simply entertain, inform or stimulate; though it does amuse, share information, and arouse. It aims to *change* attitudes, to convince, and to spur her audience to action.

2. Find one sentence which above all others states Ms. Schoonover's thesis, her core idea.

   Answer: A thesis statement broadly encompasses the central belief and attitudes desired by the speaker. A thesis serves a key beam in the structure. It is a belief which the address will elaborate and support. "Because women are no longer going to be second-class citizens in the business and career world," takes a stand. "... you should welcome this shift...," is the end attitude desired. I will not argue which of these two is the thesis.

3. Scan the speech in search of a proposition that is echoed in the address. Is it impelling? Does it touch basic drives of physical safety, ego enhancement, sexual excitation, altruistic concerns for one's fellowman? For example, the safety slogan might be considered an impelling proposition: "The life you save may be your own." Write out the one phrase or sentence in this address which most ought to make the target audience *want* to do as Ms. Schoonover suggests:

_____

_____

Answer: For me there is no one sentence that echoes more than: fear to be dispelled must be understood. After this general truth is stated ten fears of businessmen are described, hopefully explained sufficiently to create understanding. At the conclusion of this explanation Ms. Schoonover again talks about "fears of the 'old' man." Now why should this theme get to that target? The appeal is to overcoming fear of the *old* man. Not one in that audience of businessmen wants to be linked with *old* age! Here indeed, is an impelling proposition that reaches to the psyches of that audience.

4. Now what does Jean Way Schoonover really expect from her target audience? Will she be satisfied with applause? I think not. She wants action that springs from a new attitude. She is not subtle about the behavior desired. What behaviors, if performed, will she use to evaluate the ultimate effectiveness of her address? Of the 15

she listed, which do you consider most realizable? _____

_____

And which is most important?   _____

_____

Finally, let me add that Ms. Schoonover, in spite of her forceful presentation, is not so naive as to think her address will force her audience of businessmen to behave differently. Her direct attack upon the problem demonstrates that a woman can take command and can compete in the Male world. The experience and efforts of the upgrading program for women of the company which she heads, speaks loudly through her testimony. Hopefully, she has begun a dialogue about these matters, a relationship of candor, and respect.

Jean Way Schoonover

Jean Way Schoonover has been a staff member of Dudley-Anderson-Yutzey, a national advertising agency, for more than twenty years, becoming president of the firm in 1970. Mrs. Schoonover has been an account executive, account supervisor and operational manager of every major account group in the agency. The firm ranks among the top 15 and has nearly tripled in size under her leadership.

An accredited member of the Public Relations Society of America, Mrs. Schoonover was PRSA'a first national Consumer Relations Study Group chairman and is currently a member of the Executive Committee of the PRSA Counselors Section.

She was named Advertising Woman of the Year in 1972 (one of ten) by the American Advertising Federation. She is a member of the Executive Committee of the Cornell University Alumni Council and the Board of Directors of the American National Metric Council. She has also served on various committees and boards of the Council of Better Business Bureaus, United Negro College Fund, Advertising Women of New York and Women Executives in Public Relations.

Her philosophy of women in business was recently featured on the Op Ed page of the *New York Times,* in *Vital Speeches,* and will appear in the November issue of *The Saturday Evening Post.*

Mrs. Schoonover is married and the mother of a college-age daughter and two sons. She is listed in *Who's Who in America* and *Who's Who in Public Relations.*

Remarks by Jean Way Schoonover
President, Dudley-Anderson-Yutzey

It's an old saw that two heads are better than one.

It's a new saw that two sexes are better than one. . . . That's you and me, baby. And it's today . . . in corporate America . . . as peers and equals managing America's business.

Not only is it a new saw, but it's a new law. One that you and your corporations are having a lot of trouble with. And there will be more trouble before this new saw becomes an old saw. Trouble at first for the institutions who are the leaders and then trouble for those who are the laggards in American industry.

Because women are no longer going to be second-class citizens in the business and career world.

And corporate America—you—should welcome this shift, this new awakening of both women and men to the skills and the abilities of women.

Human resources, we all know, are the corporation's greatest assets. Your companies are known by your managements. You ultimately succeed or fail largely because of your people, because of the leadership of your managers. You know that better than I. That's probably why you are here.

You know also that the main unidentified or under-utilized human resource in your companies, in nearly all companies, is your women. Yes, your women. All those women sitting around in secretarial jobs, clerical jobs, assistants' jobs. All those girl Fridays.

How much do you know about them? Do you know which ones have BA or BS or MA degrees? Do you know how many have trained their bosses . . . not one, but two or three, or a succession of men who have moved upward and onward thanks to the help of their women assistants? These are America's invisible women—on the job but really unseen.

I know that men are sometimes invisible, too, both sexes often go unseen. But I'm here to talk about women and the way you see them today.

Equal opportunity for women is now a legal requirement. And it's a legal requirement that is causing consternation in many a corporate headquarters . . . anguish among the men who are trying to cope with this new edit, this new problem: the problem of women as managers, as peers, as equals in corporate America today.

In our firm, we say that we know about women, and we do. But the pain and the anguish of our clients spurred us on to learn more, much more about women, because we wanted to help our clients understand women.

So at D-A-Y a team of us, including Tom Leighton, our senior vice president for corporate counseling, and myself, have undertaken to immerse ourselves in the subject. To get a new perspective, we sought help, expert help, from psychologists and psychoanalysts, male and female.

We have learned much that has been useful as we have passed it along to our clients. Our first concern was, why? Why are you men in corporate management having so much difficulty accepting women as peers, working with women on the job.

Dr. Ed Shelly, a New York psychoanalyst, wrapped it up neatly for us one night: "It's quite simple," he said. "Men fear women for a variety of reasons."

Fear, to be dispelled, must be understood. Here are some of the reasons men fear women—here are keys to understanding; here are ten reasons why men fear women on the job.

One:

Men fear women as peers on the job—the brainworkers in particular, because they believe, and often rightly, that women are unable to free on-the-job relationships of sexual tensions.

Two:

Men fear women on the job because the culture, our business society, has not taught them how to work with women whose only relationship to them is that of co-worker, professional colleague.

Three:

Men fear women because of their physical need for women and they fear that career women will exploit their vulnerability, and that in the case of competitors, a woman's sex gives her a strong competitive "edge."

Four:

The fourth fear men have of business equals who are women is that men do not trust women because they do not trust women's emotions. Most men feel that the emotional responses of women to business problems—problems in general—are unpredictable. Because men cannot predict the responses of women to business stimuli, not with any reliability at any rate, they do not trust women in business. From a lifetime of experience, from boyhood on, the culture teaches the male members of our society the rules of the game, teaches them to predict, with reasonable certainty, the reactions of another man to a given stimulus. Women haven't learned the game. Their responses are not predictable by the men, and because they are not, women are considered untrustworthy.

Five:

Men fear women on the job because—with very few exceptions—they have had no "life models" for the business relationship between man and woman. Women are mothers, wives, sweethearts, girlfriends, relatives. Women are not co-workers and most men are afraid because they view the working woman through the tunnel of their experience with women, which is very small. Each experience is easily and rigidly "type-cast" by a culture which affords men remarkably few opportunities to learn about women other than those in stereotyped, culture-conditioned roles.

Six:

The sixth fear is man's fear of woman's superiority. Woman lives longer than man, years longer, and this actuarial truth has given rise to still other fears about woman as a physically superior being. When Masters and Johnson discovered that the "little woman" was a mythic figure sexually, that her appetite was very likely superior to the man-of-the-house, male machismo took a tumble; anxiety was produced.

Seven:

Men fear women on the job—in the professions—because of what they believe is the career woman's ability to devote herself utterly to her job. The "career man" usually has a wife, children, home, friends, church, and many other interests beyond his work; he must play many roles imposed by the culture, and this variety, this diffusion of energy, gives his female counterpart a tremendous advantage. He believes that the career woman is free to focus her full force on career goals while he is forced by the culture to spread himself thin, playing a variety of roles.

Eight:

The eighth fear men have is that they are not dealing with ordinary women on the job, in their careers, but with extraordinary women, work-freaks of some kind, demented amazons who want to be facsimile men. What they have to get used to, what we all must get used to, what *you* must get used to, is that today—thanks to The Pill, perhaps, and to new cultural values, the new woman in business is a normal, an ordinary woman, seeking to make her way in a normal, ordinary way.

Nine:

The ninth fear—and a painful one in a mature society—is this: executive America, corporate America fears women because the men who run corporate America are afraid of losing their identities. It is one of America's tragedies that we have come to believe that a man is what he does for a living. Chiefly that. If women also do what he does for a living, is he less than he was? Less than a man ought to be? Are his victories made small because women also enjoy them? What is a man in our society who loses a job? A man who loses his job loses his identity. It is this, far more than income loss—which is usually temporary—that terrifies men. It is one more reason, this critical factor of identity, why men cannot help fearing co-workers who are women.

Ten:

The tenth fear men have of women is a second-hand fear; a "second-person" fear. The tenth reason why men in corporate America fear women is the fear their wives have of the women with whom they work; the woman who serves as a co-worker, peer, equal to their husbands.

This may be the most difficult fear of all to deal with, *the fear of one woman for another.*

All those fears, my friends, are there—consciously or subconsciously—in the minds and psyches of you men in corporate America who are charged with bringing women into the management group, trying to do what you know you must do, grappling with the new problem of business and the new woman.

All those fears are also keys to understanding the problem. They are fears held by the "old" man, coming out of the old culture, the old work ethic, the old wisdom, the old waste.

Yes, the old waste of one of our nation's most precious assets . . . the human resource represented by its women. A colossal waste.

And a stunning example of the negative effect of our culture's conditioning.

America's businessmen are the best in the world, the most creative, the boldest, the most enterprising. You're the best. And yet you back off from an opportunity of historic proportions, a monumental opportunity to use, to harness virtually untapped energy; to put into the service of this culture, this business society, a totally fresh perspective—the energy, the brainpower, the perspective of the modern liberated woman who is free to work with men, free to build with them—an entirely new way of business life, where two sexes are better than one. That's you and me, baby.

But what about the women? What about our fears and our anxieties? Many of us have culture conditioned attitudes as well. If we are old school, second-class citizen type women, we will be apprehensive, reluctant to take initiative, or go out on a limb, jealous of what little power and prestige we have. Women traditionally have not been too helpful about lending support and encouragement to the women coming along behind them. They couldn't afford to, because if the younger women were to succeed, the superior might be out in the cold. We women haven't traditionally had many rungs to climb on the corporate ladder. So these "old" women may need help in broadening their views and widening their horizons.

The younger new school women's lib type women, on the other hand, may be too impatient, too aggressive, too abrasive—or so you think. And they're turning you off. You have to understand both types and be compassionate and intelligent about it.

You have to find the way in which men and women working together can create a new, more creative, more effective, more profitable management team.

And that's why we've met here.

The question we're here tonight to discuss is how can we make it happen . . . how we can get men and women together in management, understanding each other better, working together as peers and equals to complement each other's skills and insights.

Communication has to be the answer . . . an entirely new kind of communication which deals with attitudes and opinions, fears and anxieties, new perspectives and new understanding.

The first thing to do, in my opinion, is to get rid of the fears of you men in management. Destroy the myths. Talk out the problems. Bring the fears out in the open in candid . . . confidential dialogues . . . in consciousness raising sessions.

Then introduce a wholly new idea to the men in your corporate management: what's in it for me?

Here's the great insight . . . the wholly new idea . . . the sum and substance of what's in it for you or any man:

Women aren't men. Women don't act like men; women don't think like men; women aren't built like men either, baby. Women cannot—even if they try—they cannot be facsimile men.

And no one should want them to or assume they can.

Women are women and they come with women's perspectives . . . women's creativity. They offer you a freshness of viewing the situation from a new angle . . . They bring a reportorial eye . . . an objective look . . . useful new insights. Women—and we are talking about intelligent, trained, management potential women—are decision makers on the most practical level. Women are problem solvers; women are the pragmatic people who get themselves and their group through the day; they are cool in crisis; and they are by and large the value makers in our society.

So what's in it for the corporation? For the men? For you? Adding women to the team can add a new strata of excellence . . . complementing, not competing . . . working for, not against . . . making it a reality that two sexes are better than one.

I have a few specific suggestions about how to bring all this about, and here they are:

1. Hire a team of women to upgrade your work force of women. Men can't do it with the same credibility, or effectiveness, at least not yet.
2. Choose and train selected women to be role models for the other women in the company. These are the ones to watch the progress, provide the pat on the back, keep an eye on how things are going for women in the career track process.
3. Appoint a vice president for women's affairs, or at least a director of women's affairs, to coordinate what your corporation is doing and should be doing for the women on its payroll. Hopefully this would be a short term job, but it's needed now.
4. Call on the local college for assistance in planning and implementing your affirmative action program.
5. Appoint a women's advisory committee to your corporate management, composed of both employees and outsiders.
6. Require a written policy regarding women's affirmative action objectives, plus a periodic assessment and reporting on your progress.
7. Utilize the full resources of the government—on local, state, regional and national levels. The Department of Labor, the Department of Commerce, the Small Business Administration . . . have all kinds of material and personnel who can be of help.
8. Introduce an incentive program for male executives who master a course in women's affairs.
9. Offer an incentive for men and women who integrate their departments successfully.
10. Inaugurate an internal communications effort devoted to women's affairs—and the men involved in the program as well—to go to all employees. One big need is to defang the working men, the staff and line workers who are the most hostile. These men must be helped to look on women as ordinary competition, nothing special.
11. Help your employees to upgrade their perceptions of women as workers and the worth of women to the enterprise. This might include plant posters, slogans, etc. Rosie the Riveter reincarnated in the 1970s.
12. Make everyone in the corporation—men and women together—proud of your company's leadership position on this issue.
13. Invite prestigious people to be guest lecturers: women who have made a success in various careers of work situations. These should not be the first clenching type of women's libbers, but the ordinary run of the mill successful women who accept their success as standard operating procedure.

14. Start developing a case history of your company's experience in dealing with this most important issue. How you went about it, what you gained from it. It is a subject which will make your executives popular in talking to other corporate executives . . . and it will give you a sound basis on which to exchange ideas with others.

15. Finally, and most importantly, your concern and your management's concern for elevating women into management positions must be real . . . not cosmetic. It must be viewed as a permanent, organic change . . . one that effects the head and heart and bone of the company. It can't be just rouge and false eyelashes. You and your company—the men and women in your company—must change inside and mean it. One way or another, my friends, the women are going to be part of your company's future.
Help them.
Welcome them.
Learn from them.
Enjoy the difference they make.
Be a man about it!
Thank You.

Project Five-2

Outlining

Clear messages are organized logically and usually partitioned into two to four blocks. Looking at an address to a Business Leaders' Luncheon by Frank T. Cary, Chief Executive Officer of IBM does not provide an obvious organizational pattern, yet one is present.

1. Outline the major divisions of this presentation below.

2. What is his thesis? What does he want his audience to believe, feel or do?

3. Next examine Jiro Tokuyama's speech in which he explains why Japan is so formidable a competitor. What do you notice about his use of signposts? Would you make any suggestions that might eliminate confusion by his excessive use of signposts?

Business and Opinion Leaders Luncheon

F.T. Cary
October 28, 1980

In my country and in yours there is great concern about inflation, lagging productivity and the world-class competitiveness of American and Canadian business enterprises. So I'd like to say a few words about world-class competition, beginning with an outstanding example of a world-class company — IBM Canada.

When we were here in 1975 I told some of you that IBM Canada was one of the stars in the IBM firmament.

In the years since, that star has been burning more and more brightly.

Last year its revenues were 186% of those five years earlier.

In the past five years IBM Canada has added a thousand employees, bringing the total to 12,000 Canadians.

Its annual capital expenditures have more than doubled, to 300 million Canadian dollars.

Its exports have also more than doubled, going to $400 million.

And its purchases from Canadian vendors have nearly tripled. Last year they totaled 270 million dollars, providing jobs for 2,600 Canadians.

Since 1975 we've added 600 thousand square feet to our plant capacity, and we have another 300 thousand under construction. With all that, the Headquarters has grown too, and a handsome new complex is scheduled for completion in 1982 to meet their needs.

Our Canadian customers continue to be on the leading edge of data processing: pioneers in the use of scanning in supermarkets; in interactive point of sale systems in department stores; in on-line branch banking.

We are very grateful to all of you who have participated with us in this progress.

The IBM company today does business in some 120 countries around the globe, and so we're in a good position to measure world-class competitiveness among our principal companies.

It's our goal to meet competition across the entire spectrum of the information processing industry.

And so all around the world we constantly compare the price/performance of our product lines and the productivity of our employees with those of our competitors.

And whether you measure price/performance cost performance, or productivity, IBM Canada is a world-class competitor.

But the question I am asked most often is: How is IBM going to fare in the future, particularly against Japanese companies, given their national goal to export data processing equipment and their past successes in shipbuilding, autos, electronics, and other fields?

Well, let me say a little bit about that.

The quick answer is that we know IBM can compete with the Japanese companies on price/performance, cost/performance and productivity.

Ours is a technology-driven industry. We are a leader in the technology that moves that industry ahead, and we're continuing to invest a billion-and-a-half dollars a year in research and development.

Furthermore, inside the Japanese market we have a company, IBM Japan, that has been competing head-to-head with Fujitsu and Hitachi and Nippon Electric and the rest.

IBM Japan is very competitive and very successful.

When we look at our world-class competitiveness in Japan or Canada or the U.S. or anywhere else, we have one major concern.

And that is how much our competitiveness is distorted by the actions of governments.

We are always concerned with the government actions which tend to make all of the enterprises in a specific country less competitive with enterprises in other countries.

The classical actions that do this are excessive regulation, income and price policies that distort cost/performance and price/performance even though the basic productivity of employees may be very competitive.

What I am more concerned about are those government actions that discriminate between enterprises located within the same national boundaries. Examples of this are in our industry:

1. Direct government subsidies to so-called national companies for research and development. This takes place and has for a number of years in Japan, the UK, France and Germany.

2. Indirect Government subsidies through low cost loans. And procurement practices where governments buy only from so-called "national manufacturers." The definition of a "national manufacturer" is often strained and can even result in a national enterprise with a negative balance of trade getting the order over a so-called non-national with a positive balance of trade. This has been a practice in Japan, the UK and France.

3. Government barring all but national manufacturers from particular parts of the business — for example, small computers in Brazil.

4. Probably the most flagrant example is the antiquated antitrust litigation of the U.S. Department of Justice against the IBM company: (*Editor's note: this action has now been dropped.*)

   —an action that reflects a lack of awareness of the competitive nature of the information processing industry.

   —an action that seeks to break IBM into several companies and if successful would certainly dismantle IBM's world-class competitiveness.

Now I realize that all of these actions are justified by governments to protect infant industries, but when they continue longer than a decade, one has to question not only the motivation, but the economic feasibility of such policies. Particularly when one finds oneself competing with so many successful enterprises with a critical mass of resources.

So let me sum up:

The IBM company—along with many others in our industry—is trying to be a world-class competitor.

And we need governments that encourage that process—governments that become part of the solution, not part of the problem.

If governments want world-class competitors, they themselves must become world-class governments.

And more and more, despite all the difficulties, I believe that's what we're going to have in our industry, at least in Europe, Japan and North America.

Though we hear a lot of protectionist talk and work through a great deal of government discrimination, I believe these economies have become so interdependent that world-class government is in their national interest.

Some signs of improvement are evident. The French Government has begun to buy from other than national manufacturers. The Japanese Government is permitting NTT to consider an IBM proposal.

Perhaps I am an optimist. Some of you have probably heard the latest definition of an optimist: a man who fervently hopes that the future is uncertain.

But I believe my optimism is justified.

And I can't think of a better place to voice it than right here in Canada:

—a country that shares with the United States the longest, most open border in the world;

—a country that with the United States produces the largest volume of trade.

I hope you share not only my optimism but my conviction.

And I thank you for your attention.

Jiro Tokuyama

Mr. Jiro TOKUYAMA is Managing Director of the Nomura Research Institute, the leading interdisciplinary research organization in Japan.

A graduate of Tokyo University (M.A. in Economics, 1944), he continued his education at the International Seminar of Harvard University under Dr. Henry Kissinger and was a research fellow of the Rockefeller Foundation at Princeton and Columbia Universities between 1957 and 1959.

His past assignments include having been assistant to the Minister of Defense, Deputy Executive Director of the Japan Trade Center in New York, and Director of the NRI New York Office.

He is the author of several books, including *Nixon's Economic and Foreign Policy* (1969), *Corporate Mergers in the United States* (1969), *Lobbyists in the United States* (1970), and *Graduate Schools of Business Administration in the United States* (1973), all in Japanese. He is also translator of many works, including Vance Packard's *Pyramid Climbers,* Alvin Toffler's *Future Shock* and most recently *Future Without Shock* by Louis B. Lundborg, Chairman of Bank of America.

Mr. Tokuyama has been a contributing editor of the international edition of *Newsweek* magazine since early 1974.

Japan: A New Framework for Judgement and Forecast

Jiro Tokuyama
Managing Director
Normura Research Institute
Tokyo, Japan

Foreign opinion about Japan is characterized by a large number of myths and stereotypes like the "economic animal" stereotype and the myths of the "automated society," the "economic miracle," and the "samurai spirit." These myths were invented many years ago to fill the information gap created by the language barrier, and they live on even today as a very poor substitute for understanding of Japan. One effect of their lack of a solid basis in fact is that they give rise to violent shifts in foreign opinion about Japan. One such shift occurred after the oil crisis when the foreign outlook for Japan changed overnight from very bright to very gloomy.

The omnipresence of these cliches suggests that the foreign perception of Japan is a castle built on sand. As a substitute on more solid ground, I would like to suggest four factors to form a new framework for foreigners to use in judging Japan and in forecasting her reactions to world events. None of these factors is directly political or economic. Rather, they deal with the geographic and climatic environment which created the underpinnings of Japanese politics and economics, i.e., the thought pattern of the Japanese people.

First is Japan's northern monsoon agrarian culture, which contrasts markedly with the hunting/cattle-raising culture of Europe and America and the tropical culture of S.E. Asia. Japan has four distinct seasons, with summers hot and humid and winters cold and dry. Japanese of times past had little fear of starving so long as they worked hard in the spring and summer. Thus Japanese considered Mother Nature basically benign, and there was little economic need to fight with others for food. The dangers faced were the excesses of nature: typhoons, floods, and earthquakes.

The contrasts with Europe are sharp. European agricultural productivity per acre is only a fraction of that in Japan, so Europeans had to fight each other for food, and so the spirit of competition became rooted in the European character. Japanese of old had a much easier life, and so no such competitive spirit developed. Another point of difference is that northern Europeans could fight nature: bitter cold was fought with fire, wind with sturdy structures. But ancient Japanese had no way to fight earthquakes and typhoons. The result is that Japanese culture emphasized adapting to great forces, while European tried to conquer them.

The contrasts with Southeast Asia are just as sharp. While Japan is quite hot and humid in summer, Southeast Asia is more so, and the heat and humidity continue all year around. This climate saps human energy and fosters a different attitude toward the pace of work. While work in Southeast Asia was paced over the long term. Japanese worked extremely hard at times (such as the hot summer) and very little at others. Even today, Japanese work extremely hard when a big job confronts them, but not so hard when not under pressure. The agricultural environment thus created many Japanese operating methods, and thus the differences in agricultural climates of Japan and other parts of the world can be seen as the root of many modern day frictions.

The second factor is ethnic homogeneity in Japan. While European countries are mixtures of many ethnic groups, Japan has basically only one. The last major migrations to the Japanese islands occurred thousands of years ago, and in the time since all Japanese have come to share a common thought pattern. There may be large amounts of local color in sections of Japan and some linguistic differences, but the thought pattern is the same.

One result of the homogeneity of the Japanese people is that communication does not rely heavily on words. European peoples were so different culturally that rhetoric and logic were developed to bridge the gaps and enable people to cooperate with each other. But logic in Japan was tacit; it needed no distinct verbal clarification since all people were of the same culture. As a result, foreigners from Europe, Asia, and America who are all outside Japanese culture cannot understand its logic. Moreover, it cannot be explained in words, since no verbal tradition exists. One simply has to get used to it.

Another result of ethnic homogeneity is the Japanese attitude toward competition with other ethnic groups. Since ethnic groups in Europe were always competing and fighting with each other, they have no great revulsion to competition with outside groups. Indeed, many even enjoy "a good fight." But Japanese deeply fear such competition. Moreover, the European legal tradition which developed from the sublimation of the ethnic groups' fighting spirit is still basically competitive; it is A vs. B. This contrasts sharply to the Japanese legal concept, which stresses arbitration and harmony, i.e., A and B work out a settlement. Japan's ethnic composition and the contrast with other countries is thus the key to understanding another large part of Japan's friction with the rest of the world.

The third influence which has shaped Japan is population pressure. Japan's high population density is not a recent phenomenon; rather, it goes back hundreds of years. Like the agricultural climate and ethnic homogeneity, population pressures are at the root of many aspects of Japanese behavior.

First of all, population pressure accounts for a lack of personal economic opportunities. This in turn results in an emphasis on harmony in which the basic agreement is "I won't take your opportunities, so please don't take mine." In other words, the life-time employment system and promotion by seniority (rather than merit) are direct results of population pressure and the need to accommodate everyone.

Second, high population density means that individualism is impossible. In its place, the Japanese have developed an ability to work in groups far better than peoples of many foreign countries; but, on the other hand, creativity is stifled. Moreover, to keep groups functioning properly, skills at human relations are quite important, which is the reason that so much time, money and alcohol are used to keep people talking to each other. Much friction between Japanese and foreigners has occurred because the latter, not influenced by high-density society, do not realize the importance of human relations to Japanese. Population density has meant a lot more to Japan than just crowded trains.

Fourth comes the question of morality. In western societies, religion is the basis of morality with an omnicient God watching all and judging all. But in Japan, even when the emperor was considered a god, he was never considered omnicient. Indeed, no omnicient power has ever existed in Japan, so morality had to be established by some other means. But without such a God, the only moral force left is man and his opinion. Thus, morality in Japan is defined by the consensus of men's perceptions of what is right in a given situation.

As an illustration of these four factors in action, one need only refer to Japan's reaction to the oil crisis. When faced by large cuts in power, members of all parts of Japanese society reacted swiftly to adjust, with energy saving measures. It was as if Japan was suddenly confronted by the modern industrial version of a typhoon, and people simply accepted it and tried to adjust; however, some enterprises viewed it as a "hot season" to be taken advantage of. The effects of population pressure then made themselves felt as those who took too great advantage of the "hot season" were disgraced because public opinion felt that there are too many people in Japan to allow a few to profit at the expense of the rest.

Moreover, many foreigners viewed Japan's "pro-Arab" policy shift as humiliating and immoral, but the Japanese concept of morality did not see things that way. Since Japan's position on the Middle-East is actually less "pro-Arab" than that of many European countries, the real reason Japan's action was considered "immoral" was that it represented a change in policy which many foreigners consider a matter of morality. But change is not considered immoral by Japanese. There was a new situation created by the oil crisis which called for a new policy, informed by greater appreciation on a world-wide level of the importance of Arab peoples to world peace.

Had foreign opinion judged Japan in terms of the four factors I have outlined above, reaction to the oil crisis would not have been severe. These factors are absolute necessities in understanding Japan and forecasting her reaction to world events, and I hope they will be able to replace some of the cliches which have all too often substituted for understanding of Japan.

6

Interviewing

Chapter Outline

Kinds and Types of Interviews
Problem-Solving Interviews
The Informational Interviews
Planning the Interview
Structuring the Interview
Recap

Chapter Objectives

Those who complete this chapter should better understand:

1. the various types and purposes of interviews as a form of dyadic communication;
2. the various parts of the selling process;
3. how to effectively plan, structure and develop the interview;
4. how to appraise the interview.

"People under thirty-five change jobs on the average of once every eighteen months."

— Richard Bolles
What Color Is Your Parachute, 1980
Preface

"Interviewers are more influenced by unfavorable than by favorable information."

— Lois J. Einhorn, Patricia Hayes Bradley and
John E. Baird Jr., *Effective Employment Interviewing,*
1982

"...the public has a mandate for business, one that business had better heed carefully. A high 71 percent feel that management should pay less attention to short-term profits and *more* to long-term growth...For the first time, people are willing to hook their financial rewards to productivity increases. But they quickly add that they want their supervisors to treat them with far more respect than has been the case in the past. And perhaps as important as any mandate, they want to be cut into the decision-making process about their future on the job and what conditions of work and procedures on the job are set.

— Louis Harris, Poll Taker, "The Ball's in Management's Court," *Journal of Communication Management,* 1982/1, 7.

The interview is a planned and purposeful verbal exchange between two or more persons; it is a meeting consciously embarked upon to accomplish a specific purpose. Those who have studied the interview generally agree that it is "a process of dyadic communication with a predetermined and serious purpose designed to interchange behavior and usually involving the asking and answering of questions."[1]

Surely interviewing of some sort has been in existence for as long as man himself. Even as far back as the time of Christ and before, men have always had to consider the wishes and opinions of others. Man's earliest interviews and surveys were probably done by rulers to keep in touch with public opinion and desires, and by military leaders who interrogated captured prisoners.

Planned interviews are of comparatively recent origin. In 1912, for example, the government of Great Britain conducted one of its first surveys. It was a social survey of five industrial cities. More recently, the reader is probably most familiar with the public opinion interviews which have been conducted through the past century by Louis Harris, Elmer Roper, George Gallup and other research organizations.

In the past twenty-five years interviewing has been recognized as a major communication tool of industry, government, health care, and the social sciences. Today interviews are widely used to arrive at important decisions by attorneys, social workers, physicians, law enforcement officers, poll-takers, journalists, business managers, personnel directors, school counselors, pastors, teachers, government. For example, farm and crop support by the government and regulations governing the Federal Reserve System are in part predicated on the findings of interviews. The appearance of a new consumer product may be a direct result of a carefully administered marketing survey. In fact, most important economic, political, and social decisions made today are usually based on some type of interview.[2] Interviewing has become a part of our way of life and has been proven to be an extremely valuable tool.

The interview is a dyadic, one to one, form of communication. It is the most basic unit of interpersonal communication and "is best characterized as face-to-face communication with pervasive feedback and in which the role of speaker and listener are constantly shifting."[3]

Kinds and Types of Interviews

In most professions, interviews take place between superior and subordinate, for example, manager and employee, doctor and patient, lawyer and client, banker and customer etc. The individual who initiates or conducts the interview is usually referred to as the interviewer and the individual receiving the interview the interviewee. It is often difficult to distinguish the differences between the interviewer and interviewee, particularly when the interview is being conducted by individuals of similar status. In many interviews, the roles will change back and forth between the interviewer and interviewee.

There are two fundamentally different approaches to the interview: directive and nondirective. In the directive interview the interviewer determines the purpose and usually controls the pace of the interview. Information giving, information gathering, and the employment interview are examples of directive interviews. The major advantage of the directive approach is that it uses less time. The major disadvantage is that it is less flexible in its approach. Carl Rogers is credited for the development of the nondirective approach to interviewing, primarily to permit the interviewee to control the purpose, subject and pace of the interview. The Rogerian or nondirective approach grew out of the problem-solving, psychological counseling interview. The nondirective approach permits flexibility by the interviewer and a greater opportunity for the interviewee to solve his own problems.

The chief disadvantages are that in its pure form it consumes much time and is more suited to dealing with personal matters than business. Of course, and we will advocate such, that a combination of these polar extremes may be adapted to suit the functional purpose of a particular interview. The interview, like several other forms of communication, seeks a behavioral outcome: to solve problems, increase understanding, and change attitudes.

Problem-Solving Interviews

Several kinds of interviews have as their chief objective the solution to problems. A problem tends to be unimportant until it becomes your problem. Problem-solving interviews have in common the objectives of two individuals trying to find a mutually satisfactory solution to a problem.

Reprimand or Correction. The correction interview is one of the most common of the problem-solving interviews. Obviously, the correction interview is usually initiated by the superior. The purpose of the interview is to correct the behavior of a subordinate and therefore bring about some form of behavioral modification. Likely the supervisor has observed or someone has reported improper work behavior, such as failure to follow instructions, company policy, absenteeism etc. The pattern or flow of the interview should be directed toward improvement and not toward indictment of the offending employee. The interviewer should avoid questions which are hostile and create resentment. In many cases the interviewee will not even be aware of the fact that he is violating a company policy or procedure, or behaving in an unacceptable manner. It is, therefore, important for the interviewer to deal with him in a rational manner. Most employees want to behave according to accepted standards and will normally do so when properly informed. Many correction interviews are the result of ineffective induction and orientation interviews.

Performance Appraisal. It has been common practice for employers in government, business and service organizations to conduct annually an employee performance or merit review. This most often consists of some type of check list, rating scale, or other written evaluation of the employee. Following this formal rating procedure, the traditional performance appraisal interview is held. The appraisal interview naturally carries with it a high measure of emotional involvement, and consequently causes the employee being appraised to develop unnecessary levels of anxiety, defensiveness, and ego threat.[4] One way to lessen anxiety and offensiveness is in advance of the appraisal interview for the supervisor and employee to jointly confer and agree upon tangible behaviors which will be expected of the employee. Often it is wise to put these in writing and to set a future time for review of his performance. In addition, to lessen anxiety and defensiveness, the interviewer should adopt a positive style. Contemporary management today is moving more toward the problem-solving or management-by-objectives approach, and away from the critical review of an employee. The progressive manager "believes that his men's problems are his problems, and the sooner he can help solve them, the better for all concerned. The central focus of any appraisal should be the discovery of why things are as they are and how they can be improved in the future."[5]

Interviewee analysis plays a very important role in the performance appraisal interview, for no two employees are alike. The interviewer needs to communicate to the interviewee that the appraisal process is a continuous one and that only by working together can they accomplish individual and organizational goals. It is designed to provide feedback. It is this monitoring of an employee's behavior and his subsequent attention to nonproductive behavior that causes behavior modification, which eventually leads to a more satisfied and efficient employee.

Work-Production-Problem Solving. This is a very normal and frequent type of interview. It actually can be initiated by either the superior or subordinate depending on who discovers the production problem. The format usually follows the problem-solution approach. It starts by defining the production problem, analyzing it's causes and effects, establishing standards for a desirable solution, arriving at possible and preferable solution, and finally how to go about implementing the solution. When time is of the essence, the one-to-one interview is usually to the point and the course of action is stipulated by the superior.

Grievance. The neglect of grievances by American corporations have probably been the chief factor in work stoppage and plant shutdowns which occurs annually in this country. In 1974, a local auto assembly plant in Ohio, which is one of the largest in the world, was shutdown primarily because management had failed to answer some one-hundred and fifty employee grievances. The loss to the auto company ran into the hundreds of millions. A single grievance may not seem very important to the supervisor, but it might also be the complaint of a large number of employees and, therefore, should be faced and hopefully resolved to the satisfaction of all concerned. Ignored, it may lead to more severe problems. Like a cancer, if it can be removed, health may return, but unattended it may infect the total organism.

In nonunion plants usually a complaint is handled informally. In a union plant sometimes a full time staff is employed to handle complaints which cannot be resolved by a superior and subordinate. Outside arbitrators may be hired to resolve differences. The grievence interview is almost always initiated by a subordinate and if it involves a union, a set procedure is usually followed. Holm suggests this kind of interview can be thought of as a correction interview in reverse, with the employee seeking improved working conditions or behavior.[6]

Counseling. The counseling interview is a natural task for the Japanese manager, but it has always seemed to be difficult for the American manager. American managers have too often avoided the personal problems of their subordinates. Counseling interviews usually occur as a result of poor job performance, a negative attitude, or undesirable behavior on the part of the subordinate. They are normally initiated by the superior, but may be initiated by the subordinate, particularly if it is a serious personal problem, economic, social, physical, marital) affecting his job performance.

Steinmetz suggests that the purpose of the counseling interview is to "correct less than satisfactory performance, alleviate fears, or otherwise handle specific job performance problems—whether they have to do with mechanical skills or personality problems."[7] The objective of the counseling interview is to cause a subordinate to understand his problem: what's causing it and what behavioral modification is necessary to bring about a satisfactory solution. In many companies the counseling interview has taken the place of the reprimand. It is indeed a more humane approach to employee performance. The nondirective approach, advocated by Rogers seems to be the most effective in dealing with normal behavioral employee problems. In this approach, the interviewer is more of a listener-observer or facilitator rather than an advisor. When a manager is confronted with a subordinate with severe abnormal behavior, he should refer him to a professional counselor, such as a plant psychologist or psychiatrist.

One of the most important qualities of the counseling interviewer is the ability to empathize with the interviewee. Obviously the interviewer should never give advice he is not qualified to give; pry into private affairs, become emotionally involved; debate the interviewee, or expect to solve all of his problems.[8] The interviewer should do all he can to enable the interviewee to be relaxed. Once rapport has been established, the interviewee will talk about whatever he wants to talk about. Usually given time he will eventually get to his problem. The counseling interview becomes one of the most time consuming of the problem-solving interviews.

The interviewer must avoid excessive probing. Too many questions will interrupt the flow of the interview. Mirroring statements should be employed. The objective is to get the interviewee to think for himself in analyzing his problem and their possible solutions. The close of the interview should be honest and sincere. Whatever is said must remain absolutely confidential. The interviewer should offer to schedule a follow-up for the counseling interview or to be available, if and when, the interviewee desires further discussion of the issues.

The Informational Interviews

Information Giving. The three basic informational giving interviews are the job orientation, training and job-related instruction interviews. Perhaps the job-orientation and job-training interviews have been the most neglected of all the types of interviews. American business has failed to realize the importance of these types of interviews. Employee identification with this company naturally requires an understanding of what one is doing, why he is doing it, and what will become of it. Without the job-orientation and job-training discussions, business must face the consequences: employee turnover, low productivity, poor product quality, and a total decrease in business effectiveness.

Job-Orientation. The job-orientation interview often provides the new employee his first view of the organization. The purpose of the interview is to introduce the new employee to his new environment. Gomersall and Myers theorize, "Anxiety on the job is characteristically assumed to be the dependent variable, gradually dropping as competence is acquired. Might not the reverse be true? Might not competence increase as a result of anxiety being decreased?"[9] To test this idea they designed an orientation program at Texas Instruments to reduce the anxieties of an experimental group of new trainees.

A one day job enrichment orientation program designed to overcome anxieties not eliminated by the usual orientation program was conducted. The program emphasized four points:

1.   Your opportunity to succeed is very good.
2.   Disregard gossip.
3.   Take the initiative in communication.
4.   Get to know your supervisor.

By the end of four weeks, the experimental group was significantly outperforming the control group in production, job attendance as well as in learning time—an improvement in performance of approximately 50 percent. To Texas Instruments, this was a first-year savings of $50,000. On the basis of reduced turnover, absenteeism, and training time, additional annual savings of $35,000 were estimated.

Traditional orientation programs usually include a tour of the business or plant, an explanation of company policy and procedures, company benefits, and opportunities for advancement. Starting a new employee off with a proper orientation may be the difference between success and failure for the new trainee.

Job Training. Although the vast majority of North America's large corporations have quality job training programs, this is not the case for thousands of small and medium sized companies. These small and medium corporations often have capital investments exceeding a million dollars yet they have not developed quality managerial training programs at any level. About the only kind of active instruction taking place in these companies is the traditional apprenticeship and the on the job training. It is in these small and medium companies that our greatest efforts should be placed.

In most states, a barber needs 600 hours of formal training before he can become a licensed barber. Yet a first level manager often receives little formal training, but is responsible for 25 to 50 skilled employees and production that may exceed one quarter of a million dollars in a single working week. We can and must do better.

The major objective of the training interview is to give the trainee adequate information about his job and to monitor his behavior during the training period. To make the training interviews a success, it is suggested that the interviewer, working with the interviewee, establish workable goals for the interviewee and definite time limits for their accomplishment. The chances for a successful interview are much greater if a management-by-objectives program is established and followed.

Other types of information giving interviews are the medical care and job related interviews. Bernstein and Danta suggest that there is a great deal of difference between giving information and giving advice in the health care interview. Advice is generally based upon one's opinion. "Information-giving, in contrast to advice, is usually based upon relatively comprehensive study. Choice is limited to the appropriate treatment for the specific illness."[10] A physician is validly giving information when, after he has properly examined a patient and his x-ray's, he tells the patient he has a broken leg and should follow a given regimen.

Finally, one of the most frequent uses of information-giving in the health care industry is the prescription of drugs and methods of self-care. Research by Ley in 1966 suggests that between 25 and 50 percent of patients who have been given prescriptions, do not take them. These findings are similar for other types of medical advice. The research in this kind of interviewing clearly suggest a need for improvement on the part of the medical professions.

Information Gathering. The information gathering interview is one of the most popular of all interviews. Although some are brief and informal, the majority are lengthy and formal. The function of all informational gathering interviews is just about the same, to gather accurate and complete information in the shortest time span.

To conduct this kind of interview requires considerable training. For example, the public opinion survey and research interview needs to be carefully planned and conducted by trained professionals. The general purposes of the information gathering interview are to discover attitudes, beliefs, values, trends, fears, political opinions, and objective data.

In preparing the information gathering interview, the interviewer needs to ascertain just why he wants to conduct the interview. His general purpose might be to determine consumer attitudes toward a new brand of laundry soap. After the why question has been answered, the interviewer needs to determine how he will use the information. In the case of the laundry soap, a report could be compiled for a major soap manufacturer, to help determine market acceptance and potential.

In determining the specific purpose for the interview, the interviewer should specify the basic goals to be attained and the chances for their completion. Once this step is completed, an interview guide can be developed. The interview guide can serve as a check list for the various topics to be dealt with. It can help the interviewer recall relevant information, help record answers, and help in determining the appropriate question to be used. Journalists have traditionally used the "what, when, where, who, how, and why" checklist. Who do you select to interview? In practical terms one must locate an individual who has the desired information, and who is available and willing to communicate it to you.

Initially, the interviewer should establish his credibility. He should indicate the purpose, nature, and time the interview will last. He should further indicate why the interviewee was selected and what will be expected of him. At this point, he must ascertain if the individual selected will affirm his cooperation.

The body of the information gathering interview will be developed according to the type of format. The formats would range from a nonstructured to a highly structured one. The nonstructured schedule would contain little more than some topics and a few questions. This allows for a high degree of freedom by the interviewer to probe the interviewee. A moderately structured interview is more highly structured in that most of the questions for the subject areas are listed, but the interviewer still has a high degree of freedom. The highly structured interview contains all of the questions to be asked and they are always asked the same way. The highly structured format is normally employed by the researcher and the public opinion pollsters, whereas the non and moderately structured formats are generally used by journalists. The major disadvantage of the highly structured format is that there is little opportunity for the interviewer to probe. The major advantages are economy of time, training and reliability. In some cases, provided the interviewee grants his permission the nonstructured interview may be tape recorded, as are many magazine interviews of celebrities. Of course, in cases where anonymity is important tape recording is taboo.

The close of the information gathering interview should be as brief as possible, while of course expressing appreciation and affirming confidentiality when appropriate.

Exit or Separation. Although the exit interview may be classified as a data gathering interview, it may nevertheless become a problem solving interview when the employer desires to persuade the employee to stay on. Companies spend as much as twenty thousand dollars to hire, train and develop an employee, and therefore, are most reluctant to lose a good employee. Job turnover has become a high cost item to North American Corporations in the past decade. Great effort must be made to reduce this cost factor.

The exit interview is usually a voluntary situation, but in the case of a dismissed employee, it becomes involuntary. In preparing for this kind of interview, the interviewer needs to assemble all the pertinent data on the employee, such as insurance forms, appraisals, pensions, vacation pay, severance pay, and any other information a departing employee needs to know. Advising an employee of this pertinent information will help breakdown some of the barriers and relieve some of his tension and thereby put him in a more relaxed mood. McNaughton suggests that most employees leaving one job for another seldom give the real reasons for leaving. Eliciting that reason for leaving can be difficult.[11]

Confidentiality is important in the exit interview. The interviewer should indicate that he hates to see the employee go, but it would be helpful if he could give him some suggestions as to how improvements could be brought about in the company. This is a good way to get him started. To keep him talking, mild probing questions may be necessary. Listening becomes the most important task for the interviewer.

In order to get the facts of why an employee is leaving, Black suggests probes concerning his likes and dislikes about his job, about the manager and the company.

> In your preparation you should make out a checklist on his assignment which will enable you to cover such matter as: was his work a challenge; did he believe that he was properly compensated; how useful were training programs; was he kept well informed about departmental business and company policy; did he feel free to offer suggestions, even constructive criticism, when necessary; when they were useful or valid were they accepted; was he satisfied with management's programs for allowing employees to take part in outside educational opportunities, attend meetings and seminars; did he think the company provided a reasonable chance for promotion; did he find the appraisal system fair and the appraisal interview helpful; was his work assignment too demanding or not demanding enough or about right; was there too much routine work."[12]

Answers to such questions should give the interviewer a fairly clear idea of why an employee is leaving and thereby help improve the overall working conditions of the company.

In closing the exit interview it is important for the interviewer to close on a high note. The interviewer may express his own positive regard for the company and should wish him success in the future wherever he chooses to work next. This point is important, even if the employee is being dismissed. As soon as the employee leaves the interviewer should write down all the pertinent information he can remember.

Health Care. Health care interviews are, in our opinion, the most important of all information gathering interviews. They include the psychiatric interview, the psychological interview, the social worker interview, physician-patient interview, physician-nurse interview, and nurse-patient interview. One doctor described the interview this way:

> Sound interviewing technique is a most important skill for the health professional to develop if he hopes to apply his technical skills in the most effective manner possible. It is the foundation upon

which efficient history-taking rest, and the ability to obtain a good history is still regarded, even in our era of applied biochemistry, as essential if one is to treat the ill human being both humanely and scientifically.[13]

The vast majority of the interviews in the health care industry are the nurse-patient and physician-patient type. They are essential for quality medical care. Bernstein and Danta suggest that training in the essentials of interviewing are a must for the health care professional.

The nurse becomes the most important communication link between the physician and patient. Often the nurse is the one individual who cares for and about the patient and who can serve as a go between the family and the rest of the health care staff. With the shortage of health care personnel, the nurse will probably be called upon to accept an expanded role. Among the skills that will be needed, will be competence in interviewing.

Bermosk and Mordan suggest that the patient-nurse relationship goes through four phases of interpersonal communication in which the needs and behavior of the patient are identified. "These phases are (1) orientation, (2) identification, (3) exploration, and (4) resolution."[14] The awareness of her role in these phases will help the nurse plan, approach, and complete her patient interview. It is important that the nurse have a deep awareness and understanding of the patient's needs and wishes. The nurse must make an objective observation and a total exploration of the patients needs, if resolution is to occur.

The general purpose of the nurse-patient interview is "to encourage the communication of ideas, feelings, and data from the patient in an effort to identify both his immediate and long term health needs."[15] In the opening of the nurse-patient interview, the nurse gathers and interprets patient information in order to determine the basic problem. In the body of the interview the nurse applies her medical knowledge to the problem and establishes a plan of action for the patient. The interview is terminated by the nurse by assuring the patient of continued interest and support by the entire medical staff. The content, depth and direction will always be dependent upon the climate the nurse establishes with the patient.

Journalistic Interview. Interviewing skills are a must for the journalist-reporter. News stories relate to action, and action involves people. As we indicated earlier the journalists is concerned with the five w's: what, who, when, where, and why. Finding who was involved and what happened is most important.

Presson believes the successful journalists is one who "(1) can decide which person to interview, (2) can set up the interview to his advantage (3) can ask the questions the reader would ask if he were there, (4) can detect any other interesting items that the reader would like to know about, (5) can write the story in clear, concise language so the reader can understand easily."[16]

Success and achievement in the journalistic interview is learning to ask the right questions in order to get the right answers. In planning the interview it is important to research your subject to its limits. Background research aids in planning questions and developing the story line. A checklist of questions will be helpful and is much more reliable than your memory.

In conducting the interview, time will be an important factor, but it is important that one keep the interviewee talking. No two interviewing situations are exactly alike, so it is important for the interviewer-reporter to be flexible, quick and ready for anything that might occur. Being well prepared is the best advice for the journalistic interviewer.

Research and Public Opinion Survey. Many Americans rely upon what "others think." The hundreds of public opinion polls conducted annually by various research organizations help this society determine and modify its norms. The increasing sophistication of the polling business has increased the dependence upon them by business, labor and government alike. They help decide many important questions for these groups. Harry Field, former director of the National Opinion Research Center, suggests that the burden of being worthy of public confidence falls on the individual interviewer. "For the heart of public opinion surveys is the thousands of personal interviews gathered from people in all walks of life."[17]

In planning a survey, it is most important that the population sample be a true cross-section of the population being studied. For example, if you are surveying the adult population of the United States and 7 percent of the adults reside in Chicago, then 7 percent of your national sample better come from the Chicago area.

> Basic to the making of any public opinion survey is the scientific fact that the views of a very small number of persons faithfully reflect in accurate ratios the opinions of the entire population—provided that the persons interviewed (the sample) represent an accurate cross-section of all the people, a miniature population drawn to scale.[18]

Most surveys conducted by the leading research organizations are national in scope. That is people are interviewed all over the country.

Kendall surveyed blue collar workers from a downtown section of Albany, New York, for their frequency of speech making. The United States Census in 1970, indicated that Albany's population was 115, 781, of whom 40.9 percent or 47, 354 people were defined as blue collar workers: Thus, 202 interviews had to be conducted in order to generalize to the entire blue collar population of the city at a confidence level of + or − 3 percent."[19]

In addition to the problem of sampling the researcher must deal with validity. The validity of the questionnaire used in gathering the data is crucial to the validity of the conclusions that are derived from the survey. If the data are not accurate, generalizations cannot be accurate. As is true with the computer, garbage put in, results in garbage put out.

Again, we suggest that the purpose and objectives of the interview be explained before the interview. Next he should explain how the respondent was selected and who is sponsoring the research and should assure the respondent of confidentiality. "The interviewer's job of asking questions from the questionnaire is comparable to the scientific technician's role of applying a measuring instrument in a standard manner. It is through the use of carefully worded questions transmitted to the respondent verbatim that we achieve much of the standardization in the interview."[20]

Applicant Assessment. The applicant assessment interview is one that most all Americans are familar with, but fear the most. Why do they fear it? They fear it because they do not understand what it attempts to do. The applicant assessment interview is a normal, necessary business contact. The purpose of the interview is to elicit enough information regarding the abilities, skills, and knowledges of the applicant to permit a valid decision to be made regarding whether the job applicant possesses enough of the abilities, skills and knowledges required by the job. It also provides the applicant an opportunity to learn if the job sought is one in which he can find satisfaction. When this information has been obtained, the purpose of the interview has fulfilled its purpose.

The criteria for evaluating applicants may be lengthy. Yet the basic criteria may be few. Martin for the Hughes Aircraft Corporation suggests that their supervisors ranked achievements, ambition, discipline and goals as the most important.[21] These criteria would, of course, vary from company to company and from interviewer to interviewer, but most personnel directors would probably agree that the four mentioned above would be at the top of their list. Other behaviors sought often include the following: initiative, ability to communicate, appearance, general intelligence, grades attained, health, age, and integrity.

The success of an interview is not measured by the amount of information which has been obtained but rather by the amount of *pertinent* information which has been obtained. In general, the information which is pertinent to the employment interview is information regarding the individual's accomplishments in the past, particularly those most closely related to gainful employment. Facts regarding the individual's personal problems and adjustments are of interest only insofar as they bear upon his probable adjustment to the job.

Various standardized inventories and tests are available to the assessment interviewer to assist him in evaluating the interviewee's drives, needs, attitudes, self-concept, personality, values, goals, interests, hobbies, abilities and skills. Austin suggests that there are three basic levels of information obtainable in the selection of an employee: "The first and most concrete data are events in the applicant's history. Secondly, observable responses, the actual behavior during the interview; and finally inferential knowledge that an astute interviewer can gain from careful, sensitive observation."[22]

Before conducting the applicant assessment interview it is important to examine all available information on the interviewee's resume, application form, qualifications, and letters of recommendation etc. In opening the interview it is important to establish some level of rapport. Herman reports that in the old days there were two basic styles of employment interviewing: commonly referred to as "sweet and the sour."

> In the sweet approach the idea was to establish a warm, friendly relationship between interviewer and interviewee as quickly as possible. The object then, after winning the applicant's confidence, was to get him to relax. Thereafter it was merely a matter of asking the right questions and listening closely for what might be revealed in the answers. The sour style, more often called the stress approach, was less frequently used, at least by premeditation. Its premise was that since the candidate would likely be subject to stress situations in the course of his job, it was a good idea to test his reactions beforehand. (One early clue to whether the interview was to be sweet or sour was where the interviewer sat. If he came out from behind his desk and settled down beside you, the chances were good that you were to be approached sweetly. If he remained entrenched behind his desk — unless he was an amateur or just lazy — it meant the battle lines were drawn.[23]

A friendly, tactful approach to the interviewee assures him that the interviewer is interested in his case and has no ulterior motives in the probing questions. At this point, he should assure the applicant that he may respectfully decline to answer any questions which get into an area he feels is irrelevant to his work. Concern for a candidate's privacy may help establish rapport. This opening process should not take more than a minute or two.

Previous to the interview, the assessment interviewer should have decided what facts he wishes to determine and just what it is he wants to accomplish by the interview. Only then is it possible to lay out a general question format to be followed in the interview. When the applicant discusses his qualifications at some length, he gives not only the information directly sought by the interviewer's question but additional details and cues to further data as well.

The interviewee should be encouraged to ask questions, because such questions may reveal important items of information about the job or company. The interviewer should be sure that the interviewee understands the meaning of all questions. Questions should be presented in clear, simple terms and one at a time. Avoid a machine gun approach, trick questions, yes or no questions, leading questions, or questions that have already been answered in the resume. Questions should be put in a straight forward manner. Clever or shrewd questions are to be avoided. Avoid cross-examination which may work to the disadvantage of the applicant's position. The interview should be a discussion between equals. The interview is not a contest, but a cooperative effort.

Not only is the formulation of questions important, but the interpretation of answers is equally so. The interviewer must be sure that he understands the answer just as he must be sure that the interviewee understands the question. The most important single principle for good questioning is to have thoroughly in mind the purpose of the interview.

The termination of the interview should not be abrupt, but it should conclude when enough information has been gathered. If the interviewer has kept in mind the purpose of the interview and has followed a procedure designed to obtain and impart certain specific information without allowing too many or too excessive wanderings, then the interviewee should also be aware that the end of the process has been reached. He will then also be prepared for the termination of the interview and a few final remarks should serve to bring it to a close. The interviewer should close the interview in a neutral manner and suggest the proper follow-up procedure.

For taking part in the selection interview, we suggest you read "Making the Most of Your Job Interview" which can be obtained from the New York Life Insurance Company.

Socialization into a work organization begins by matching recruits with organizational needs and values. It is a transactive process, usually in the form of resume evaluation and interview.

The Job Winners. Because the process is communicative, study of the job interview is a vital topic of investigation. Einhorn through content analysis studied the rhetoric within video taped job interviews which were successful and unsuccessful (1979).[24] She analyzed the tapes to check how frequently some 93 rhetorical behaviors were in evidence either verbally or nonverbally. These were clustered under basic principles: (1) job candidates should convey positive images of themselves, (2) identify with their interviewers, (3) offer well supported arguments, (4) organize their thoughts coherently, (5) phrase their ideas in clear and appropriate language, and deliver their messages effectively.

What distinguishes the winners from the losers in the job hunt? The research into this question discovered a number of differences in the way those who are hired, compared to those who are not, performed in the job interview.

- Those who are successful convey positive images where the unsuccessful do not. That is to say the successful had clearly defined career goals which were realizable with the prospective employer. They wanted careers not jobs. Those who did not get hired failed to describe a position they wanted and their career goals for the future. Some waffled among many alternatives such as graphics, buying, sales and going on to graduate school. Employers are not interested in hiring candidates who cannot define what they want.

- Those who are successful identify with the prospective employer and seek a specific job with a certain firm whereas those who fail to get the jobs appear to be shopping around as though they were looking for an attractively packaged job which could be picked from among many on a department store shelf. Shopping around turns the interviewee into screener, a role reversal that does not wear well with personnel.

Those who get hired openly express their interest in the firm for which they are interviewing over other possibilities. They show enthusiasm for what they learn about the firm. Those who do not get hired fail to find anything that they can say complimentary to the prospective employer.

- Those who get hired researched the prospective employer. They gather information about the firm from friends, library, and from the organization's public relations department.

- Those who get hired articulately talk about the qualities they possess which may benefit the prospective employer. They rate themselves positively with such traits as analytical skills, flexibility, initiative, leadership and organizational skills. The successful make a good argument for their being hired. They are able, modestly, to present testimonials as to their competence and reliability. Those who fail to get jobs discount their assets and sometimes accentuate their faults.

- Those who are hired are better communicators. They ask appropriate questions. They are more certain and have less "um hums," "okay," "yeahs" and "nos." They don't need prodding. They take control of their side of the interview. They expand more upon their answers and laugh more than do those who do not get hired. Those who do not get the jobs use more ambiguous and negative language such as "I guess," "pretty good," "awful," "dull" and "difficult." Those who get hired are more assertive and affirmative using such words as "progress," "improvement," "advantage," "enjoyment" and "success." The successful are able to use the jargon and technical language of the job. They combine their words with clarity whereas those who don't get hired often speak with jumbled thoughts, and piece their sentences together with many "ands." The successful applicants are active listeners. They look at their interviewers without staring and they nod at what they hear. The difference is significant between those who get hired as compared to those who don't have successful interviews.

If you want to get ready for a job interview, and it is stupid not to, one of the best ways to prepare is to construct answers to expected questions and to prepare questions to ask the interviewer. Howard Mitchell, Director of Manpower and Development of the Corporate Personnel Department of Monsanto, suggests questions appropriate to four stages in the job interview process:

- **Self-Exploration**
  What are my strengths and weaknesses?
  What are my main interests?
  What is my objective for working?
  What is the quality and depth of my education?
  What is my relevant work experience?
  In light of my abilities and interests, what kind of a job and career do I want?

- **Appraising the Appraiser**
  What products and services does the firm he represents provide?
  What is its record of financial success?
  Is the company growing, maintaining a steady level of business, or declining?

How to write a resume

by Jerrold G. Simon, Ed.D.
Harvard Business School

International Paper asked Jerrold G. Simon, Ed.D., psychologist and career development specialist at Harvard Business School, who has counseled over a thousand people in their search for jobs, to tell you how to go after the job you really want.

If you are about to launch a search for a job, the suggestions I offer here can help you whether or not you have a high school or college diploma, whether you are just starting out or changing your job or career in midstream.

"What do I want to do?"

Before you try to find a job opening, you have to answer the hardest question of your working life: "What do I want to do?" Here's a good way.

Sit down with a piece of paper and don't get up till you've listed all the things you're proud to have accomplished. Your list might include being head of a fund-raising campaign, or acting a juicy role in the senior play.

Study the list. You'll see a pattern emerge of the things you do best and like to do best. You might discover that you're happiest working with people, or maybe with numbers, or words, or well, you'll see it.

Once you've decided what job area to go after, read

"'Who am I? What do I want to do?' Writing your resume forces you to think about yourself."

more about it in the reference section of your library. "Talk shop" with any people you know in that field. Then start to get your resume together.

There are many good books that offer sample resumes and describe widely used formats. The one that is still most popular, the *reverse chronological*, emphasizes where you worked and when, and the jobs and titles you held.

How to organize it

Your name and address go at the top. Also phone number.

What job do you want? That's what a prospective employer looks for first. If you know exactly, list that next under *Job Objective*. Otherwise, save it for your cover letter (I describe that later), when you're writing for a specific job to a specific person. In any case, make sure your resume focuses on the kind of work you can do and want to do.

Now comes *Work Experience*. Here's where you list your qualifications. <u>Lead with your most important credentials</u>. If you've had a distinguished work history in an area related to the job you're seeking, lead

off with that. If your education will impress the prospective employer more, start with that.

Begin with your most recent experience first and work backwards. Include your titles or positions held. And list the years.

Figures don't brag

The most qualified people don't always get the job. It goes to the person who presents himself most persuasively in person and on paper.

So don't just list where you were and what you did. This is your chance to tell *how well you did*. Were you the best salesman? Did you cut operating costs? Give numbers, statistics, percentages, increases in sales or profits.

No job experience?

In that case, list your summer jobs, extracurricular school activities, honors, awards. Choose the activities that will enhance your qualifications for the job.

Next list your *Education*—unless you chose to start with that. This should also be in reverse chronological order. List your high school only if you didn't go on to college. Include college degree, postgraduate degrees, dates conferred, major and minor courses you took that help qualify you for the job you want.

Also, did you pay your own way? Earn scholarships or fellowships? Those are impressive accomplishments.

No diplomas or degrees?

Then tell about your education: special training programs or courses that can qualify you. Describe outside activities that reveal your talents and abilities. Did you sell the most tickets to the annual charity musical? Did you take your motorcycle engine apart and put it back together so it works? These can help you.

Next, list any *Military Service*. This could lead off your resume if it is your only work experience. Stress skills learned, promotions earned, leadership shown.

Now comes *Personal Data*. This is your chance to let the reader get a glimpse of the personal you, and to further the image you've worked to project in the preceding sections. For example, if you're after a job in computer programming, and you enjoy playing chess, mention it.

"Talk about a hobby if it'll help get the job. Want to be an automotive engineer? Tell how you built your own hot rod."

Chess playing requires the ability to think through a problem.

Include foreign languages spoken, extensive travel, particular interests or professional memberships, *if* they advance your cause.

Keep your writing style simple. Be brief. Start sentences with impressive action verbs: "Created," "Designed," "Achieved," "Caused."

No typos, please

Make sure your grammar and spelling are correct. And no typos! Use 8½″ x 11″ bond paper–white or off-white for easy reading. Don't cram things together.

Make sure your original is clean and readable. Then have it professionally duplicated. No carbons.

Get it into the right hands

Now that your resume is ready, start to track down job openings. How? Look up business friends, personal friends, neighbors, your minister, your college alumni association, professional services. Keep up with trade publications, and read help-wanted ads.

And start your own "direct mail" campaign. First, find out about the companies you are interested in–their size, location, what they make, their competition, their advertising, their prospects. Get their annual report–and read it.

No "Dear Sir" letters

Send your resume, along with a cover letter, to a specific person in the company, not to "Gentlemen" or "Dear Sir." The person should be the top person in the area where you want to work. Spell his name properly! The cover letter should appeal to your reader's own needs. What's in it for him?

Quickly explain why you are approaching *his* company (their product line, their superior training program) and what you can bring to the party. Back up your claims with facts. Then refer him to your enclosed resume and ask for an interview.

Oh, boy! An interview!

And now you've got an interview! Be sure to call the day before to confirm it. Meantime, *prepare yourself.* Research the company and the job by reading books and business journals in the library.

On the big day, arrive 15 minutes early. Act calm, even though, if you're normal, you're trembling inside at 6.5 on the Richter scale. At every chance, let your interviewer see that your personal skills and qualifications relate to the job at hand. If it's a sales position, for example, go all out to show how articulate and persuasive you are.

Afterwards, follow through with a brief thank-you note. This is a fine opportunity to restate your qualifications and add any important points you didn't get a chance to bring up during the interview.

Keep good records

Keep a list of prospects. List the dates you contacted them, when they replied, what was said.

And remember, someone out there is looking for someone *just like you.* It takes hard work and sometimes luck to find that person. Keep at it and you'll succeed.

Jerrold Simon

What is the company's record for providing continuous employment?
What is the reputation of the company's management?
What is the quality of the company's personnel policies and practices?
Is this a company that I would be proud to work for?

- **Prescreening Process**

What are the specific responsibilities of the job for which I am being interviewed?
What qualifications, education, ability, and interests are considered necessary to do the job satisfactorily?
Where is the job located?
Does the job require travel, and if so, how much?
What is the general salary range for the job?

- **Final Interview**

What are my future career opportunities with the company?
Does the company have a promote-from-within policy?
What professional and management development assistance does the company provide?
What advanced degrees or specialized education does the company consider important for my future progress?[25]

Planning the Interview

Preparation time often is short but interview success rarely results from an impromptu approach. The following steps should be taken in order to assure the successful achievement of the established goals:

1. Establish your purpose and objective. The purpose and objective of the interview will be primarily determined by the type or class of interview involved. If the interview is primarily information gathering, determine precisely the type of information you are seeking. If it is a sales interview, predict if the sale must be closed on the first call or if its purpose rather is to establish a working relationship with the interviewee. A professional interviewer should be able to switch gracefully to a secondary objective or goal if the primary objective is blocked or not attainable.

2. Analyze the interviewee and the situation. Your analysis of the interviewee is of prime importance and some experts suggest it is the most important step in interview preparation. You must consider the interviewee's attitudes, beliefs, motives, values, and his personal characteristics. Is he likely to be cooperative or argumentative? What is his position in relation to yours and does this cause a status problem? If it is a problem-solving situation, is he conscious of the problem, and if so, what is his attitude toward a solution? When possible, gather as much information as possible about the interviewee. The type of interview, of course, influences the planning. An analysis of a work-production interview would be completely different from that of an exit interview. Such factors as the amount of time available, possible interruptions, and the over all results to be achieved must be considered. In certain types of interviews, it is helpful to notify the interviewee in advance of the subject and purpose of the interview.

3. Develop your strategy and tactics. Once we have established our purpose and have analyzed the interviewee and the situation, we are ready to develop our approach. The strategy of an interview will have certain information or points which the interviewer wants to communicate to the interviewee and facts, ideas and opinions that he wants to obtain from the interviewee. "Together these points and items cover the content to be discussed, and your interview plan will list them in the sequence in which you think they should be taken up."[26] Just as in preparing a speech, the various points to be considered should be assigned time limits. Your analysis of the interviewee and the situation will dictate the points used, their order, and the questions employed. Pretest questions. Developing and asking questions is an art and improves with practice.

4. Meeting resistance. Resistance can be expected in some types of problem-solving, informative and attitude-chance interviews. In the problem-solving interviews, a solution recommended by the interviewer or company policy frequently may be resented by the interviewee. In an exit interview, where the interviewee has been terminated, one normally will have to deal with considerable antagonism. The grievance interview by its very nature frequently will contain serious employee objections and resistance. In some performance appraisal interviews, the interviewee will not always agree with the interviewer's analysis of his development and therefore, resists vigorously. Although there is no set formula for discovering or dealing with objections and resistance, the interviewer can do his best to put himself in the interviewee's position, and from that point vicariously better understand his attitude. In the sales interview, the experienced salesman has learned to classify major objections into such things as price or value. The experienced salesman welcomes objections, because they help him isolate that resistance to the sale. Resistance may be offset by inoculation. The interviewer brings up expected objections and inoculates against resistance before the interviewee has the opportunity by suggesting appropriate counter arguments. Being prepared for resistance is half the battle.

5. Establishing the time of the interview. In many kinds of interviews there is no opportunity to establish the time of the interview, but common sense dictates that certain times are more appropriate than others. For instance, if a manager has had a particularly difficult work week, it might be desirable to put off a work-production interview until the first of the next week. Health care interviews obviously should be held while the patient is awake. No patient should be awakened for an interview at the crack of dawn. Professional salesmen more so than most interviewers realize the importance of timing in an interview. They like to call on a client when he is least occupied.

6. Arranging a comfortable environment. Often the type of interview will determine where it will be held, but even if this is the case, the environment should be clean, clear, private, comfortable, and clear of all distractions. Chairs should be arranged so that each person can see the other and feel comfortable. The interviewer should try to hold all distractions to a minimum. Managers can help reduce anxiety on the part of their subordinates by going to the subordinate's office for an interview, instead of making him come to his office. Offices can be serious barriers, so a neutral environment might be more acceptable. The professional salesman usually prefers to meet his client on neutral ground. A large number of sales interviews take place every year in bars and on golf courses. Clients are more relaxed in these environments and, therefore, more receptive to a new product or point of view.

7. Motivation for the interview. There are several things the interviewer and interviewee can do to motivate themselves for an interview. They can be well prepared, well attired and physically ready for the interview. They can have a positive mental attitude toward the outcome of the interview. Dress or attire should fit the role. An interviewee going for a job, should gather all the information he can on the interviewer and his particular company. He should be able to introduce his credentials at the proper moment. A notebook of materials should be at his elbow. If planned carefully, he can expect success.

Structuring the Interview

Although the nondirective interview has little organization, they do have a beginning, body and conclusion. The same is also true of all structured informative, problem solving, and attitude change interviews. The opening. The amount of time that is spent in the introductory phase of the interview will be determined by the purpose of the interview and the amount of time that is necessary for the interviewer to establish this rapport. Introductory remarks should put the interviewee at ease and lead into a permissive atmosphere and consequently alleviating possible interviewee insecurity or defensiveness.

Rapport begins with simple courtesy and by exercise of a few common social amenities—a genuine hello and handshake, a question inquiring about the client's welfare. The interviewer may talk briefly about matters of mutual interest, or search out common ground. The interviewer too must be at ease. We read each others' muscles. After the interviewee is relaxed, the main purpose of the interview should be established and made clear.

The interview should be conducted at a language level understood by the interviewee. Many professions have a language of their own, and professional jargon often is not comprehensible to the average individual. Eye contact is important for establishing good rapport. Before getting into the body of the interview the interviewer should make a total effort to instill confidence in the interviewee. The interviewer should make it clear that he is there to help.

There are many complications and uncertainties that might occur in the introductory stages of the interview: Possible personality differences, language barriers, status differences, biases, anxiety, prejudices and any number of complications that may arise. An important aspect of the introductory stage of an interview is an opportunity for ventilation of feelings. "He should know that he will have the opportunity to express himself, to raise questions, or to say things which he feels should be included in the interview."[27]

Do not let the opening be obvious as a device, and do not let it consume an unnecessary amount of time. Under all circumstances both parties must realize that they are meeting for a purposeful conversation. The opening must be designed to help this realization.

The Body of the Interview

After we have established common ground with the interviewee, we are ready to attempt our main purpose. The body of the interview is the general business section of an interview. This is where issues are developed, where questions are asked, and ideas exchanged. The interviewer will also be expected to answer any questions raised by the interviewee during the interview.

As we develop our sequence of questions, it is important to develop questions that are brief, simple in language, and convey intended meaning. The interviewer should make every effort to use material that will be familiar to the interviewee. He should not assume the interviewee is well versed on all matters.

Questions generally fall into one of the following classes: Open or Closed and Primary and Secondary.

Open-Ended Questions

Open-ended questions are generally broad in nature and permit the interviewee great freedom in his answer. Many interviews start with open-ended questions. Such as, what do you think about our company? How do you feel about management by objectives? Tell me about your first job? What advantages do you see in this new approach to management? "Open questions may reveal what the respondent thinks is important, and he may volunteer information you might not think to ask for."[28] Open questions may bring out an interviewee's interests, desires, needs, prejudices etc. The major disadvantages of the open question are time consumption and evaluating results.

Closed Questions

The closed question can be moderately or highly restrictive, depending on the degree of information being sought. Most closed questions include the various possible answers. The closed question can be answered by using a rank order, yes or no, or a scale or continum. The closed question is often used in research and survey interviews. There are many advantages to using the closed question: The interviewer has more control over the interview, and he can ask more questions in less time. It takes less training to use them, and they are less threatening to the interviewee. The results of closed questions are easier to analyze and tabulate than answers to open questions. The major disadvantages of the closed questions especially the yes-no variety are that they do not allow for degrees of answers but only polar extremes. You also may get too little information because the interviewee has very little opportunity to volunteer potentially important information.

Examples of closed questions: How many years have you been at your present position? How many years of education did you receive? At what level would you expect to be in ten years? What is your present income? Who do you bank with?

Primary Question

Stewart and Cash suggest that we can also classify questions as primary and secondary. "Primary questions introduce topics in an interview or new areas within a topic."[29] A primary question may be either open or closed, as long as it introduces new material.

Secondary Question

Secondary questions attempt to elicit more information from a previously stated primary question. Secondary questions are often referred to as probing questions and follow-up questions. Interviewers employ these probes and follow up questions when a primary question is not answered completely or seems vague. An interviewer can double check the answer from a primary question by employing a "reflective probing" type of question. For example: Why do you feel that way about the company? What did you do after it happened? How did you feel about him after the incident? Tell me more about it?

Another type of secondary question is the summary or mirror question. The mirror question reflects or summarizes a series of questions and answers to insure a more accurate understanding of what the interviewee has stated. For example, a drill press operator may use a mirror or summary question on his foreman to see if he clearly understands the information he communicated to him concerning a new job set-up. "Let me see if I understand this operation. I first place the part into the press upside down. I drill four three-eighth inch holes. Then I insert the four bolts." Employing the secondary question effectively requires considerable training and skill.

Directional Questions

Directional questions are usually referred to as leading or loaded questions. These kinds of questions should be avoided unless you are a professional interviewer. The directional question is often employed in the attitude change or sales interview. The directional question can proceed from mere leading to the loaded variety. An example of the leading would be: Do you oppose the Theory X type of manager like most of your associates? You like to travel, don't you? An example of the loaded variety: How do you feel about those asinine labor unions? Don't you think that productivity is considerably more important than experience in a free enterprise system?

Closing the Interview

Knowing when to close the interview is usually no serious problem for the professional interviewer; however, for the young manager, salesman or counselor it may be a problem. In the information giving interview, the interviewer will usually know when he has given all the information he intends to give. This is also true in the information gathering interview, in that the interviewer has a good idea when he has obtained all the relevant information.

Many interviewers attempt to set time limits on their interviews; however, this does not always work. For example in a problem solving interview it is impossible to terminate the interview until both parties have mutually agreed upon an acceptable solution to the problem. The salesman realizes that the sales interview is ready to be terminated only when the interviewee is showing signs that he is ready to buy.

A basic guideline that an interviewer can follow in closing the interview is to ask the question: Will further discussion contribute any more significant information? If not, the interview should be gracefully terminated. Closing the interview can be easy if a set pattern is followed. First the interviewer should summarize the items that were discussed, secondly, what conclusions were reached on each item, and thirdly, what action need be taken by either party. Occasionally, he may ask the interviewee to make a summary and then will add items which he feels were accomplished. In either case, the one who does not do the summarizing should be invited to "playback" what the other said and to concur or modify that summary. When an interviewer has gone through all of these steps, he will have effectively closed the interview. All that would be required would be a statement concerning a follow-up interview, providing a follow-up seems advisable to either the interviewer or interviewee.

Recap

The interview is a planned verbal exchange between two or more individuals and attempts to accomplish a specific purpose. As a form of communication, the interview has been in existence for thousands of years; however, the planned interview is of comparatively recent origin. Most major professions today recognize the interview as a major communication tool. In short, interviewing has become a part of our way of live.

Most interviews are classified as either problem solving, persuasive or information giving or receiving. The success of an interview is usually determined by the amount of planning and preparation that go into it. Establishing your purpose and objective is essential.

As in other forms of communication, it is important to analyze your audience so you can develop your strategy. Questions are the major tool of the interviewer and they are structurally either open ended or closed.

The interview should be terminated when both parties feel that no significant information remains to be discussed.

Negative Factors Evaluated During the Employment Interview Which Frequently Lead to Rejection of the Applicant as Reported by 153 Companies[30]

1. Poor personal appearance.
2. Overbearing—overaggressive—conceited "superiority complex"—"know-it-all."
3. Inability to express himself clearly—poor voice, diction, grammar.
4. Lack of planning for career—no purpose and goals.
5. Lack of interest and enthusiasm—passive, indifferent.
6. Lack of confidence and poise—nervousness—ill-at-ease.
7. Failure to participate in activities.
8. Overemphasis on money—interested only in best dollar offer.
9. Poor scholastic record—just got by.
10. Unwilling to start at the bottom—expects too much too soon.
11. Makes excuses—evasiveness—hedges on unfavorable factors in record.
12. Lack of tact.
13. Lack of maturity.
14. Lack of courtesy-ill-mannered.
15. Condemnation of past employers.
16. Lack of social understanding.
17. Marked dislike for school work.
18. Lack of vitality.
19. Fails to look interviewer in the eye.
20. Limp, fishy hand-shake.
21. Indecision.
22. Loafs during vacations—lakeside pleasures.
23. Unhappy married life.
24. Friction with parents.
25. Sloppy application blank.
26. Merely shopping around.
27. Wants job only for short time.
28. Little sense of humor.
29. Lack of knowledge of field of specialization.
30. Parents make decisions for him.
31. No interest in company or in industry.
32. Emphasis on whom he knows.
33. Unwillingness to go where we send him.
34. Cynical.
35. Low moral standards.

36. Lazy.
37. Intolerent—strong prejudices.
38. Narrow interests.
39. Spends much time in movies.
40. Poor handling of personal finances.
41. No interest in community activities.
42. Inability to take criticism.
43. Lack of appreciation of the value of experience.

44. Radical ideas.
45. Late to interview without good reasons.
46. Never heard of company.
47. Failure to express appreciation for interviewer's time.
48. Asks no questions about the job.
49. High pressure type.
50. Indefinite response to questions.

NOTES

1. Charles J. Stewart and William B. Cash, *Interviewing* (Dubuque: W. C. Brown Company, 1974), p. 3.
2. Stacy Adams, *Interviewing Procedures* (Chapel Hill: The U. North Carolina Press., 1958), pp. 3-4.
3. Stewart and Cash, *Interviewing,* p. 4.
4. Jack R. Gibb "Defensive Communication." *Journal of Communication,* 11, 1961, p. 141.
5. Stewart and Cash, *Interviewing,* p. 177.
6. James N. Holm, *Productive Speaking for Business and the Professions,* (Boston: Allyn And Bacon, 1968), p. 218.
7. Lawrence L. Steinmetz, *Interviewing Skills for Supervisory Personnel* (Reading, Mass: Addison- Wesley Co., 1971), p. 3.
8. James M. Black, *How to Get Results From Interviewing* (New York: McGraw-Hill Book Company, 1970), pp. 160-61.
9. Earl R. Gomersall and M. Scott Meyers, "Breakthrough in On-the Job Training," *Harvard Business Review,* (July-August, 1966), pp. 63-70.
10. Lewis Bernstein and Richard Dana, *Interviewing and the Health Professions* (New York: Appleton-Century-Crofts, 1970), pp. 44-45.
11. Wayne L. McNaughton, *Personnel Journal,* Vol. 35, 1956, pp. 61-63.
12. Black, *How to Get Results From Interviewing,* pp. 160-61.
13. Robert Senescu, M.D., Chairman, Department of Psychiatry, University of New Mexico School of Medicine.
14. Loretta Bermosh and Mary Jane Mordan, *Interviewing in Nursing* (New York: MacMillian and Co., 1964), p. 4.
15. *Ibid.,* p. 9.
16. Hazel Presson, *The Student Journalist and Interviewing* (New York: Richard Rosen Press, 1967), p. 13.
17. *Interviewing for NORC* (Denver, Colorado, National Opinion Research Center, University of Denver, 1954), p. 2.
18. *Ibid.,* p. 3.
19. Kathleen Edgerton Kendall, "Do Real People Ever Give Speeches?" *Central States Speech Journal,* (Fall, 1974), p. 233.
20. Leon Festinger and Daniel Katz, *Research Methods in the Behavioral Sciences* (New York: Holt, Rinehart and Winston, 1953), p. 357.
21. Robert A. Martin, "Toward More Productive Interviewing," *Personnel Journal,* 50 1971, pp. 359-61.
22. David Austin, "Is the Interview an Analog?" *The Personnel Administrator,* 17, January-February, 1972, pp. 13-25.
23. Stanley M. Herman, *The People Specialists* (New York: Alfred A. Knopf, 1968), p. 105.
24. Lois Einhorn, "The Rhetorical Dimensions of Employment Interviews: An Investigation of Communication Behaviors Contributing to Applicant Success," PH.D. Dissertation, Indiana University, 1979.
25. Howard M. Mitchell, "What Should You Ask the Company Interviewer?" *SAM Advanced Management Journal* (Winter 1977), pp. 55-61.
26. Holm, *Productive Speaking for Business and the Professions,* p. 288.
27. Steinmetz, *Interviewing Skills for Supervisory Personnel,* p. 31.
28. Stewart and Cash, *Interviewing,* p. 58.
29. *Ibid.,* p. 58.
30. "Making the Most of Your Job Interview," *New York Life.*

Project Six-1

Simulating the Interview

Study Guide

These sample role-playing simulations are provided for in-class simulation. The simulations represent a variety of interviewing situations and therefore, can be modified by adding more detail to the specific cases. The interviewer and interviewee can be evaluated by class members by using the "Interview Appraisal Form."

PROBLEM SOLVING

Appraisal

MOVING UP

Richard Allen

You are working in the Development Engineering Department of the Treadwell Tire Company. You joined the company 2 1/2 years ago as a trainee, and were promoted to your present job eight months ago. This is your first real chance since leaving college to prove what you can do as an engineer.

You learned in the company's training program that it is important to impress favorably whomever you contact on the job if you expect future promotions. Your job is challenging, and you feel that many important things must be learned before you move on to a better position in the company.

In an effort to further your relationship with management personnel, you have joined the local chapter of the Engineer's Professional Society, which many of the company's executives also actively participate in. You have met and talked to a few of the executives as a result of this affiliation.

The company has a policy of discussing employee's performance at least once each year. This is currently being done in the Engineering Department, and you have been told to report to Mr. Andrew's office at 1:00 P.M. today for your appraisal.

Jim Andrews

You are the manager of the Development Engineering Department at Treadwell Tire Company. It is your job to discuss your employees' performances annually. Before the employee is called into the office, you complete a Merit Rating Form that you discuss with the employee.

Richard Allen's form has been completed, and you have rated him highly on all traits except one which is judgment. Judgment is described on the rating form as the logic of thinking and timing of expressions. You have rated Richard Allen as being fair in this particular trait because two executives have reported to you that they did not like the forward manner in which he approached them at the recent meeting of the Engineer's Professional Society.

You feel that this unfavorable impression, created with executives of the company is just cause for grading Dick down in this particular area. You must justify your rating to the employee if it is to be effective and if he is to benefit from the appraisal.

You feel that Dick has an excellent quality of getting along with people and communicating personally with them. This is an important part of his job, and you want to impress on him the importance of using good judgment without inhibiting his aggressiveness when it is necessary. Dick is coming into your office now for his rating.

INFORMATION GATHERING
Exit

AN EXIT INTERVIEW

You are Esther O'Neil, an employee of the Lamson and Smithers Company, where you work in the general office, doing routine filing and typing. You have been employed there for 17 months since your study at the McCoard Business College was completed. You are 20 years old, and have the interests of an average girl of your position. Your company is a small manufacturer, employing a total of about 500 people.

During your service at L & S your work has been satisfactory so far as you can tell. Mr. McGee, the office manager who is your boss, has never told you otherwise—nor has he ever told you that your work was good. As a matter of fact, he never expresses appreciation to any of the workers in the office. He is a middle-aged man, rather sour in demeanor, who never speaks to those in the office unless it is to give an order. He does smile and speak graciously, but only when he wants you to do something extra. Then he forgets it. His main purpose in life seems to be to please his boss, the vice president. McGee is always extremely cordial and helpful to anyone who is his superior.

As a result of McGee's general attitude, the office is not a warm and friendly place to work, and you have gotten a feeling of being no more important and human than an adding machine. So when you had an opportunity to go to work for the Conley Company at the same salary for the same kind of work, you took it, since you had been told that it was a pleasant place to work.

You have just picked up your last pay check from L & S, with a note that Mr. Burbank in the personnel office would like to talk to you before you leave. Therefore, you are on your way in to see Mr. Burbank.

You are Walter Burbank, age 29, employed in the personnel office of the Lamson and Smithers Company, a small manufacturing concern employing a total of about 500 people. One of your duties is to talk to employees who are leaving the company to try to find out the reasons.

This is an important function, since the cost of training and developing an employee is not inconsiderable, and the management would like to keep personnel turn-over as low as possible by determining why employees leave.

You have been notified that Esther O'Neil, a filing clerk in the general office is leaving, and has put a routine request in her pay envelope, asking her to see you before she leaves.

You know nothing about Miss O'Neil other than what is on her personnel record, which shows that she has worked at L & S for 17 months, was a graduate of McCoard Business College, is 20 years old, and her work record bears no unfavorable comments.

Mr. McGee, general office manager, has asked for a replacement for Miss O'Neil in his usual friendly way. He is a middle-aged man, rather precise in manner, who is known for running a tautly efficient office. However, he is always cooperative with his superiors, and friendly with you when he asks for assistance from Personnel.

There could be many reasons to account for Miss O'Neil's departure—the usual from getting married, or finding a better paying job, to going into a different line of work—but your assignment is to find out for the record.

Miss O'Neil walks into your office—a youthful looking girl.

The Employee

You are Phil Adamson, a young man in your middle twenties, and have spent the last four and a half years working for Consolidated Stores, Inc., a large national organization. Although Consolidated is known principally for its chain of retail stores, it has other concerns, including two manufacturing plants and substantial real estate interests. This has been your only employment since you graduated from college with a degree in retailing. Two days ago you gave the district store supervisor notice of your intention to resign from your present position as manager of one of Consolidated's smallest stores in Poughkeepsie, New York.

You have been generally satisfied with your progress since joining Consolidated, becoming a store manager after only three years with the Company. In fact, you feel your progress has been better than average. Thinking back to your employment interview with Mr. Heiser, Director of Personnel, you recall his saying that after spending a year in the training program, the average new employee requires several years' experience in other store positions before being considered capable of managing a store.

The decision to resign your position was not an easy one to make, but you feel that conditions in the store have become intolerable. Joe Scott, your district supervisor, is an impossible man to work for. When you were assigned to the Poughkeepsie store as manager, the store had lost about $50,000 for the year, largely as a result of unwise extension of credit. Although you have managed to correct that situation, you have been unable to replace the credit manager, an old timer who has been in the Poughkeepsie store for twenty years but who has become incompetent in his job. Because you have to devote so much time to the supervision of credit functions, you have been unable to do the many other things you feel are necessary to substantially increase store profits. Scott has been extremely critical of you ever since you took over the store. He has been unreasonable in his requests and has not kept his word on many things. Just last week, he severely criticized you in front of your employees and some store customers. It was this last incident that led you to your decision to resign. Because you and your wife are from the East and would prefer to remain in that area, you do not see any other solution to your problems.

You have been asked to come to the home office in New York City for an interview with Mr. Heiser. You feel you know what this is for and that Mr. Heiser is going to want to know your reasons for leaving. You are wondering what to tell him since you know that Jack Barry, the former Kingston store manager, reported his troubles with Scott at the time he resigned two months ago and has been unable to get a comparable job since. The grapevine has it that Barry was considered to be a troublemaker by the company.

The Personnel Director

You are John Heiser, 56, Vice President and Director of Personnel for Consolidated Stores, Inc. With the exception of a very brief period after college, you have been in personnel work all of your business career. You came to Consolidated as Manager of Service Personnel twenty-one years ago. Since that time you moved up the ladder to the job of Director of Personnel. Three years ago you were given additional status and recognition by being elected a vice-president of the company. This represented the highest level ever reached by a personnel man in the history of the company.

One of your main concerns during your many years in personnel work has been the problem of employee turnover. You have devoted a good deal of your time and energy in times past to this problem—determining its causes and developing programs to minimize it. Of nagging concern has been an increase in employee turnover during the last two years, particularly in the Eastern District. You feel that some good store personnel have been lost, and you do not like to see that happen.

Because of your concern, you asked Ted Sorenson, the Manager of Store Personnel, to personally interview all exempt store personnel who resigned. After examining his reports for the last six months, you came to the conclusion that Sorenson was not getting to the heart of the problem. Accordingly, you decided to interview the next man yourself. Even though it has been three years since you conducted an interview of this kind, you feel you still have the touch and are confident you will uncover the basic problem.

You are rather surprised to find that Phil Adamson, the Poughkeepsie, New York store manager, is the latest employee to resign. His record has been very good since he started with the company four and a half years ago. Not many men rose to the rank of store manager in a little more than three years as he had done. When you hired him, you felt he showed real potential. Perhaps he had been moved ahead too fast and was not ready for the burdens of store management.

INFORMATION GATHERING
Applicant Assessment

SO YOU NEED A JOB

John Roberts

You are an accountant in your forties who has spent twelve years working for the Hardshelled Metalworking Associates. Twice during the past five years a departmental headship has been vacant and both times an outsider was brought in to fill the position. In each instance you felt qualified and deserving of the promotion. The third time the same thing happened you went to the boss to protest what seemed to you an injustice. A bitter argument followed, and you were fired. You are now about to talk to Howard Jones, who is the personnel manager for the All-Metal Stamping Company, which is in a line of business similar to the job you held so long.

You have a degree in accounting from Ohio State University, a record of successful work in two positions prior to going with the Hardshelled outfit, and at the last place you made several suggestions for improved accounting procedures which reduced office costs.

You are not quite sure what you will say if Mr. Jones asks you why you left your last job. How should you handle that problem? You certainly want the job, because the pay is even slightly better than you have been receiving, you have a family to support, and you must keep up your payments on the house and car.

Howard Jones

You are the personnel manager for the All-Metal Stamping Company, and have a vacancy to fill in the accounting department. The job will require a full knowledge of accounting procedures, some initiative, and loyalty to the company. There is not much immediate opportunity for promotion from the position at the present time and whoever is hired will be in a dead-end for some years at least. The accounting department has a good morale, and the workers get along well together and with the department chief.

Mr. John Roberts is coming to see you about the position. You know little or nothing about him except that he is slightly more than forty years old, has a family, and in general has a good reputation in the field of accounting. He would probably make a good man for your job, except that at his age he might be eager for promotion. Why he left his former employer is uncertain, but he certainly is looking for another position or he wouldn't have called you in answer to your classified ad.

It would be a relief to be able to fill the vacancy you have with a steady, capable, and loyal man.

THE PAY RAISE

John Wagner (The Boss)

I am John Wagner. I've been the office manager at Clauss Cutlery for fifteen years.

One of my jobs is to evaluate the work of my office employees. Recently, Gloria Wild was given a five-cent-an-hour pay raise.

I use an Efficiency Chart to evaluate the tasks of each employee. If results are found to be satisfactory, then employees are given pay raises at the end of each twelve month period.

Miss Wild has met all the requirements for a pay raise. Upon completion of her duties, she helps Miss Evans with her work for at least forty-five minutes every day.

Joan Evans should have had a pay raise two months ago. Joan doesn't show much interest in her work, takes four coffee breaks a day instead of the allowed two, and constantly needs help to get her work finished.

I've said nothing to Joan about a pay raise. Also, it is a company policy to keep all employee salaries and pay raises a secret. It serves for better relations.

Miss Joan Evans (The Employee)

I am Joan Evans. I work as a billing clerk at the Clauss Cutlery Company. I've been with the company for approximately fourteen months without a pay raise.

John Wagner is my boss. He is the office manager and seems to take interest in all of his employees.

Gloria Wild, also a billing clerk, has been with the company for only twelve months. Last week, word leaked out that she received a pay raise. When I asked Gloria how much of a raise she got, her reply was, "I can't tell."

Our job classifications are the same, I've been with the company two months longer than Gloria, and now she gets a raise and I don't.

My only solution is to go to Mr. Wagner and ask him why I didn't get a pay raise. If I don't get a raise next week, I'm going to quit.

PROBLEM SOLVING
Grievance

AN ADJUSTMENT CASE

Fred Moore—Manager of a "Goodstone Store"—one of the retail units of the Goodstone Tire and Rubber Co., a combined filling station, auto accessory and appliance dealer.

Your products are sold under a warranty, including Goodstone Tires, which are guaranteed for 20,000 miles against road hazards, including cuts and blowouts. The warranty is pro-rata, which means that if a tire runs 10,000 miles before trouble develops the purchase price toward a new tire or the tire may be repaired free of charge if repairable.

One of your customers, Martha O'Reilly, a teacher, purchased a set of 4 tires 2 months ago, and is seeking an adjustment this afternoon on one which has been damaged beyond repair. Inspection will show that the carcass of the tire was broken by some kind of hard blow.

Martha O'Reilly—A teacher who commutes 15 miles to work. She must depend on her car, and two months ago bought 4 Goodstone tires at the local Goodstone Store to ensure dependable transportation. The tires were guaranteed against road hazards including cuts and blowouts for 20,000 miles.

Yesterday in parking her car at an angle Martha bumped the curb too hard, the casing was broken (she later discovered), and this morning the tire was flat. Not only was the inconvenience of changing the tire and being late for work annoying, but it was doubly so because the tires were purchased to avoid such inconvenience, have been used for only two months and run only 2,000 miles. Martha drives to the Goodstone store after school to get a new tire in place of the one which failed before the guarantee had run out.

THE LITTLE ROCK BASKETBALL TEAM

I am Rick Dyer, new basketball coach at Little Rock High.

Little Rock High School has an enrollment of 300. Due to a rather unsatisfactory basketball season, they have changed coaches. Rick Dyer, the new coach, is preparing for the opening game. Mr. Templeton, township trustee, who hired Dyer because he thought he could produce a winning team, is an ardent fan, and is very proud of his son, Bob, who, the previous season played quite a bit of first team basketball. Bob now is a senior and, because two of last year's regulars have graduated, his father seems to expect that he will be a member of the first five this year.

Dyer is changing the style of basketball. He plans to concentrate on teaching the squad his new style this season and make as good a showing as possible, but is looking ahead to next year. He wants speed and teamwork. Two sophomores who lack experience but show great promise of developing into skillful players are his principle concern; one of the boys, Dick Ballard, is the son of a political rival of Mr. Templeton. Because Bob Dyer is a senior and not an outstanding player, coach Dyer seems it not advisable to waste time trying to develop him, and at the last practice, two nights before the opening game, Dyer announces the starting lineup, and Bob is not included. Bob is keenly disappointed.

Mr. Templeton the next day telephones Mr. Dyer and asks him why his son is not on the starting line-up. Not wishing to discuss the problem over the telephone, Mr. Dyer asks Mr. Templeton to come to the school to talk over the whole basketball program for the season.

Dyer believes he has made the selection which will be best for the team. He intends to use Bob as a substitute, and he will get a chance to play a great deal of basketball during the season. He knows Mr. Templeton is sincerely interested in the welfare of the team and believes he overestmates Bob's ability, as any fond father is likely to do. Furthermore, when he was hired as coach, Mr. Templeton told him to proceed in his own manner, but to put a winning team on the floor.

I am John Templeton, township trustee.

Little Rock High School has an enrollment of 300. But to a rather unsatisfactory basketball season, they have changed coaches. Rick Dyer, the new coach, is preparing for the opening game. Mr. Templeton, township trustee, who hired Dyer because he thought that he could produce a winning team, is an ardent fan and very proud of his son, Bob, who, the previous season played quite a bit of first team basketball. Bob is now a senior, and because two of last year's regulars have graduated, his father expects that he will be a member of the first five this year.

Mr. Templeton is sincerely interested in the welfare of the team, and when Dyer was hired as coach he told the latter to proceed in his own manner, but to put a winning team on the floor.

At the last practice, two nights before the opening game, Bob Templeton comes home to report that he had not been named to to the opening line-up. He is keenly disappointed.

Mr. Templeton has spoiled his son by making a habit of taking his part in all his school difficulties. Therefore, the next day he telephones Mr. Dyer to tell him he had looked forward to seeing his son start the opening game, and to ask why Bob was not included in the opening line-up. Dyer made little or no attempt to answer the questions, but invited Templeton to come to the school to talk over the whole basketball program for the season.

Templeton is irritated.

PROBLEM SOLVING
Work—Production

DRILLING EXTRA HOLES

John Smith—Foreman—Ford Motor Company

Tom Jones is a well liked worker in your section of the plant. He always gets his work done well and correctly. Tom has been a personal friend of yours for 15 years ever since high school. The superintendent came up to you last Frieday and told you Tom Jones seems to have a lot of free time. You told him that he is a good worker and gets his job done early but his production is the same as the rest of the men. The superintendent feels this is a good opportunity to add more work to Tom's job. He is told he must now drill two extra holes in the door panel. This takes away all of Tom's free time. His attitude seems to have changed. He often needs help to keep up and he is quick to jump at someone for just a simple offering of advice. The superintendent sees this and tells you to try to clear up the situation or else he will have to fire Tom. You call Tom aside from his job one day.

Tom Jones—Laborer—Ford Motor Company

Up to two weeks ago you really enjoyed working here. You obtained a quick speed on your door job which enabled you to have free time. This free time never interfered with your work or quality. John Smith is your foreman and one of your old high school buddies. He came up to you a week ago and told you more work was added to your job. You would now have to drill two more holes into each door panel. You felt this was not quite fair but kept your feelings locked inside you. Tension mounted and your work slipped so badly that you often needed help during the week. But you felt that it didn't matter because you had more work than the rest of the men. You are called into the office by the foreman, John Smith.

PROBLEM SOLVING
Reprimand

THE COMPANY CAR

I am Elmer Hill (The Boss)

I am riding in a company car with Al Jackson, one of our newer employees, Al is driving. We have been going through a good deal of heavy traffic and it appears that we won't get back to the company garage by 5 p.m. (our quitting time). It is a very warm day, and both of us have had a busy schedule. This is the first time that I have been in a coompany car with Al. He has had the use of company vehicles about a year. I have never had any official complaints about his driving except that Roy Burns, one of my older staff men, remarked one day that he had a "pretty fast ride with Jackson," and laughingly wondered if he were a hot rod enthusiast. I had answered that considering the emphasis we were getting these days on safety that I would prefer that all our men would be safe-driving enthusiasts.

Al handled himself quite well this afternoon in the meeting we attended. He certainly has done a nice job in our group. I like his energy and initiative, although he obviously needs a great deal more experience. I understand Al is engaged to be married. (At this moment, Al has swung the car into a right hand lane in order to make a right hand turn at the intersection. Another car is directly ahead of us approaching the intersection. As it reaches the corner the light changes to "red" and the car stops. There is a sign nearby indicating the right hand turns are permitted at all times. Al starts to blow the horn on our company car, and, before I can stop him, leans out of his window and shouts at the driver to keep his eyes open and to get his xxxxxx car out of the way. The driver, with an angry look at us (and the company name on the car), turns the corner, whereupon Al "guns" our vehicle on around him and on toward the garage.

I am Al Jackson (The Employee)

I am driving a company car with Elmer Hill, boss of our group, as a passenger.

It's near the end of a rough day and with all the heavy traffic on the streets we will probably be 15-20 minutes late in getting to the company garage. Of all the nights to have a prompt date with Helen! I figured I could meet her at 5:00 p.m. and we could take a look at the furniture she had picked out before the store closed at 5:30. Now she'll be standing there waiting for me at the store and I have no way of getting in touch with her. Of all the rotten luck! We have so darn many things to take care of before our wedding day. And look at these fool drivers! I can't understand why all these people who never seem to be in a hurry have to get out on the streets at the busy hours. There ought to be a law against them.

We certainly had a full day. I'll have to admit that I like this job more and more. And Mr. Hill seems like a top-notch fellow, too. Even though I'm pretty new he seems to give me every chance to tackle a job my own way. And I've always liked to get things done in a hurry.

At this moment I see the corner approaching where I want to make a right hand turn. I swing into the right lane just behind another car—one of those "pokey" drivers. This is one of the corners where you can turn right at any time. There's a sign saying you can. The light's turning red and I'll bet that d—m fool will stop. Sure enough, he does. Well, if I lay on the horn enough he'll pull around. (Honk repeatedly and then shout out the window.) "Hey, you! Why don't you keep your eyes open when you drive? Get that xxxxx car out of the way!" Honestly, I've never seen such dumb drivers. (The driver gives an angry look and turns the corner, whereupon you shift gears and rush past him.) A guy like that really burns me up!

UNION-MANAGEMENT SITUATION

You are *Joe Smith,* the union steward in plant 1. The plant superintendent is John Dawson, whom you know is not favorable when it comes to unions. In fact, he is very antagonistic most of the time. Some of the union members think that he discriminates against workers who are strong union members.

Recently you and the other men in your plant have been violating the parking rules in the company parking lot. Some of the men have parked where they are not supposed to: in places that have been assigned to others, and in the exits and entrances of the parking lot as well. This morning even you noticed that some of the men had been especially careless as to where they parked their cars. Each section of the parking lot is clearly marked as to who has a right to park there. However, some of the signs have been broken recently, and have disappeared.

Nothing has been said by the plant superintendent up to now. However, right now you are handed a note saying he wants to talk to you.

You are *John Dawson,* superintendent of plant 1. You have noticed that the employees, and mainly the union men, have not been parking in the places they are supposed to park in. They have even been blocking the exits and entrances, making it difficult for people to get in and out of the lot. Each spot in the lot is clearly marked as to who is permitted to park there.

You are not a prolabor man. You think that sometimes the union men try to take advantage of the company, and hide behind the grievance procedure if the company tries to take action against them. However, you are a fair man and always listen to the "other viewpoint."

Up to this point you have said nothing about the men parking their cars in the wrong places in the lot or about parking in the exits and entrances. You have been pressed with work that had to be gotten out . . . now you have that work done. Last week some important men from a company that purchases great deal of your products came to visit the plant. They were unable to get in several entrances to the parking lot because of cars being parked in the way, and when they did get in they had to walk a considerable distance to get to the plant because the visitors' parking lot was full. You later checked and found that many cars in the visitors' lot belonged to union men . . . they had stickers on the union seal on the back window. This morning you saw Joe Smith, your plant's union steward pull in and park in the president's spot. This is the last straw, you think to yourself, and sit down and write a note asking Joe Smith to come to your office. Some time passes, you look up, and Joe Smith is at your door.

ARRIVING LATE

I am Carl White (The Boss)

I am Carl White, supervisor of an office in the "A" Department.

Jim Webber is a young man in my office group. Jim has been with the Company for a little over 3 years. For as long as I've known him, he has seemed like a nice lad, interested in his job and cooperative. He has a good future, I'm sure.

Lately, however, Jim has developed some rather bad job habits. For one thing, he comes in late almost every morining. At first it was only 5 or 10 minutes. This past week it has been 20 or 30 minutes on an average. Then he seems to leave very promptly at our closing time.

Jim may have picked this habit up from Ed Olson. Ed has been with us 35 years and is one of the fellows who has been pretty much in the same job. Ed's desk is next to Jim's and, although they don't work on the same projects, I see them talk a lot together. Ed is going to retire next year and I just don't know what to do about his work habits after all these years.

But I do know that I want Jim Webber to get "on the ball." I think I'll have to talk with him when he gets in this morning (he's already late) and straighten this thing out!

I am Jim Webber (The Employee)

I am Jim Webber. I work in Carl White's office in the "A" Department. I have been with the Company for 38 months and like the job and the opportunity it offers.

Carl White is my boss. He seems like a nice fellow and helps me whenever I have a serious problem. Other than that, we don't spend much time together.

Ed Olson, the man at the next desk, is one of my best friends in the office. Although we do different types of work, he's been able to give me a lot of information about the Company. Ed has been around over 35 years and seems to know a great deal. There are some things I've wondered about, however. He seems to get in late every day and takes a pretty long lunch hour.

Of course, I guess I'm having a little trouble about that myself. I used to ride the Main Street bus to work every day. I usually caught the one that got me to the office right about our starting time. Once in a while, we'd be little off schedule by traffic or I'd be held up by the crowded elevators.

Because the bus was always so crowded, I decided to join a car pool and ride into town with the fellows on my block. It's certainly a lot easier and takes far less time. The only problem is that they don't have to be at work quite as early as I do and it gets me in a little late. Then I have to be ready promptly at closing time to meet the car pool.

Mr. White hasn't said anything about my being late like this. Maybe he doesn't mind as long as I get my work done.

WHO NEEDS GLASSES

(Employee)

I am Joe Zaritsky. I've got a wife and two girls at home, and I work on a lathe at the Melmac plant. The shop is just an avergae place, but I feel at home with the fellows I work with, and we get along pretty well with Al Stebbins, the foreman. Of course he's an old grandfather of a fellow, always wanting us to follow the rules—like keeping our safety glasses on while we're running the work. I know he means all right, but nobody thinks we should take the rules too seriously. I didn't wear glasses today, but neither did anybody else—and nobody was hurt.

Here comes Al now, looking like he wanted to talk to somebody, while we're all here in the washroom cleaning up for the end of the shift. Probably he'll pull the fellow over into the corner so the gang won't hear—but they'll all be waiting outside or asking tomorrow morning what the conversation was about. It's a good gang—they're all interested in each other. Well, it looks as if Al wanted to talk to me. Good thing I was early at the washstand today.

(Foreman)

I am Al Stebbins, shift foreman in the lathe section of the Melmac plant. Been foreman right here for 15 years, and have a pretty good crew of men—no fight or fusses. They all seem to get along well enough, and they even treat me all right. The trouble is they don't seem to have enough respect for shop rules, particularly safety rules. I don't like to crack down, but they ought to follow the rules more carefully.

I noticed Joe Zaritsky doing some close work today without his safety glasses. He shouldn't do that—it's against the rules and he might get hurt. Everybody's in the washroom getting ready to go home now. Guess I'll find him and talk to him about it. Too bad if he'd lose an eye, with a wife and two little girls to support. I'll just pull him aside where the others cannot hear and talk to him about the rules. There he is already through washing up.

PROBLEM SOLVING
Counseling
THE FRUSTRATED SUPERVISOR

Role for Jim Wells, Division Supervisor:

You are the supervisor of a division employing about 75 men and women and 6 first-line supervisors. You like your job, and the supervisors and employees who work for you, and you feel that they cooperate with you in every way.

This morning you noticed that one of your first-line supervisors, Bill Jackson, was rather late in getting to work. Since Bill is very conscientious and was working on a rush job you wondered what had happened. Bill is thoroughly dependable and, when something delays him, he always tries to phone you. For this reason you were somewhat concerned and were about to call his home when one of Bill's men, a young fellow named Joe Blake, came in. Joe is a good natured kid, just out of high school, but this time he was obviously angry, and said that he was not going to work for Bill another minute and was going to quit unless you got him another job. Evidently Bill had come in, started to work, and then lost his temper completely when young Joe didn't do something quite right.

Although Bill occasionally has his bad moods, it is unlike him to lose his temper this way. This latest rush job may have put him under too much pressure but even so his outburst this morning seems difficult to explain on any reasonable grounds. You feel, therefore, that something must be seriously wrong and if you can get Bill to talk about whatever it is that is bothering him you may get the situation straightened out. In any case you are determined not to get into an argument with Bill or criticize him in any way. Instead you are going to try to get him to talk about his troubles, listen to what he has to say, and indicate that you understand how he feels about things. If Bill seems more angry than Joe's mistake would reasonably justify, you might suppose that there is something more behind all of this and Bill would probably feel a lot better if he got it off his chest. If Bill is thoroughly angry with Joe, you may suggest that Joe be fired in order to demonstrate that you have not taken Joe's side in the matter.

You talked with Joe for several minutes and, after he had told his side of the story, he felt better and was ready to go back on the job. You just phoned Bill and asked him to drop around when he had a chance. Bill said he'd come right over and is walking toward your office now.

Role for Bill Jackson, First-line Supervisor:

You have just come to work after a series of the most humiliating and irritating experiences you have ever had. Last night your next-door neighbor, Sam Jones, had a wild, drunken party at his house that kept you awake most of the night. Jones is a blustering, disagreable man who has no consideration whatever for others, so when you called him at about 3:30 a.m. and told him to be less noisy, he was abusive and insulting. Things quieted down later on, but when you finally got some rest you overslept.

Since you were in the midst of a rush job at the company, you skipped breakfast to hurry to work and, as you were leaving the house, you noticed that someone had driven a car across one corner of your lawn and had torn out several feet of your new hedge. You were certain that Jones or one of the drunks at his party had done it so you ran right over to Jones' house, determined to have it out with him. He not only denied everything, but practically threw you out and threatened to knock your teeth out if you didn't shut up and behave yourself and you know that he is big enough to do it.

When you came to work, more than an hour late, your nerves were so ragged that you were actually shaking. Everything conceivable had gone wrong, and then the last straw was when you discovered that Joe Blake, a young high school recruit, had made a mistake that delayed you several hours on your rush job, or at least it would have if you hadn't caught him in time. Naturally, you gave him a good going over for his carelessness. Blake said he wouldn't take that kind of abuse from anyone and walked out on you. You noticed that he went in to see your supervisor, Jim Wells. Obviously he is in there accusing you of being rough on him. Well, you don't like that kind of an attitude in a young squirt either, and if he had gone in there squawking you'll make him wish he'd never been born. You have had all you can stand and the big boss had better not get tough with you because he'll have one hell of a time getting the job done without you. Jim had that snivelling brat in there and talked to him for quite a while before he phoned you to come in. Gabbing when there's work to be done—that's certainly a hell of a way to run things. You are on your way to Jim's office now and have no intention of wasting time on words.

NOT PROMOTED

I am Joe Brown (Superintendent)

Bill Green has been an employee with our company for 10 years. His work has always been top rate until recently. He was a good machine operator and seemed to be always a top man in production. Three weeks ago a foreman's job opened up in the department. John Gray, a fellow machinist of Bill Green, got the job. At the time we were trying to decide on one of the two men for the opening of the foreman's position. John Gray was also a top rate man in production even though he had only 7 years with the company. My decision to make John Gray a foreman was based on his qualities of getting along with his fellow employees and getting a job done without too much instruction from a supervisor. Too, he had more previous experience with another company on the same type of work we were doing than Bill Green.

These were qualities that Bill Green lacked even though he was a top rate man with our company. Since he didn't get the foreman's job, he has taken the attitude of not caring about his job anymore. His production has fallen off and he is careless in standard of work he puts out on his machine.

Bill is a good worker and I hate to see this happen. How can I explain to him about John getting the foreman's job? How can I tell Bill about the qualities he lacks for a higher position with the company and still "straighten him out" to become a top rate producer again?

I am Bill Green (Machinist)

I am Bill Green. I work for Superintendent Joe Brown. After working for this company for 10 years and being a top production man on my machine, I thought my opportunity for advancement had finally come. I got it through the department "grapevine" that John Gray and I were being considered for a foreman's opening in the department. I felt sure that the job would be mine because I had more seniority than Bill and always was top producer on my machine. I didn't bother with the other employees, I "minded my own business" so to speak. I always checked with the foreman for instructions before starting a job so that nothing would go wrong. John Gray seemed to just go ahead without consulting the foreman. He was always talking and "kidding" with the other employees, sometimes I wondered how he got his work done.

If that is the kind of man they want for foreman, I may as well give up waiting for an advancement. Why should I "break my neck" on this job, the company and superintendent don't appreciate me anyhow. I'll produce less just like some of the other employees around here do. There is no future with this company for me; I'll probably have to await another 10 years before I'm considered again for a foreman's job and chances are that someone else will get the job just as it happened now.

The Old Man Problem

You are Archie Hoskins, 26, a supervisor in a steel mill, where you have worked for three years.

Dave Leshinski is one of the workers on your shift. He is an older man—as a matter of fact he will be eligible for retirement in about two years. The problem is that he has shown an increasing record of absenteeism over the past two years, so that now he fails to show up for work about once a week on the average—sometimes twice. His record shows that the longest number of absences has occurred on Mondays. But you can't keep the shift running efficiently if all the men aren't there.

You have spoken to your manager about Leshinski, and he has simply told you to fire the man. But you're a bit sorry for Dave, who is an unhappy looking figure as he grows older—so maybe you'd better talk to him first. You just can't fire him off-hand.

You are *Dave Leshinski*, age 63. You have spent your entire working life in the steel mill in which you are now employed. It has been a relatively satisfactory life—you have a little home, your son is married and working on a space project in California, and you have little cause to complain, although your wife's illness and death about two years ago used up most of your savings.

But since your wife died, it has been lonely around the house. A handy bottle, though, has enabled you to do a lot of forgetting, especially on week-ends. It's comforting. Yet, drinking has caused you to fail to report for work an increasing number of times,. a fact which you are rather vaguely aware of. Just a hang-over now and then. But you are a peaceful man, so you just sleep away. Still, you don't much care a lot whether you get to work or not. As a matter of fact, the only reason you keep on working is that you will be eligible for a retirement pension when you reach 65—if you do reach that age. But your expenses aren't too great and you can probably get along.

Your shift supervisor, Archie Hoskins, a young man, says he wants to talk to you. He's a nice fellow, who isn't hard to get along with. True, you don't talk to him much because the work goes along all right most of the time. What does he want to talk to you about now—something that can't be discussed over the machines. Are you getting too old to do the work? Does he want to put you on another shift? Or is he going to dress you down for those absences?

Project Six-2

Job Interview Round Robin

In this chapter six principles differentiated between those who were hired from those rejected. This activity is designed to practice those principles.

Step 1. Adapt the resume you prepared in Project Four-1 to a specific business or professional organization. Select this organization realistically. One way to do this is to secure from your college placement office a list of organizations which send recruiters to your campus.

Step 2. Prepare a one page description of the organization you select.

Step 3. Prepare a sheet of questions you would ask if you were a personnel recruiter from that organization.

Step 4. Now bring your *resume,* the *organization description,* and the *list* of *questions* the *interviewer* might ask to class.

Class 5. The course instructor will next pair the students who will flip a coin to see who is the interviewee and the interviewer. The person who is the interviewee gives his/her organization description and list of interviewer questions to the classmate with whom he/she is paired. The interview then proceeds. Each interview is allotted 20 minutes. Then the pair reverses roles. On the following period the class is paired again, this time with different partners.

Step 6. Especially prepare to demonstrate your ability in each of the six winner categories:

- Convey a positive image
- Identify with the interviewers
- Offer well supported arguments
- Organize thoughts coherently
- Phrase ideas in clear and appropriate language
- Deliver your message effectively

7

Selling an Idea, Product or Service

Chapter Outline

Selling Can Be a Noble Profession
The Selling Process
Post Sale Activity
Recap

Chapter Objectives:

Those who complete this chapter should better understand:

1. The vital role salesmen of ideas, products and services play in a society, and the ethical responsibilities of those in this role.
2. The steps in the selling process: the motivational sequence involved, preparation, approaches, presentation-demonstration selling benefits, handling objections and most importantly closing skills.
3. That selling is not a one shot process but rather developing a relationship based on character, service and quality.

> "And before you leave the marketplace, see that no one has gone his way with empty hands."
> —Kahlil Gibran, *The Prophet*

Advertising Themes

1886   "Drink Coca-Cola"
1905   "Coca-Cola Revives and Sustains"
1929   "The Pause that Refreshes"
1970   "It's the Real Thing"
1975   "Look Up America"
1982   "Coke Is It"

"'Coke is it!' means Coke is the premier pop, which certainly is arguable, and arguing the point—if advertising can be called argument—may coin money for Coke. But advertising generally may be producing diminishing returns. About $34 billion was spent on national advertising last year—more than $400 per household—but the visual and audio clutter is canceling itself. About 1,500 advertising messages come within the average American's range of vision and hearing every day. There are nearly 600 network-television commercials a day. There often are nine consecutive 30-second commercials (usually at least $100,000 apiece in prime time) in the middle of an hour show. Four and a half minutes is time enough to make a sandwich, which many people probably do.

Proctor & Gamble, the leading advertiser, spent more than half a billion dollars on TV last year. Soft-drink makers spent $307 million. But inflation has increased price consciousness, and recent history has increased skepticism about all claims. Competition often makes products so similar that you have cases like the mouthwash that advertises its unbreakable bottle rather than what is in the bottle. Much advertising is aimed more at incresing a product's market share than at expanding the market. The Coca-Cola Co. spent $109 million on TV last year, not primarily to make you thirsty or to get you to buy its products rather than shoes or beer, but primarily to get you to buy its products rather than other sodas.

—George F. Will
Newsweek, May 10, 1982, p. 98

Life for most of us is a constant effort to influence others through persuasion or attitude change. Almost every day of our lives we attempt to get people to accept our ideas, attitudes, beliefs, and values. In fact, one of the major reasons we communicate is to influence each other. We seek to influence each other because we are trying to modify attitudes, beliefs, and values.

Attitudes, beliefs, and values are what psychologists call "hypothetical constructs." While an attitude is (nothing more than) a person's evaluation of other people, ideas, and things, a belief is the way a person views reality. Values are "our enduring conceptions of the nature of good and bad. Whereas attitudes and beliefs are normally subject to modification and change, values tend to remain constant over much greater periods of time."[1] Attitudes, beliefs, and values are generally acquired through reinforcement, generalization, and identification with reference groups. Throughout life our attitudes, beliefs, and values are always subject to change.

The most common form of attitude change is the sales presentation. Attitude change and selling have similar objectives in that they both attempt to influence thought and conduct. Attitude change deals with influence in any direction and has a broader objective than selling. Selling deals with influence in a specific direction.

Selling Can Be a Noble Profession

Selling is the oldest profession known to man. Several million men and women make their living as outside salesmen, while an even greater number make their living selling within wholesale and retail establishments. The selling profession has been the brunt of more humor than any other vocation, but the history of this profession is probably the richest of any of our occupations. Historically, we find salesmen were "drummers," who, with a wagon and an Indian, made their way through the villages of America sweet-talking the locals into buying medicines guaranteed to cure everything from the common cold to old age.

I can remember as a youngster growing up in Southern Ohio, the medicine man paying a visit to the local fairgrounds.* Although his wagon was not drawn by horses, his product and presentation skills were, I am told, very similar to his predecessors. As America was developing, so were the inventories of the drummer. The supplies of medicine were supplemented with new fabric and gadgets of all kinds from "back East." The "drummer" was a general store on wheels. He was a showman, and his style of dress was bright and unusual for his day.

As the villages grew along the rivers and crossroads of America, they spawned merchandizing units called stores. The drummer was now considered a traveling salesman. He traveled by buggy, train, and later automobile, calling on the proprietors of stores in a fixed territory. The major difference between the traveling salesman (of today) and his predecessor is the specialization of the products.

Of course, we cannot mention types without citing the door-to-door salesman. We tend to view this breed of salesman as not very bright — a somewhat ordinary man who made colossal mistakes, got his foot caught in doors, and felt the teeth of every dog in the neighborhood; and who usually made a sale by some haphazard turn of events. It is no wonder that we have come to look upon the role of the salesman as something just a little short of respectable. Yet some of the country's leading corporate executives started their careers as door-to-door salesmen.

While it would be foolish for anyone to assume that today's salesman is just a "chip off one of these old blocks," it would be just as foolish for us to ignore the rich heritage these early vendors have left to us. It was they who broadened the horizons of the residence of small villages by bringing unheard of products from far-away places. These early salesmen taught us the power of dramatizing and demonstrating. Many of these fast-talking, loud-dressed fellows laid the foundations of modern sales psychology. Let's take a brief look at the true role of the modern salesman in terms of how far he has come and where he is expected to go. Until he understands his real function, he can never develop the pride that is justly his.

---

*In this chapter, the occasional use of "I" in anecdotes is referring to this text's second author John Miller.

Emerson once said, "What you are speaks so loudly, I cannot hear what you say to the contrary." A good salesman has simply been a "good man selling." Upon the salesman's integrity, honesty, decency, and desire to serve, selling has marched upward through the years, packing its punch in every facet of our living. With these demonstrated qualities, salesmanship has become an honored word among men and selling a proud profession to which we owe much. List the things we value—cultural, political, social, and spiritual lives—and I'll show you a salesman behind each.

Politicians Are Salesmen. Were it not for salesmen, we would be a nation of horses and buggies. Actually, were it not for revolutionary salesmen, we would not be a nation. One-third of the colonists were solidly on the side of the British and one-third of them didn't care, so it was up to the remaining third to persuade the undecided to fight the revolution. From time immemorial, man has not accepted change unless he were influenced or persuaded to do so. Such influencing and persuading is selling.

While the label of salesman is not ordinarily applied to the farmers, lawyers, and merchants who debated and persuaded their neighbors in the various Continental Congresses, the intent and end result of their actions were, nonetheless, salesmanship. Washington, Jefferson, Adams, Paine, Franklin, Jay, Hamilton, and Hancock were salesmen: some of the most effective salesmen in the history of this Republic. In fact, much of the progress on this planet has been the result of salesmenship by the likes of Fulton, Whitney, Bell, Edison, Westinghouse, Wright, Ford, and thousands of other great men and women.

Even after the Republic was well on its feet, it took men like Jackson, Lincoln, and others to keep it going. It is still being sold, both at home and abroad. With our promotion of democracy in the far corners of the earth, we are but returning the compliment to the venerable salesmen who gave the idea its original impetus.

Political and social reform and the struggle for civil rights have helped us to distinguish between effective and ineffective leadership. Statesmen have been master salesmen. The words of Lincoln, Roosevelt, Johnson, King, and Young have been trusted and accepted; and their influence has shaped the lives of many Americans. In the political world, the difference between being perceived as effective or ineffective is measured by the politician's ability to sell himself and his programs.

Salesmen Are Educators. Explorer, scientist, educator, statesman—all these have salesmen. Today, the salesman is still an educator. Our space program, military defense and reindustrialization will all mean new products, new ideas, and new methods of doing things; and they will all have to be sold by salesmen. Many of our salesmen today are educators. Political and industrial leaders are educating the citizens of their respective communities on the need to rebuild their core cities; and this effort has achieved great success in such cities as Detroit, Baltimore, Cincinnati, and St. Louis. Even the scientist has to be an educator salesman. Today's products are marvels of mechanical fabrication. They have to be explained, explained in a language that can be understood by superiors, coworkers, subordinates and sometimes the media and general public.

The saleman knows who his ancestors were. His heritage is a proud one. Looking beyond the drummer, the pitchman, and the huckster, a thorough history gives us a portrait of dignity, honesty, integrity, zeal, sincerity and wisdom. The salesperson's heritage is not one of gimmicks and quick-fire strategy. What the finer of their predecessors sold, they sold because they were good men. Their lives were persuasive. They knew full well that a good idea can perish if it becomes associated with a shoddy personal character. A farsighted salesman has always been a man selling ideas for tomorrow and not just a vendor taking orders for today.

Until recently in many business organizations the salesman was considered as an adjunct to production, a more or less necessary evil, a function which could be cut when the going got tough. More properly the salesman is seen as the last step in production. Without the salesman, the production cycle is not complete. No product — automobile or pair of jeans — is a product until it is put to its intended use by a customer. Up until that time, it is nothing more than a potential. The production cycle has not been completed. Appliances in warehouses or in dealers' showrooms are only potentially useful. Services not yet purchased also fall in this category. It is the salesman who makes a product out of the potential! Therefore, he is a very real and very necessary last step in the production cycle.

The Selling Process

Kirkpatrick suggests that "salesmanship is showing a prospect how he can get greater satisfaction from the money he spends — it is aiding the prospect to make a wise buying decision — it is helping."[2]

The Sales Interview. In conducting the sales interview, the salesman sells benefits, not just products or services, because the buyer is buying satisfaction, not merchandise. A buyer may appear to be buying a car, but he actually is buying safe, low-cost transportation. If you were to observe America's greatest automobile salesman, Joe Girard, you would notice that he does not sell cars, but family dreams.[3] A buyer does not buy a new television set; he buys home entertainment. The typical life insurance policy is in reality "death" protection; but if a salesman is to be effective, he has to put "life" into the policy. One creative salesman put it this way:

> A life insurance policy is just a time-yellowed piece of paper with columns of figures and legal phrases until it is baptized with a widow's tears. Then it is a modern miracle, an Aladdin's Lamp. It is goods, clothing, shelter, education, peace of mind, comfort, undying love and affection. It is the sincerest love letter ever written.
>
> It quiets the crying of a hungry baby at night. It eases the aching heart of a bereaved widow. It is a comforting whisper in the dark, silent hours of the night. It is new hope, fresh courage and strength for the mother to pick up the broken threads of life and carry on. It is a college education for sons and daughters. It is a father's parental blessing to the children on their wedding day.
>
> It is the function of a father's hopes and plans for his family's future. Through life insurance he lives on. There is no death. It is a plan that exalts life and defeats death. It is the premium we pay for the privilege of living after death.[4]

Success is achieved in the sales interview by knowing the product or service, then bringing the two together. Most sales presentations follow a problem-solution or need-satisfaction format. The sales interview should attempt to appeal to the psychological wants and needs of the buyer. His product or service should be the satisfier. The basic needs or motives are profit and economy, comfort and convenience, health and safety, pride and prestige, and the need for affection.[5]

A Motivational Framework. There are many organizational schemes around which one can build a sales message. The standard pattern is the one that is motivational in sequence:

1. Talk about those things which will capture the attention of the prospect.
2. Feed out the information and ideas which then will create a desire or need.
3. Now shift your materials to show how your product or service will satisfy the desire or need.
4. Help the prospect visualize what it will be like to possess the product or service.
5. Build a bridge to action by attempting to close the sale, asking the prospect to try the product or service.

This pattern requires an adjustment for each new prospect, since obviously what captures the attention of one may be pretty dull stuff to another. Adaptation of materials within this pattern therefore is dependent upon the individual prospect. Adjustment of materials is likewise dependent, to some extent, upon the salesman. This is to suggest that not all techniques of capturing attention are equally effective for all salesmen to use. The sales interviewer should have a reservoir of evidence to support his case.

The process of selling is simply the process of communicating along certain well-patterned avenues of motivation and persuasion.

Preparing. The first step in the process is called by some writers the preapproach. This can best be described as the planning stage of the process. In planning a sales interview, a salesman must do some preliminary work. His responsibility in any sales interview is to achieve, on the part of the prospect, three things: (1) information about, (2) a liking for, and (3) confidence in the company which manufactures his product or provides his service. Also he wants to promote good will toward the product, service itself, and and the salesman representing the company.

There is some truth to the assertion that 20 percent of a salesforce sells 80 percent of the goods and services in that organization. At least it is indisputable that some salespeople sell much more than other salespersons doing the same jobs. One of the major causes for this most probably is lack of product knowledge. Every salesperson should test his/her product knowledge by asking the following questions: How well do you know your product and market competition? Preparation does not merely mean reading about only one subject. It means thinking in terms of the kinds of sales resistance one is likely to meet.

Think of your customer first. Every successful salesman we have met has developed this power of forgetting himself and concentrating on the other fellow — on his wants, needs, interests, and problems. A salesman must see the product or service through the customer's eyes. Remember the prospect thinks of himself as the most important person in the world. Treat him that way. The more references you can make to the prospect, his possessions, his job, and his plans, the more interest your talk will have for him. Use as many "you" phrases in your presentation as you can think of.

Use these "you" phrases:

> You're right...
> You have a good idea there...
> Your problem...
> Your needs...
> You benefit by...
> You gain...
> Your satisfaction...

As in most other types of interviews, the question is the primary tool of the salesman. The customer's greatest interest in the *you* you talk about.

Use these questions:

Is this what you want?

What is your opinion?

Is this your problem?

What is your real reason?

Why do you say that?

Why not work up a list of "you" questions as they might apply to what you might be selling.

In planning your presentation, use words that your prospect can understand. The problem in using unknown words finds illustrative support in the story of the plumber who wrote the U.S. Bureau of Standards that he found hydrochloric acid fine for cleaning drains and was it harmless? Washington replied, "The efficacy of hydrochloric acid is indisputable, but the chlorine residue is incompatible with metallic permanence." Completely mystified, the plumber wrote back that he was mighty glad the Bureau agreed with him. The Bureau replied with a note of alarm: "We cannot assume responsibility for the production of toxic and noxious residues with hydrochloric acid and suggest you use an alternate procedure." Slightly confused but still appreciative, the plumber immediately posted another letter indicating continued happiness that the Bureau agreed with him. Whereupon Washington exploded: "Don't use hydrochloric acid; it eats hell out of the pipes!"[6] At long last the Bureau used words he could understand.

The most effective picture-producing vocabulary is an active one. Active words are verbs, words that show action taking place. Why not list the action words you normally use? For every one of them, find a substitute that suggests even more action. In the preapproach, you learn as much as you can about your prospect, his problems, his company, and his business.

Do a buyer analysis. Many sales authorities are against the idea of developing a totally canned sales presentation because it lacks flexibility. Rather, professional salesmen today outline their presentation and then put that to memory. Like plays in a basketball game it is good to memorize certain phrases and sentences, particularly the first few lines you will use. But the plays one uses and the sequence of the material presented in a sales talk must be in keeping with the concerns expressed by the prospective buyer. This style of planning allows for more flexibility in tailoring the presentation to a specific buyer.

Edward Hegarty, former Director of Sales Training for the Appliance Division of Westinghouse Electric Corporation, used to suggest in his sales workshops a salesman should ask three questions:

What will I say first?

What will I show?

What will I ask for?

If you answer these questions before you make your call, you will be better organized than most salesmen. Most salesmen work hit or miss. And you won't fail because you plan to fail, you'll fail because you won't plan.

The Approach. The approach is very important to a salesman because it helps establish the receptivity of the buyer and thus provides clues about how difficult it will be to close the sale. The basic objective of the approach is to generate the prospect's interest and help him see that he needs some advantage which he does not enjoy now.

The late sales master, Jack Lacy, often suggested that the first thirty seconds you spend with the prospect are by far the most important moments you will ever spend with him. Making a good impression, surveying the situation, and stirring the feelings of the prospect are the three main goals a salesman should have in mind during the first few moments of the sales interview.

Early credibility is a must. By credibility we mean his intelligence (such as product knowledge), trustworthiness, and the good will.

The salesman needs to secure control of the interview early, and maintain it throughout. He needs to be customer oriented. Many sales experts suggest that a buyer benefit be used early, such as: My product can save you time, money, and labor.

Sales Presentation-Demonstration. After the salesperson has successfully asserted the buyer will benefit, he/she must demonstrate these benefits and advantages and then get buyer commitment. Since the actual convincing is done in the presentation, this is the point at which the buyer decides to buy (or not to buy). The close is merely working out the details.

The common denominator of every selling situation is: "What's in it for me?" If you have not satisfied the "what's in it for me," there is no close. In stating buyer advantages, it is important to state them in terms of buyer motives. It is important to have a large supply of product advantages and always make them definite and specific. Unfortunately, product advantages alone are not enough to guarantee your success as a salesman. You also have to know how to use these advantages with each prospect. It is the artistic use of these advantages which helps determine whether you will be a success or a failure.

Selling is an art because it entails a creative use of materials and unique adaptation to different people. If selling rather was a science, we could simply prescribe a sure-fire formula. But although there are formulae, none are sure-fire. Selling is an art.

It is important to understand what a benefit or advantage really amounts to. Simply put, a benefit or advantage is a personalized value about your product or service which answers the "What's in it for me" question. When used as a natural part of your presentation, benefits give the prospect sound personal reasons for buying from you. The salesman's job, then, is to provide this personalization as he discusses the product or service. Tie your product or service to the needs, interests, and wants of the prospect, using the advantages or benefits that he will receive as the knot!

Benefits must be based on factual information, and they must be proved. Most benefits are obtained from the product, the service itself, or the organization you represent. In the case of a product benefit, you usually refer to the product's special features or advantages. *Special features* are the physical characteristics of the product, such as the correcting device on a typewriter. *Product advantages* mean those performance characteristics derived from the special features, such as lower maintenance cost or better mileage. You need to prove each of your product advantages. Logical reasoning and concise facts must be presented. Most companies supply their salesmen with proof of product advantages in the form of statistics, research findings, testimonials, and case histories. While serving as a spokesman for the Exxon Oil Company at their various dealer trade fairs, I was impressed with the myriad of statistics, research findings, and customer testimonials that their Atlas Products Division made available to their dealer's. Exxon's biggest problem was getting their dealers to use the information they made available to them.

One of the most effective ways to prove a product's advantages is simply to demonstrate it. A demonstration shows how a product is built and what it can do for the customer. Your sales presentation should be simple and complete, but with positive statements of what the product will do for the buyer. The objective of the presentation-demonstration is to get buyer commitment or action on each product advantage presented. Getting this early makes the buyer action-minded and will influence him to buy the product rather than to reject it. Action is usually obtained by employing closed primary questions, always attempting to get a "yes" answer. However, a skillful salesperson is careful not to ask so many questions seeking a yes response that he appears to be trying to manipulate the prospective buyer. When strong, enthusiastic agreement is achieved on several buying motives, that is a signal to try and close the sale.

Handling Objections. Sales resistance is a normal behavior of consumers because most consumers have unlimited wants but limited purchasing power. All objections are signs of customer resistance and, as such, vary greatly both in degree and cause. Viewed pragmatically, an objection is any customer statement, action, or reaction which keeps you from obtaining his commitment. The primary reason for customer objections is rooted in the human tug of war between his desire to have something not possessed against a reluctance to give up something to acquire it. Each prospect is a unique individual with attitudes, emotions, instincts, hang-ups, and a mind uniquely his or her own. As all of these factors work together during the decision-making process, a balancing act occurs in his or her mind. Every product advantage or benefit you give the prospect is being balanced against a question which hasn't been answered in his or her mind.

One of the mistakes that some salesmen make when an objection comes up is to react defensively. Here again, we're dealing with the human factor; but this time it's the salesman. Salespeople's natural tendency is to defend themselves when under attack. A salesperson's intellect tells him customer objections are normal and that he should not allow this resistance to deter him from his task. But his emotions may take over to defend his product and his reputation. Some common sense rules that you can follow when encountering an objection are: 1. Treat the objection with respect, even though your first thought is that it is way out in "left field." 2. Listen carefully to the objection. You must understand the objection before you can properly deal with it. 3. Do not interrupt while the customer is stating his objection. In some cases, the customer may talk himself out of his own objection. 4. Always maintain a positive attitude. When a customer brings up an objection, he is usually saying, "tell me more."

Objections can be classified into four areas. They concern themselves with: (a) the customer's need for the product, (b) the price of the product, (c) the features of the product, or (d) the services that the company may offer in connection with the product. To prepare for handling objections, effective salesmen list the major objections that they encounter most frequently in these four basic categories. Next they write down a positive statement which they can use to *anticipate* each objection. It is important that a salesman not be caught off guard and often when prepared he is able to get a positive point across before the customer has a chance to raise his objection.

Encouraging customers to voice their doubts and objections, however, can be extremely helpful to a salesman. They are a prospect's way of saying, "I need more information on a particular aspect of your presentation." These requests permit the salesman to expand his presentation and further attempt to convince the prospect he needs the product. Objections should be welcomed, not feared. A prospect should be encouraged to bring up his objections because only then can they be dealt with.

As in the demonstration, the question is very important in dealing with objections. The "why" question is one of the salesman's strongest allies: When a prospect brings up an objection, a salesman should ask them why: "I'll think it over." "—Why?" "I can't afford it." "—Why?" By asking the "why" question, the salesman can usually identify the major road-block.

Sales experts agree that there are many ways to handle objections. One popular method is simply to ignore it and hope it will go away. If it is not really important, the prospect will also forget it. Another tactic is to postpone the objection until you have had enough time to explain your sales story. Time has a tendency to reduce resistance. Occasionally a salesperson must admit he does not have the information at hand. But if he does so, he should promise to find the information if he possibly can. Probably the most popular method for handling objections is the indirect answer, often referred to as the "yes,...but" method, or the "...however" method. This method permits the salesman to agree with the objection and then follow with a "but" or "however" as a point of departure into a different area for consideration. This is a give-and-take technique and is a way to introduce the positives which outweigh the negatives.

Objections should always be capitalized on by the salesman. An objection should never just be answered, but should be used to bring up more buyer benefits. This will convert the objection into a reason for buying and give justification for purchase. Again, the best way to deal with objections is to prevent them from ever coming up. This can be done by incorporating the answer to the major objection you normally encounter in your presentation. To a professional salesman, an objection is never a serious problem; it's just a temporary detour. He handles it by classifying it, and then disposes of it by using the proper technique. He then moves right back into his presentation. A word of caution: the hard sell turns off many people. Moreover, such pressure may force a customer to buy who really should not; subsequently he may become a dissatisfied customer who will trade elsewhere in the future.

Closing the Sale. The close is the final stage of the sales interview. It's the climax of the salesman's presentation. Most salesmen have more difficulty with the close than any other part of the sales interview. Actually, the close should be the easiest part of the interview, if the convincing process employed during the interview was successful. When the sales interview nears the closing stage, it should no longer be a question of if the prospect is going to buy, but how the prospect will handle the transaction. Therefore, one should never try to close until he has done an effective job of persuasion during the presentation-demonstration.

The purpose of the close is simple. You are trying to get the prospect to give expression to the decision he made during presentation-demonstration. The goal is to make it easier for him to say "yes" than it is for him to say "no." Even more importantly, the close is a time to assist the customer in making a wise decision, even if that decision is not to buy.

When to Close. If a salesman has made an effective presentation, he then must decide at what point to attempt a close and what method he will employ. In most situations, customers give signals which show they are ready for the close. Some of these signals are physical, such as repeated assembly and disassembly of your product, looking over the product advantages, or working out some rough cost figures as to how he might finance the purchase. More often, these signals appear verbally in the form of questions about such things as delivery, service, and guarantee. Some buying signals are not quite so obvious and require a closer awareness on your part. These might include favorable changes in his facial expression, shifting his position in order to pay closer attention to what you are saying, or a sudden relaxing in his chair while smiling at you because his favorable decision has just been made.

In the early days of selling, there was a belief that there was an exact moment in the sales interview when the close was possible. This method proved ineffective over the years, and a more contemporary method was developed which we now call the "trial close." The purpose of the trial close is to test the buyer's degree of readiness. Actually, closing starts with the beginning of the interview. Time is both your and your customer's most important resource, so it is important to close as soon as possible. A salesman can attempt a trial close at any point in the sales interview; and if he is not successful, he merely resumes his presentation as though nothing ever happened.

Kirkpatrick suggested that there are two types of trial closes: (a) oral, and (b) physical. The oral trial close is in the form of a question: "Do you want this delivered, or would you care to take it with you?" "Would that be cash or credit card?", "Do you prefer the deluxe or the economy model?" In the physical trial close the salesman actually starts to execute the sale without asking the customer's permission to do so. Automobile and insurance salesmen are very good at the physical trial close. They start filling out the sales contract before the customer has decided to buy; and before the customer realizes what is occurring, he is closed.

If you should receive negative or noncommitting replies to your trial close questions, you should accept these for what they are — minor points of resistance or genuine doubt which must be resolved. Instead of being thrown off-track by these responses, use the information gained to adjust your presentation. Then try another trial close question to see if the customer is now ready to buy. Remember trial close questions can be used anytime during your presentation so long as they do not become annoying. As you can see, the trial close is an essential ingredient of a successful closing attempt. In most cases, the trial close allows you to make the best possible use of the limited time you have with your prospect. In some cases, a trial close will pay off right at the beginning of a call. If the buyer knows what he wants and is ready to buy from you, he will frequently accept your trial close as your final close and give you the order right then and there. If, on the other hand, the buyer does not need or cannot use your product at the present time, he will appreciate your not wasting his valuable time. By departing politely on a minor point with the door still open, he probably will be more inclined to call you when and if he does need one of your products.

The Assumptive Close is probably the best known and easiest to employ. As the name implies, you make the assumption that the customer has decided to buy. The rest of your presentation involves handling minor details that must be cleared up to complete the sale, such as: "Do you prefer the brown or blue suit?"; "Do you prefer twenty-four or thirty-six month financing?" An ice cream salesman once asked me if I wanted two or three dips. Actually, I only wanted one dip; but he never asked me if I only wanted one, so I took two. It should be noted that the assumptive close completely by-passes the need to ask for a favorable decision. Since up to that point in the sales call you and your prospect are in agreement, and since he is not placed in a position where he has to say either "yes" or "no," in most cases he will continue to agree with you.

A very similar method is the *Minor Point* or *Closing on a Choice* method; only in this case, the prospect has not made up his mind. The way you ask for a choice is what is important in employing this technique. By asking the prospect to choose between two positive alternative decisions concerning your product or products, he is really being placed in a position to say either "yes" or "yes." The salesman might ask: "Which home do you feel would fit your needs, the colonial or the ranch?" "Will you have to have this by Monday? Our regular delivery for your area is Wednesday. Would you be home on that day?" It should be noted that with the closing choices, the prospect's attention that was focused on whether to make the larger commitment is usually eliminated, while he focuses on which "yes" agreement he wishes to make.

Another frequently used method is the *Last Chance* method. This method is based on the assumption that if a prospect is interested in something and then is informed that it is the last item, they will act on it with greater speed than he might otherwise. During my college years, I used to spend my summers working as a desk clerk in a resort hotel. If a customer would come in late at night to inquire about a room, invariably if I informed him that I only had one vacancy, I would immediately register that customer. Needless to say, I did not lose many late-night customers. Frequently, you hear customers ask if an item will be here tomorrow or if this is the last day of the sale. Clerks usually indicate that the item will probably be gone or that it will return to the regular price tomorrow.

Another popular method of closing is the *Return Back* method. In this method the salesman concedes a reason for not buying and then turns back to more buyer benefits: "That is a good point, but...", "I am glad you mentioned that, however...", "This is an interesting point, but when you consider..." One other method is the *Special Feature* method. Frequently a product will have a special feature that its competition cannot match. For many years IBM was the only company that could offer its customers several typing elements for a single typewriter. I recently purchased a new car because of a special feature—front wheel drive.

Summarizing the Advantages is another effective closing method. It is essentially a review of the major selling points covered during your presentation. It is particularly effective after a lengthy presentation. Just as a lawyer uses a summary to remind the court of his most logical or convincing points of proof, the key is to emphasize those points which created the most interest during your presentation.

The *Emotional* close cannot be separated, nor should it be, from the logic appeal. Often we want a product as a result of an emotional appeal to fear, sex, pride, or death. The life insurance and the funeral industry are very successful utilizing this method.

Finally, if none of the above closes seem to work, use the *Direct Appeal*: "You need the product. You want the product and deserve it. You can afford it, so let me ship it out to you Monday." When all buying conditions are favorable, there is nothing more natural than asking directly for your prospect's order.

A sale is a living thing. It is ever changing, always growing, continuously evolving until it reaches its culmination in the close. Although we may talk of the various parts of a sale as if they existed independently of one another, this distinction is for the purpose of study and analysis only. The individual portions of a sale are only selected moments in a dynamic two-party experience. The true secret of a natural closing lies in the salesman's own attitude and outlook on himself as a human being and on the customer as a person who must make an intelligent decision.

Post Sale Activity

At the moment a customer says "yes," psychologically speaking, the trade is out of balance. The customer has given the salesman his consent. He has only a promise of performance in exchange. Nevertheless, often after a decision to buy, that customer suffers. He/she is beset with separation pain—that is the pain of parting with his money. Also he may suffer anxiety about possibly having made a bad choice.

To correct this imbalance, the salesman must immediately offer customer reassurance. Reassurance reinforces the customer's action. Reassurance helps solidify the customer's choice. Reassurance coupled with a promise of success from the newly purchased product helps the customer to look forward to the long-range value he will receive from the purchase.

Service. It is important for the salesman to properly follow-through. When accepting an order, a salesman must be alert never to fall into the trap of promising something he is not sure he can deliver. The moment a customer says "yes," a salesman's responsibility shifts. Now instead of simply working for his company, he also works for the customer as well. If a salesman has many customers, he should plan on a simple, well-organized method of note-taking and reminders to help him in his follow-through. The salesman's knowledge of product's use can add real value after the purchased items have been delivered. If you intend to be a professional salesman, you must service your customers to the best of your ability.

Turning Satisfied Customers Into Prospectors. If you intend also to grow in your role as a salesman, then it is necessary to use your satisfied customers for referrals. When a salesman is out of customers, he's only out of money. When he's out of prospects, he's out of hope. Many salesmen fail to prospect through their satisfied customers simply because of neglect.

When Joe Girard (the afore-mentioned World's greatest salesman) completes the sale of an automobile, he gives the satisfied customer fifty of his business cards. Each customer, naturally, has a wide range of contacts. These occur in his personal life and in his business life. On the back of each card, he prints the name of the satisfied customer. As he delivers a new automobile, he asks the customer who referred him and then sends twenty-five dollars immediately to the person who referred that new customer. Joe Girard feels that if a customer has enjoyed a pleasant, mutually satisfactory relationship with a salesman, he will naturally be happy to help him.

As we crisscross the United States speaking to a variety of groups, we make it a point to give public relations brochures about our work to every individual who might need or know someone who might need a speaker or organizational consultant. We make it a point to leave brochures with groups after we complete an address, for satisfied listeners are our best salesmen. A good salesman should view each individual customer as a single element in a constantly expanding system of prospects.

Recap

Selling is a matter of influence in a specific direction—to secure action upon an idea or purchase of certain goods or services. Selling, therefore, is linked to the marketplace of ideas, to educating and politicking, as well as to business.

The skillful salesperson sells benefits. S/he understands how the buyer thinks and feels and links what is for sale to her/his target customer. Selling is an art of adaptation.

Closing a sale, of course, is an end goal. But even more important, generating consumer goodwill is both a short range and long term objective. Manipulative techniques may win the sales battle but lose the respect of the customer.

Selling is not a simple matter of exchange. Rather it is a most vital transaction of earning trust, which is so necessary for any society. Happy sales.

Notes

1. James C. McCroskey, Mark Knapp, and Carl Larson, *An Introduction to Interpersonal Communication* (Englewood Cliffs, N.J.: Prentice-Hall, Inc., 1971), p. 60.
2. C.A. Kirkpatrick, *Salesmanship* (Cincinnati: Southwestern Publishing Company, 1966), p. 46.
3. Joe Girard, *How to Sell Anything to Anybody* (New York: Warner Books, Inc., 1977).
4. Charles E. Irvin, *How to Sell Yourself* (New York, N.Y.: The American Press, 1957), p. 69.
5. Kirkpatrick, *Salesmanship,* p. 176.
6. Stuart Chase, *The Power of Words* (New York: Harcourt, Brace and Company, 1954).

Project Seven-1

The Sales Campaign

Study Guide

During most of the seventies, Merrill-Lynch's advertising theme was "Bullish on America." Ogilvy and Mather, the agency which created the campaign, created the image of a herd of bulls charging across a plain.

Transfer of the Merrill-Lynch account to Young and Rubicam brought a new theme—"A Breed Apart." Joseph T. Plummer, an executive vice president and director of Y & R research, argued the rationale for this change was that their research revealed Merrill-Lynch customers' perceived of themselves as achievers. Therefore, words like "innovative, resourceful, brute strength, and finesse," supported by a lone bull weaving through a maze of hedges or profiled against the horizon carry more appeal to the targeted buyers.

The thundering herd, Plummer reasoned, was geared to "belongers," "traditionalists," and "flag-wavers."

Norman Berry, executive vice-president, creative head of Ogilvy and Mather, (perhaps quite understandably defensive about the earlier theme "Bullish on America") sees the current campaign quite differently—"an old, tired bull wandering through a shop or maze" as incongruous with what a bull symbolizes.

1. Which selling theme do you favor? Why? What are the strengths of each?

2. Imagine you have been asked to create a new theme and campaign for Merrill-Lynch. Prepare your description and rationale in a one page proposal below.

Project Seven-2

Consumer Profiles

Study Guide

Modern marketing theory sees the marketplace as consisting of overlapping buying segments. Science Research Institute, a giant think tank that at one time was linked to Stanford University, has authored a market research program titled VALS. The system categorizes the buying public by life styles:

Need-Driven Consumers. These are money restricted consumers who are struggling to buy the basics, approximately 11 percent of the population. This group is divided into two categories: Survivors—who are old, poor, depressed and far removed from the cultural mainstream and Sustainers, who are relatively young, angry, crafty, struggling on the edge of poverty and willing to do anything to get ahead. Many single female heads of households fall into this category.

Other-Directed Consumers. This category covers two-thirds of the adult population, what makes up Middle America. Other-directed people conduct their lives so that others will think well of them. This large segment of society may be partitioned into three subcategories: Belongers who are traditional conservatives, conventional, nostalgic, sentimental, puritanical and un-experimental. Emulators who are eager to make it big; they are ambitious, upwardly mobile, status conscious, macho and competitive, but they also are distrustful and angry, with little faith that they will get a fair shake from the Establishment. Achievers, who are the leaders in business, the professions and government are materialistic, concerned about efficiency, fame, status, the good life, comfort and luxury.

Inner-Directed Consumers. This group presently is growing and will amount in the next ten years to 28 percent, according to SRI. These inner directed people primarily buy products to meet their own needs rather than to please others. Three types of inner-directed life styles make up this group: I-am-me's, who are generally young, narcissistic, impulsive, exhibitionistic, dramatic, fiercely individualistic and inventive. Experimentals, a more mature version of the I-am-me's, who want direct experience and vigorous involvement. They are concerned with inner growth and naturalism. The third group are societally conscious individuals. These are attracted to simple living, and the cause of environmental conservation.

SRI suggest that another small segment exists, yet too small to be a significant target consumer group; this group they have labeled Integrated. Integrated individuals are fully mature in a psychological sense, tolerant, assured, self-actualizing and have a world perspective. (This summary is based on descriptions in "A New Way to View Consumers" in *Dun's Review,* August 1981 and other materials supplied by SRI.)

1. Look at the several competing enterprises such as the Hyatt Corporation vs. Marriott Corporation, Burger King vs. McDonald's, Sears vs. Penny's, and General Motors vs. Nissan Motors. Describe in VALS terminology how these enterprises differ in their customer appeals in their ads, their decor, and styles.

2. How helpful do you believe it is for marketing divisions of an organization to have a category system and design their sales campaigns accordingly? In teams, do a little field research on how sales persons in your community *analyze, categorize,* and *adapt* to their customers and public. Visit businesses such as car sales, restaurants, entertainment, and hospitals. Each team should prepare and present a report not over one page in length. The category systems which emerge from this field research may then be compared with VALS in a class discussion.

Project Seven-3
FAB

The 3M Company and many others train their sales forces in FAB—Selling **F**eatures, **A**dvantages and **B**enefits. This means knowing your product.

What is it?

What does it do?

What does it mean to the customer?

1. Can you apply the FAB guidelines to a product? For practice, select a common object you would like to get rid of or make a profit on such as a used book, shirt you no longer want, typewriter. Now prepare
   a. a list of its features,
   b. a list of advantages, and
   c. a list of benefits to a person who might buy it.
   Sometimes its even more fun to sell a service, such as teaching a classmate how to dance.

2. Don't offer your product before a need has been "expressed." Here's an example of what *not* to do:
   Seller: Are you completely satisfied with the output of your present system?
   Buyer: Not entirely, it's a little slow.
   Seller: Then what you need is our new Super XKL. It puts out 300 percent more.
   Buyer: But its not worth $3000 extra dollars.

3. Next study the advice below about how to deal with resistance:
   - Listen—it lessens the objections raised.
   - Express empathy for how they feel.
   - Acknowledge what is raised that is logical.
   - Ask yourself what caused this resistance
     —lack of information
     —lack of awareness of the problem
     —bias
     —unrevealed commitment
   - Then ask a question that can be answered successfully by referring to a benefit your product or service provides.
   - Next use other questions: open, mirror, guided vs. yes/no. Check to get prospect's response.
   - Then offer evidence, comparison.
   - Again check to get prospect's response.
   - Close sale when and if the prospect signals he or she is ready.

4. Now practice. In pairs, take turns using the FAB system to sell that product.

Project Seven-4
Classroom Flea Market

One sales experience that is clearly face-to-face buyer-consumer activity is the flea market. The merchant must select, display, and price a product. She or he must show or demonstrate features, advantages and benefits of the product. Too often in the classroom students do only one sales presentation. A classroom flea market provides audiences for several presentations by each student and in a relaxed festive atmosphere.

Step One. Each student selects a product and makes a poster listing its major Features, Advantages and Benefits, as you did in Project Seven-3.

Step Two. One third of the class sets up their products at various points in the classroom, hall or outside. The rest of the class mills about from site to site listening to each merchant's presentation.

Step Three. Sealed bids are then handed to those merchants whose products are desired. The high bid gets the product. And the process begins again for the next group.

Step Four. Debriefing. What sold? Why? What presentations were particularly fun and persausive? Why?

8

Organizational Dynamics

Chapter Outline

Chapter Objectives

Those who complete this chapter should better understand:

1. the dynamics of groups within organizational structures;
2. the different types of groups and phases of interaction;
3. individual-member characteristics within the group;
4. how leadership emerges in the group structure;
5. why agenda and procedure are important to group effectiveness;
6. the pressures to conform to group norms.

"...employees are the prime movers in recommending new tools, methods and techniques. That's where our Participative Management Program has been a tremendous help...this program...makes every employee a member of the management team."

—Motorola, Inc., 1982

"Most of the decision-making groups in industrial relations are in the form of *ad hoc* meetings to deal with certain subjects. Some industrial relations-related subjects such as executive compensation, retirement and higher level grievance handling involve the use of established committees."

—Donald P. Crane, "The Case for Participative Management," *Business Horizons,* April 1976, p. 19.

233

Murphy's law holds that if anything can go wrong it will. Other such kindred laws as Parkinson's (work expands to fill the time) and Peter's Principle (the tendency to promote to a level of incompetence) all grow out of the frustration of human interaction within organizations. Peter Drucker, the dean among management consultants, suggests that the symptoms of malorganization are: (1) too many levels of management, (2) reoccurrence of organizational problems, (3) too many meetings attended by too many people, (4) overstaffing and (5) assistants whose job it is not to have a job.[1]

Within organizations, people function both as individuals and as members of various groups, departments and divisions. A manager often represents his unit to other units and upper levels of administration. At the production level, employees must interact cooperatively, or else time, materials and energy are wasted. Advancement in our careers and satisfaction with our jobs will depend upon how effectively we are able to work in groups and upon how effectively our group functions within our larger organization.

In this chapter, we, therefore, will examine the dynamics of groups within organizational structures. Maier, who has dedicated his career to understanding group behaviors within the business environment, likens the behavior of persons in organizational units to a starfish. When the nerve ring of the starfish is surgically cut in sections, the behavior of one ray can still influence others, but not in an integrated manner. If opposite rays are stimulated, for example, that starfish may become locked for a time and in some cases may split the creature, destroying it. A starfish with an intact nerve ring, on the other hand, functions in a coordinated locomotion under the control of a dominant ray. The behavior of all rays together is superior to the activity of anyone, even a dominant ray.[2] The same is true of individuals in groups. The product of a well coordinated group often will be superior to any one member.

The components of group communications which are addressed in this chapter are: (1) definitions, types, and phases of group interaction, (2) member characteristics, (3) leadership and roles, (4) procedures and formats of problem solving, and (5) conformity and commitment.

Definitions, Types and Phases

Definitions. Almost all of us were born into families and spent our early years as members of this *primary* group. We were taken to community gatherings, to church or temple, to school. We aspired to belong to and be like people who belonged to other groups, *reference* groups, which for good or ill had influence upon us, even though we may have not belonged. When we belong to teams, clubs, gangs, fraternities, sororities, we are in the *in-group*. Occasionally, we declare that others are not one of us—they are in the *out-group*. About every community has certain circles which are the "in" group for the upper class, and other organizations of subcultures which are the "out" group for the rich.

The business of living, from the simplest tribe to the most complex civilization, is dependent upon the commitment of people to invest energy in collective efforts—to work together in a social contract for the common good. Ours is not a nation of individuals, but of interpersonal, *interdependent* relationships, of committees, organizations and institutions.

What then is a group? A group is a collection of people who frequently interact in the hopes of achieving interdependently what they cannot achieve singly. They define themselves as members and are defined by others as members. They take on a group personality, think in terms of we and they, and speak as a body to outsiders.[3]

Types. Some groups are as informal as the Monday morning quarterbacking during the coffee break; others are as formal as the Congressional Committee governed by Robert's *Rules of Order.* Some are public with an audience; others are closed and private. Some are one-time only affairs; others are continuing; some small, some large.

I Casual-Social	II Interpersonally Supportive	III Learning	IV Decision-Making and Persuasion
Examples	Examples	Examples	Examples
Street corner gang	Divorce anonymous	Great books discussion group	Committees and task groups
Gourmet club	Group therapy	Classroom	General Motors Board of Directors
A clique who bowl	Religious worship	Photography club	

Figure 8.1

Phases. Through what phases do groups progress? Relationships which are gratifying move from informal loose structure toward regular meetings, procedures, and organizations designed to perpetuate themselves. Several people, for example, who like foods from different countries may decide to visit a Japanese restaurant together. If the food and drink are good, the group may decide to eat out together once a month. If the activity indeed proves to be beneficial, an organization may be born. Questions such as membership, leadership, dues, and program arise. If the club matures, review and evaluation of its purpose and practice may take place.

Central in any coming together of two or more people are the interpersonal concerns of inclusion, control and affection.[4] In the early stages, concerns about being included are high. Primary tension may arise during this orientation time, when people wonder how well they will be accepted by others. The desire for knowing one's standing in the group and the evolving nature of the group leads to formation of some structure. But who will lead?

The second concern is control. Who will take charge? Or, if a leader is externally assigned, the question of control may be lessened in those members with low need to control. However, if the need to control dominates in several of the members, or if the assigned leader is incompetent, a struggle for control will preoccupy the membership. Usually the struggle is relatively subtle. Those who talk less usually are counted out of contention. Those who dogmatically take extreme positions, even though articulate, are slowly eliminated from leadership. Those who appear to want to lead and who seem to most typify the majority in the group tend to emerge. Most groups by the end of the second or third meeting have reinforced leadership behaviors in someone whom they approve.[5] Dependence upon that leader will be particularly heavy if others in the group wish to abdicate leadership roles.

The leader must minister to the task at hand, as well as attend to the interpersonal concerns of the membership. Often, one in the group seconds his suggestion and encourages support. He may serve as lieutenant and a leader of morale. Occasionally a counterforce will emerge, a leader of grievances. Such an individual may be high in his needs to dominate (to advise, direct, initiate) but low on affiliation, and therefore he analyzes, criticizes, disapproves, judges, and resists.[6]

Groups within organizations sometimes are temporary task groups or committees, but most often are configurations of people which have in the past and will in the future continue to work together. It is particularly fitting therefore to examine these continuing relationships as one might see a small society, a society which moves in time into different stages of development. To have meaning a group must have a sense of its identity, a structure and task. The phases which groups tend to work through include:

- Orientation—a time of defining, testing and securing member commitment, group norms; dependence upon the leadership, initial search for cohesiveness, and struc-· ture.

- Conflict—a time of frustration over defining purpose, mission, roles and sometimes trial balloons to function without leadership, possibly coalitions or cliques.

- Functional Goal Striving—securing resources and skills, integrative-negotiative efforts; clarification of purposes, role assignments and implementation of internal member controls; and efforts to interact with external political realities. If the group survives, rather than disbands or retreats into ritualistic inactivity, periodic review of themselves takes place.

These three phases are divided into Task and Relationship concerns in Figure 8.2.

Discussion does not progress in a linear fashion, rather interaction generally proceeds in a reach-test spiral.[7] One member makes a suggestion. The others in the group may ask questions, and comment upon that suggestion. Group members tend to circle about a suggestion clarifying, modifying, elaborating, sharing their ideas and feelings about that suggestion. The circling is more than a matter of deliberation about the suggestion. It is a time in which the members seek to discover common values and meaningful relationships.

After a time of encircling a suggestion, the group may accept it, and someone will reach forth with another idea. Or the suggestion may be rejected or dropped and a new topic proposed. In either case, the group will again circle back to rediscover an anchor in the common values and reason for their relationship. This backward and lateral movement serves as both a time for restablishing the group's interpersonal relationship and for deliberation upon the pros and cons of an idea. The extensive work of Robert F. Bales, largely concerned with small groups untrained in special discussion skills, reveals a similar pattern. He found approximately one half of all contributions consisted of answers, and the other half of questions and reactions. He suggests that if enough time is not allowed for giving opinions, for questioning and reactions to occur in the meeting, members will carry away tensions that will eventually operate to vitiate an apparently successful, but actually superficial, decision.[8] Bales also established that within the course of a group meeting, no matter whether it be the first third, middle third, or final third, that the verbal and nonverbal interaction involves both task and socioemotional communications.

A world-famous team, the Anheuser-Busch Clydesdales, emerging from the main gate of Grant's Farm near St. Louis. A Clydesdale team has represented Anheuser-Busch since 1933 and a design of the Clydesdale team and a beer wagon has been a registered trademark since 1971.

Phot reprinted with permission from Anheuser-Busch, Inc., St. Louis, Missouri.

The attention of individuals in groups fluctuates between the task at hand and their feelings about the people with whom they are working. (These tensions are represented in Figure 8.2.) A group, whether it be a committee or departmental unit, moves from attention to identity, structure, roles, norms (what might better be understood as developing standard operating procedures) to control. The items above the line in the diagram represent those visible, tangible agenda concerns. Those items below the line represent those less talked about, personal concerns about human relationships.

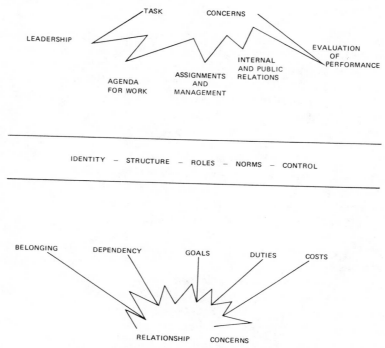

Figure 8.2. Phases of group interaction.

Member Characteristics

Working with people may be unpleasant. In volunteer groups, such as church boards or civic organizations, morale is low when attendance is poor. In such cases, a leader runs from rather than for office. Chairpersons are drafted not elected.

Business also has its difficulties. Many executives behave destructively in decision-making conferences. In an extensive study, Argyris tape recorded 265 decision-making conferences in six companies with 150 employees in the smallest to 40,000 in the largest. The behavior of 165 top executives was then analyzed from the tapes, observations and interviews.

An executive's behavior in a conference was scored according to how many times he (a) owned up to and accepted responsibility for his ideas or feelings, (b) opened up to receive others' ideas or feelings, (c) used a style of behavior which supports individuality, (d) helped others to own up and take risks, or (e) the opposite of these behaviors.

Executives generally were found to own up to their own ideas. However, rarely were they observed taking risks or experimenting with new ideas or feelings. Nor did they, except on a few occasions, help others to own up, be open and take risks. Moreover, rarely were they observed using a style that supports individuality. They avoided expression of feelings. That is to suggest that in the 265 different taped meetings, the executives focused "on getting the job done" but little or no time was spent analyzing or maintaining their group's effectiveness. The executives seemed to place a premium on rationality and played down feelings and emotions.

The top executive committees were rated by subordinates as low on openness, trust, risk taking and ability to deal with conflicts. Conversely, they were high on conformity.[9]

Conflict. It should be said and loudly said that working with groups means working with conflict. People do differ. People do take sides. Some people are disagreeable. Some are more likeable than others. This phenomena is particularly true for groups which must work together for a long period, perhaps years. A group in which members are afraid to voice disagreements is in more trouble than one in which disagreements are openly expressed. Discussion may help people work through conflict.

Characteristics. Suppose for a moment that you were able to pick an ideal group. Who would you choose? Obviously you would first select persons with abilities and skills to get the job done. Next, likely you would want to select members who liked to work with people. Two personality characteristics have been found to be particularly suited to groups: extroversion and tolerance for ambiguity. By definition extroverts like to work with people and in groups. This extroversion is apparent in a willingness to talk, laugh and to choose seats which encourage interaction (opposite others, central, head positions and close to others).[10]

Extroversion appears to be related to the amount of participation. One study in which the most talkative member of a group is given the solution to a problem resulted in the group's acceptance of it; but when the solution is given to the least talkative member who subsequently reveals it, the group rejects it.[11] Talkative participants do seem to have their ideas accepted more than less talkative members, and the highly energetic, outgoing participator frequently is perceived as the group's leader.[12] Overly talkative persons who dominate take far-out positions and are dogmatic, however, after a time are rejected from leadership positions. A word of caution may be necessary at this point. That is to suggest that introverts may also make strong group members, especially when the rewards to belonging to that group are high and when their particular skills are needed.

A second characteristic important to success is tolerance for uncertainty. Uncertainty obviously is inherent in group deliberations. Persons trained in discussion should have a higher tolerance for dealing with uncertainty and disputable issues. In short, they should learn to expect differences and conflict. Persons who perceive situations to be "black and white" either are by nature rigid, or lack training and experience in group dynamics.

A productive task group does not just happen. It results first from luck or a wise choice of members with skills suited to the task; second, it frequently is a product of training for working in groups; and, third, it is the result of personality characteristics such as extroversion and a tolerance for ambiguity. Finally, if there is sufficient motivation, a group may find it is compatible and productive.

How to improve your vocabulary

By Tony Randall

International Paper asked Tony Randall—who is on The American Heritage Dictionary Usage Panel, and loves words almost as much as acting—to tell how he has acquired his enormous vocabulary.

Words can make us laugh, cry, go to war, fall in love.

Rudyard Kipling called words the most powerful drug of mankind. If they are, I'm a hopeless addict—and I hope to get you hooked, too!

Whether you're still in school or you head up a corporation, the better command you have of words, the better chance you have of saying exactly what you mean, of understanding what others mean—and of getting what you want in the world.

English is the richest language —with the largest vocabulary on earth. Over 1,000,000 words!

You can express shades of meaning that aren't even *possible* in other languages. (For example, you can differentiate between "sky" and "heaven." The French, Italians and Spanish cannot.)

Yet, the average adult has a vocabulary of only 30,000 to 60,000 words. Imagine what we're missing!

Here are five pointers that help me learn—and remember— whole *families* of words at a time.

They may not *look* easy—and

won't be at first. But if you stick with them you'll find they *work!*

What's the first thing to do when you see a word you don't know?

1. Try to guess the meaning of the word from the way it's used

You can often get at least *part* of a word's meaning—just from how it's used in a sentence.

That's why it's so important to read as much as you can— different *kinds* of things: magazines, books, newspapers you don't normally read. The more you *expose* yourself to new words, the more words you'll pick up *just by seeing how they're used.*

For instance, say you run across the word "manacle":

"The manacles had been on John's wrists for 30 years. Only one person had a key— his wife."

You have a good *idea* of what "manacles" are—just from the context of the sentence.

But let's find out *exactly* what the word means and where it comes from. The only way to do this, and to build an extensive vocabulary *fast,* is to go to the dictionary. (How lucky, you *can*— Shakespeare *couldn't.* There *wasn't* an English dictionary in his day!)

So you go to the dictionary. (NOTE: Don't let dictionary abbreviations put you off. The front tells you what they mean, and even has a guide to pronunciation.)

2. Look it up

Here's the definition for "manacle" in *The American Heritage*

Dictionary of the English Language.

man·a·cle (mân'ə-kəl) n. Usually plural. **1.** A device for confining the hands, usually consisting of two metal rings that are fastened about the wrists and joined by a metal chain; a handcuff. **2.** Anything that confines or restrains.—*tr. v.* **manacled, -cling, -cles. 1.** To restrain with manacles. **2.** To confine or restrain as if with manacles; shackle; fetter. [Middle English *manicle,* from Old French, from Latin *manicula,* little hand, handle, diminutive of *manus,* hand. See **man-²** in Appendix.*]

The first definition fits here: A device for confining the hands, usually consisting of two metal rings that are fastened about the wrists and joined by a metal chain; a handcuff.

Well, that's what you *thought* it meant. But what's the idea *behind* the word? What are its *roots?* To really understand a word, you need to know.

Here's where the detective work—and the *fun*—begins.

3. Dig the meaning out by the roots

The root is the basic part of the word—its heritage, its origin. (Most of our roots come from

"Your main clue to remembering a word is its root—its origin."

Latin and Greek words at least 2,000 years old—which come from even earlier Indo-European tongues!)

"'Emancipate' has a Latin root. Learn it and you'll know other words at a glance."

Learning the roots: 1) Helps us *remember* words. 2) Gives us a deeper understanding of the words we *already* know. And 3) allows us to pick up whole families of *new* words at a time. That's why learning the root is the *most important part of going to the dictionary.*

Notice the root of "manacle" is *manus* (Latin) meaning "hand."

Well, that makes sense. Now, other words with this root, <u>man</u>, start to make sense, too.

Take <u>manual</u>—something done "by hand" (<u>man</u>ual labor) or a "handbook." And <u>man</u>age—to "handle" something (as a <u>man</u>ager). When you e<u>man</u>cipate someone, you're taking him "from the hands of" someone else.

When you <u>man</u>ufacture something, you "make it by hand" (in its original meaning).

And when you finish your first novel, your publisher will see your —originally "handwritten"— <u>man</u>uscript.

Imagine! A whole new world of words opens up—just from one simple root!

The root gives the *basic* clue to the meaning of a word. But there's another important clue that runs a close second—the *prefix.*

4. Get the powerful prefixes under your belt

A prefix is the part that's sometimes attached to the front of a word. Like—well, *prefix!* There aren't many— less than 100 major prefixes— and you'll learn them in no time at all just by becoming more aware of the meanings of words you already know.

Here are a few. (Some of the "How-to" vocabulary-building

books will give you the others.)

PREFIX		MEANING	EXAMPLES	
(Lat.)	(Gk.)			(Literal sense)
com, con, co, col, cor	sym, syn, syl	with, very, together	conform sympathy	(form with) (feeling with)
in, im, il, ir	a, an	not, without	innocent amorphous	(not wicked) (without form)
contra, counter	anti, ant	against, opposite	contravene antidote	(come against) (give against)

Now, see how the *prefix* (along with the context) helps you get the meaning of the italicized words:

• "If you're going to be my witness, your story must <u>corroborate</u> my story." (The literal meaning of *corroborate* is "strength together.")

• "You told me one thing— now you tell me another. Don't <u>contradict</u> yourself." (The literal meaning of *contradict* is "say against".)

• "Oh, that snake's not poisonous. It's a completely <u>innocuous</u> little garden snake." (The literal meaning of *innocuous* is "not harmful".)

Now, you've got some new words. What are you going to do with them?

5. Put your new words to work at once

Use them several times the first day you learn them. Say them out loud! Write them in sentences.

Should you "use" them on *friends?* Careful—you don't want them to think you're a stuffed shirt. (It depends on the situation. You *know* when a word sounds natural—and when it sounds stuffy.)

How about your *enemies?* You have my blessing. Ask one of them

if he's read that article on pneumonoultramicroscopicsilicovolcanoconiosis. (You really can find it in the dictionary.) Now, you're one up on him.

So what do you do to improve your vocabulary?

Remember: 1) Try to guess the meaning of the word from the way it's used. 2) Look it up. 3) Dig the meaning out by the roots. 4) Get the powerful prefixes under your belt. 5) Put your new words to work at once.

That's all there is to it—you're off on your treasure hunt.

Now, do you see why I love words so much?

Aristophanes said, "By words, the mind is excited and the spirit elated." It's as true today as it was

"The more words you know, the more you can use. What does 'corroborate' really mean? See the text."

when he said it in Athens—*2,400 years ago!*

I hope you're now like me— hooked on words forever.

Tony Randall

A considerable amount of research, although somewhat conflicting, supports the finding that highly-cohesive groups are more productive than low-cohesive groups.[13] One industrial study discovered that when teams were composed of teammates who chose each other, productivity went up and morale was high.[14]

Groups with members who behave in compatible ways get more accomplished well and enjoy their work more, than do those who behave in incompatible ways. However, there is some evidence that groups whose members are similar in their personality profiles are not so successful at problem solving as are groups with heterogeneous personality profiles.[15] Shaw's summary suggests, "When group members have a variety of opinions, abilities, skills and perspectives, the probability is increased that the group as a whole will possess the characteristics necessary for efficient group performance."[16]

Leadership

What affect does leadership have on group behavior? Probably the most influential figure in a group is the leader. His style of leadership and his procedures greatly affect the quality of solutions and the group's morale. Early attention to leadership centered on three types: authoritarian, democratic, and laissez faire. The authoritarian is assertive, tends to rally support from the group for his opinions and dominates a meeting. Authoritarian-natured persons, when not in positions of leadership, generally like to be led by an authoritarian type. Democratic leaders seek to discover the will of the group and through joint deliberation produce quality decisions. Laissez faire leadership in the extreme is no leadership, complete permissiveness, and "I don't care if we do anything or not."

Theory X and Y. Two theories of leadership of organizations labeled X and Y were developed by McGregor.[17] X type leaders believe average people are lazy, dislike responsibility, are selfish, gullible, and resistant to change. Y type leaders believe that man is self-motivating, desires responsibility, is not passive or resistant to change, and that management's job is to create a climate which can help people assume responsibility and have a say in their organization.

Obviously, most leaders are not such polar opposites as X and Y. A contingency model developed by Fiedler postulates that different styles of leadership are more acceptable with different kinds of tasks. Generally, a situation is more favorable for a leader (a) when he has good personal relationships with his subordinates, (b) when the task is well structured (i.e., when workers know what to do and there are correct ways of doing it), and (c) when he occupies a strong position of power. A situation is unfavorable when the opposite of these three factors is true. When a situation is either highly unfavorable or highly favorable a task-oriented leader is more effective. When a situation is moderately difficult, a relationship-oriented leader is most effective.[18] That is when the going is tough, or very pleasant, a leader is more acceptable and effective who vigorously addresses the task. When things are in between, a leader is more effective who attends to the recognition of others and acts in a participative manner.

Groups are usually subunits of larger organizations and are part of a hierarchy. Leaders are most often assigned. Those at the top, who are chosen by a Chief Executive Officer are the king's men. The "king" has power to reward or punish. A natural desire arises to protect that king, but also to expect from him equal love and dispersion of favors. A rivalry among those at the top may develop, to court his favors, and/or for those who are jealous to conspire to cut him down. The leader may also act to defend himself against attack. He may fire (exile) or promote a rival to a powerless position, such as awarding an ambassadorship to Skimm (in Freudian terms, castration). A group may be society's answer to strong leadership. It is the followers' way of demanding a say and a just share of those things held by the leader.

Roles. Groups need both task leaders, those whose chief attention is to getting the job done, and socioemotional leaders, those who look after harmony and morale. The effectiveness of both task leaders and socioemotional leaders depends upon many factors. The task leader must be particularly strong in competence, articulate and able to present well his group's concerns to superiors and outsiders. A socioemotional leader must earn the confidence of his group and find his own job satisfactions in seeing others succeed. He is particularly concerned about promoting good interpersonal relationships among the others.

Extensive research has led to the conclusion that good managers are characterized by three factors: motivation, participatory management, and interpersonal competence—that combine to a style which balances production and people. In Hall's words, "Good managers challenge people, bad ones comfort them."[19] A long time scholar of industrial organizations adds a word of caution, "Old-fashioned authority has some advantages, which have been forgotten, and to organize participation on a large scale leads us into the difficulties of any democratic system. . . . There are extraordinary limits on possibilities of participation because of the time people have available."[20]

Groups, also, need members to function in a variety of leadership roles played by different members at appropriate times. When the members share responsibilities for various needed functions, the named leader may function more democratically. Roles may *facilitate* or *disrupt*. *Maintenance* roles particularly help hold a group together: morale builder, harmonizer, humorist, energizer, supporter, etc.

Procedures and Formats

One of the most essential functions of a leader is development of procedures. The first of these is proposing and following an agenda. It is wise for the leader to check with group members about items which should go on the agenda and priority items. Next he must help the group discover ways of operating. When the group is small, for instance, it is good to make decisions by consensus. As a group increases in size there are many questions of procedure, such as: Should we have a formally worded motion before we vote? Should we vote by voice, hand, or secret ballot? Should important matters be delayed for a meeting and/or go to a mail ballot? Often there are delicate matters such as: How should employees be evaluated for promotions? How should complaints and grievances be handled? How can fair ratings be obtained? How should funds and equipment be allocated? Substantive matters such as these demand developing procedures in which the group has confidence in their fairness.

Rarely are there leaderless groups. Almost always a leader emerges, or more frequently one is assigned at the outset. The format used, and the style of leadership likely will influence productivity and morale. Leaders to be effective need knowledge and practice of skills in *discovery* of quality solutions and skills in securing *acceptance* of solutions. Frequently, a number of solutions can do the job but the problem is whether the group will accept one of them.

A strategy to secure participation and acceptance developed by Maier suggests that a leader should:

1. Not present *the problem,* but instead ask the group whether they have any problems.
2. Recognize all suggestions, but influence direction in thinking by asking for further suggestions.
3. Protect individuals from criticism of the group members by interpreting all remarks in a favorable light. Avoid blame for anyone.
4. List all suggestions. Do not get bogged down on early simplistic remedies. Seek to combine.
5. Not reveal your preference.
6. Keep good leads before the group by asking probing questions about them.
7. Work to eliminate undesirable features from a solution.
8. Make your objectives that of resolving group differences.[21]

Every man's ego is on the line. We cannot treat ideas as though they were anonymous. Language is personal and ideas are precious. A careless rejection of an idea and flippant criticism of someone's work are an attack on a person's feeling of worth. This may imply but should not be construed to mean that all ideas are of the same value and that no work is inferior. Rather it suggests that if we want a task force with high morale and an eagerness to see a continuing program through, then each idea should receive respectful, reflective consideration. If the reflective thinking pattern can become a group habit, perhaps opinions will not be so ego-bound, but rather will be presented with every expectation that they will be modified, expanded upon and/or replaced by other opinions.

Business organizations are particularly concerned about developing procedures and structures which will bring out the best in the management—employee relationship and, of course profits. A number of team building efforts are tried at many levels: in autonomous crews in mines, hospital teams, line variations in which a crew is responsible for completely assembling an auto, and profit centers. Some of these experiments of group decision-making and planning are successful, some are not. But the trend is in the direction of group decision making within organizations. Inland Division of General Motors, for example, for some ten years has operated with 25 to 75 member teams. Rotating chiefs, who specialize in manufacturing, product engineering, or production serve as boss for four months each year when the product cycle is especially demanding their expertise. A nine-member "board of directors" serves each of the teams at which other members may discuss problems such as quality control. Inland testifies positively about their structure.[22] Structures in organizations can be developed to increase member involvement and interaction.

Carl E. Larson, "Forms of Analysis and Small Group Solving." *Speech Monographs,* Vol. XXXVI (November 1969), pp. 452-55.

Basic Question: Do some problem solving formats produce more correct answers than others?

Treatment: Thirty-two groups composed of 4 or 5 college men each discussed four different short industrial relations problems. Each discussion was limited to 20 minutes. Experts had identified a best solution for each problem. The four different analysis forms were: (1) No Pattern. (2) Single Question. The analytic procedure was to discover what is the single question, the answer to which all the group need to know to accomplish its purpose? And following this the group examines subquestions and their answers. (3) Ideal Solution Form. This analytic procedure asks (a) Are we agreed on the nature of the problem? (b) What would be the ideal solution from the viewpoint of all parties concerned? (c) What conditions within the problem could be changed so that the ideal solution might be achieved? and (d) Of the solutions available to us, which one approximates the ideal solution? (4) Reflective Thinking. This form considered the following: (a) What are the limits and specific nature of the problem? (b) Causes and consequences of the problem. (c) What things must an acceptable solution accomplish? (d) What solutions are available to us? and (e) What is the best solution?

Results: Number of correct answers arrived at:

On 4 problems +	No Pattern	Single Question	Ideal Solution	Reflective Thinking
	15	24	26	19

The single question and the ideal solution forms were superior to the reflective thinking and no pattern. The reflective thinking form also produced more correct answers than did the no pattern.

Implications: People tend to function more locally and possibly more amicably when they have a structure. One must be cautious in generalizing from this one study that longer— term problems will be solved more accurately or more creatively by these forms.

Figure 8.3. Does an agendum of procedures help?

Conformity

Civilization justly fears the rampage of the mob. History has witnessed it in the aggressive sweep of armies led by Alexander the Great, Attila the Hun, the Crusaders, Napoleon, and Hitler; in the crowds tearing down a monarchy such as in the French Revolution or, more recently, the Red Guard in China, and the riots in our own cities after the death of Dr. Martin Luther King, Jr. Western civilization suffered its witch trials, an estimated 300,000 women were burned as witches;[23] and this country had its lynch mobs. There is ample evidence that some men will perform antisocial acts in crowds that they will not perform alone. Many, if not all men, respond to the violence within themselves when joined by like minds, and particularly so under authoritarian leadership.

Social scientists discovered a like tendency in the small group to go along with the judgments of most others. In the thirties, Sherif demonstrated that a person's estimates of the distance between two lights in the dark were influenced by other subjects' estimates.[24] With no way to ascertain a standard distance for the lights in the dark, subjects tended to rely on the judgment of others. It is reasonable, when faced with ambiguous data, to turn to those who seem to agree. A landmark study followed in which Asch learned that about one-third of naive subjects, when alone, would deny their own "eyes," to agree with incorrect estimates by several others who had preceded them.[25] The task was to compare the length of several lines. Asch had programmed the confederates to each give a wrong judgment about which lines were longer, shorter or matched. Only when the subject had the support of another person could he stick with and trust his own perception. When this tendency to consider agreement of the majority as a right answer proved to be common, as Asch proved, the very real danger of group conformity was established.

Numerous studies including cross cultural studies have confirmed this phenomena. A recent study, representative of this type, extended the experiment into judgments of controversial statements. American students were compared with Chinese students in Hong Kong. They were each brought into a small committee room in a university student center to join with five other students who were secretly confederates to the experimenter. The alleged purpose of the assembly was to poll the students upon such statements as:

1. Aggression and warfare are basic parts of inherited nature.
2. It is just as well that the struggle of life tends to weed out those who cannot stand the pace.
3. In the interest of population control, world governments should forcefully regulate the number of children that families can have.
4. Laws should be enacted to make both marriage and divorce easier.

The naive subject was first asked to indicate his opinion somewhere between -10 to $+10$. After he gave his opinion, each confederate would state a number near the opposite end of the continuum. For example, if the subject put his position at a -9, then the confederates would put theirs at $+8$, $\times 9$, or $+10$. After all had given their positions, each would be asked to state his reasons for so doing with the naive subject being the last to explain his/her position. Usually when it got to that point, the naive subject would hesitate and hedge, and question his own judgment. Upon being given the opportunity to revote, the subject frequently would shift toward the five confederates. In fact, there were a total of 30 shifts for the American students and 113 for the Chinese. Moreover, the hesitancy to answer greatly increased when the subject discovered his position to be so different each time. One other interesting phenomenon occurred. A number of the subjects became more firm in their position opposing the majority, i.e., should they have been a $+3$ and the majority were about a -3, then the subject sometimes shifted more positively, perhaps to a $+5$ or $+6$. Americans did this more than Chinese (70 as compared to 7 anticonformity shifts).[26]

Now, what dare we conclude from all of this? It is safe to conclude that in the face of majority judgments, a person alone may bend his opinion to agree with the majority and some few will disagree more strongly with the majority. In either case, in the face of the majority it is difficult for many persons to stick to their opinions. Once we are aware of this tendency in many of us to bow to social pressure, it should forewarn us and help us not to compromise our convictions. It should make us more aware that a simple vote does not make it right. Possibly it should caution us not to take an early vote prior to our discussion and deliberations.

In particular, Janis examined the Cabinets of Presidents Johnson and Kennedy in times of crisis such as the escalation of the bombing in Vietnam despite repeated setbacks and failures, the disastrous Bay of Pigs invasion, and the brinkmanship with Russia over placement of missiles in Cuba. Janis discovered "in-groups" such as the Cabinet came to believe they can do no wrong and they isolate themselves and their leader from adverse opinion. They tell anyone with a critical argument to not "rock the boat. We've got to all pull together." Janis stated his main principle of groupthink in this way:

> The more amiability and *esprit de corps* there is among the members of a policy-making ingroup, the greater the danger that independent critical thinking will be replaced by groupthink, which is likely to result in irrational and dehumanizing actions directed against outgroups.[27]

In a carefully devised field test of relationships among groups (in this case boys at a summer camp), Sherif discovered that rivalry soon developed. Competition caused name calling and a tendency to underestimate the other group, a phenomena which Janis noted in his groupthink study. Sherif, in addition, discovered that groups which had become rivals and spiteful toward each other could rediscover each other as friends. For example, when crises were "accidentally" engineered (the breakdown of a truck or, on another day, insufficient funds to rent a motion picture) the warring groups pulled together to get the truck back in running order, and pooled funds to get what they could not afford singly. Sherif termed this motivational determinant a "superordinate goal."[28]

How might a group, especially, a policy making group which demands great loyalty of its members and which has a real team spirit, arm itself against shallow reasoning, foolish decisions, and sometimes cruel behavior toward out-groups? To be warned of this danger, again, is to be partially armed against it, but Janis proposes several more tangible safeguards:

- The leader should request that the group be critical of his ideas and play the devil's advocate. Key leaders might adopt an impartial stance and probe many possibilities.
- Outside experts may be invited to examine plans of action and to sit in on meetings.
- Occasionally the group might be split into two groups to examine a proposal critically.
- Scenarios of how outgroups might respond should be written.
- Reviews of "second chance" meetings should be conducted to provide opportunities to reconsider decisions, when time permits.
- Avoid averaging, coin tossing, majority vote, bargaining, and such conflict reducing techniques. Do not feel that if one person loses, he must later be rewarded.

Differences are natural. Seek them out and try to involve everyone in the decision process. In a wide range of decisions, there are greater chances for a more adequate solution.[29]

There are dangers in groups in spite of the general superiority of group decisions over individual ones. The dangers include conforming to the assumed correctness of the majority; taking risks and doing what our cooler, more rational self would not; and "groupiness" causing us to isolate our leaders from negative criticism and causing us to censure our doubts. Of course, we must add to this the high cost in time which an overdependence upon management by committees may cause.

Battle for Quality

Scarcity of energy, the phenomenal success of foreign companies, and economic recessions have combined to make corporate leaders extremely introspective. When business is hurting, that's when questions are asked about what's wrong with the way we are managing and how can we do better? On the other hand, when times are prosperous, unions tend to be greedy about getting a bigger share of the pie. But when times are tough and unemployment is high, labor too is asking what can we do to help our companies survive and compete?

These, then, are the motivating conditions in the economic environment which have popularized interest in employee participation. The idealistic values held dear by the American system have always to some extent been in conflict. Our extremely individualistic values have warred against our democratic ideals. Our distaste for authority has been in conflict with our pragmatic commitment to hierarchical organizations. Because for most of our history America has ridden the industrial crest, these values were allowed to ebb and flow. Our more recent history has periodically seen labor or management confront each other over tangible rewards, struggling in contract disputes. Only rarely have management and labor come together other than in adversarial postures.

Issues of survival have now spelled out a new agenda for management and labor. That agenda asks: how can we develop better working relationships in order to do battle in the world marketplace?

In Japan, government and corporate teamwork and employee commitment appear to explain much of their economic success and excellent product quality. The "made in Japan" in a few short years has changed from a label that stood for shoddy merchandise to a stamp of quality. Japanese companies have institutionalized employee involvement in quality and productivity matters at even the shop floor level, in work groups called Quality Circles (QCs).

Hard record keeping has documented in that country, and in this where QC programs have been established, billions of yen and millions of dollars in savings.[30] Quality Circles consist of small groups of employees from the same work area who meet voluntarily on a regular basis to identify, analyze and solve quality and other problems in their work. A plant usually trains its managers, supervisors and employees involved in group communication skills: brainstorming, creativity, problem analysis, record keeping, and how to make proposals for change to management. A trained facilitator coordinates circle activity in a plant and helps assure follow through on QC proposals.*

Experience with QC's show that a high percent of their recommendations are adopted by management. The QC movement and other widespread use of employee participation programs by other names bear powerful testimony to the theme of this chapter, that is: those in professional and industrial careers need to develop group process skills.

---

*For further information see John E. Baird, Jr.'s three *Quality Circle* manuals (Participant's Manual, Leader's Manual, and Facilitator's Manual) available from Waveland Press, Inc., P.O. Box 400, Prospect Heights, Illinois 60070.

Recap

Advancement and satisfaction of those who elect careers in business and most other occupations are related to skills in working in groups and upon how well one's group functions within the larger organization. We are interdependent people. That awareness and acknowledgement of interdependence to achieve group or organizational goals is what defines a group as a group. Groups tend to move through phases of working out problems of group identity, structure, roles, norms, and control. The concerns of a group fluctuate from task to interpersonal relations. This concern is demonstrated by the way a group tends to proceed in a spiral-like pattern in its deliberations. Ideas are initiated and encircled. And the group often will return to previously agreed upon positions as if to find an anchor in common values.

Members who possess tolerance for ambiguity and who like to work with people find group interaction more satisfying than do individuals who lack these characteristics. This is particularly so because groups inevitably have conflicts and frustrations in resolving problems.

Leadership which is flexible and adapted to situations, is most effective. That is in very difficult or very easy circumstances very directive leadership is needed and accepted. But a more people-centered, permissive leader is more acceptable in ordinary situations. Leadership which challenges is more productive than leadership which comforts. Groups and organizations need functionally shared leadership. That is to suggest some leaders who are task centered and others are more people specialists. Many various maintenance functions are needed to create climates which are open and conducive to individuality.

Problems are better solved when approached in a scientific structured way. Solutions are more accepted when those who must implement them are involved in their solving.

Group pressures make conformists of many. An awareness of these pressures and structures designed to make critical opinions welcome are effective in preventing shallow thinking and "groupthink."

NOTES

1. Peter Drucker, *Management Task, Responsibilities, Practices* (New York: Harper and Row, 1973), pp. 546-49.
2. Norman F. Maier "Assets and Liabilities in Group Problem Solving: The Need for an Integrative Function," *Psychological Review*, 1967, 74, pp. 239-49.
3. Some works deliberate at length concerning definition such as Marvin E. Shaw, *Group Dynamics: The Psychology of Small Group Behavior* (New York: McGraw-Hill, 1971), Chapter 1; also Doran Cartwright and A. Zander (eds.), *Group Dynamics Research and Theory* (3rd ed.; New York: Harper and Row, 1968), Chapter 3, pp. 45-73.
4. William C. Schutz, *FIRO: A Three Dimensional Theory Of Interpersonal Behavior* (New York: Rhinehart, 1958).
5. Ernest G. Borman, *Discussion and Group Methods* (New York: Harper and Row, 1975). Chapter 10 describes findings concerned with emergent leadership in groups with no assigned leader.
6. David W. Johnson, *Reaching Out: Interpersonal Effectiveness and Self-Actualization* (Englewood Cliffs, N.J.: Prentice Hall, 1972), p. 35.
7. Thomas M. Scheidel and Laura Crowell, "Idea Development in Small Discussion Groups," *Quarterly Journal of Speech*, Vol. L (April, 1964), pp. 140-45; and "Feedback in Small Group Communication." *Quarterly Journal of Speech*, Vol. LII (Oct., 1966), pp. 273-78.
8. Robert F. Bales, "In Conference," *Harvard Business Review*, Vol. 32 (March-April, 1954), p. 45.
9. For further information see Chris Argyris, "Interpersonal Barriers to Decision Making," Part II, *Harvard Business Review*, Human Relations Series Part II, No. 21096, pp. 84-97; and Chris Argyris, *Organization and Innovation* (Homewood, Illinois: Richard D. Irwin, Inc., 1965).
10. Mark Cook, "Experiments on Orientation and Proxemics," *Human Relations*, Vol. 23 (Feb., 1964), pp. 61-76.

11. H. W. Recken, "The Effect of Talkativeness on Ability to Influence Group Solutions of Problems," *Sociometry,* Vol. 21 (Dec, 1958), pp. 309-21.

12. E. J. Thomas and C. F. Fink, "Models of Group Problem-Solving," *Journal of Abnormal and Social Psychology,* Vol. 68, No. 1 1961), pp. 53-63.

13. Shaw, pp. 201-204.

14. R. H. Zelst, "Sociometrically Selected Work Teams Increase Production," *Personnel Psychology,* (Autumn, 1952), pp. 175-86.

15. L. R. Hoffman and N. R. F. Maier, "Quality and Acceptance of Problem Solutions by Homogeneous and Heterogeneous Groups," *Journal of Abnormal and Social Psychology,* No. 2 (1961), pp. 401-407.

16. Shaw, p. 228.

17. Douglas McGregor, *Human Side of Enterprise* (New York: McGraw-Hill, 1960) and *Professional Manager* (New York: McGraw-Hill, 1960)

18. Fred E. Fiedler, *A Theory of Leadership Effectiveness* (New York: McGraw Hill, 1967), pp. 45-46; and Fiedler, "Style or Circumstance: The Leadership Enigma," *Psychology Today,* March 1968, pp. 38-43.

19. Jay Hall, "What Makes a Manager Good, Bad or Average," *Psychology Today,* Vol. 10, 1976, pp. 52-55.

20. "Conversation with George C. Homans," *Organizational* Dynamics Vol. 4, Autumn 1975, p. 46.

21. Norman F. Maier, "The Quality of Group Decisions as Influenced by the Discussion Leader." In Maier (ed.), *Problem Solving and Creativity* (Belmont, Calif.: Wadsworth Publishing, 1970), p. 361.

22. "GM's Test of Paticipation," *Business Week,* Feb. 23, 1976.

23. *The World Book Encyclopedia,* 1964, XX, p. 311. "Historians believe that the church put to death about 300,000 innocent women between the years 1484 and 1782."

24. Muzafer Sherif, *The Psychology of Social Norms* (New York: Harpers, 1936). The autokinetic effect is unique in that there are no right or wrong answers. People vary in their estimates.

25. Solomon Asch, "Studies in Independence and Conformity: I a Minority of One Against a Unanimous Majority," *Psychological Monographs,* 70, 16 (1956).

26. Robert D. Meade and William A. Barnard, "Conformity and Anticonformity Among Americans and Chinese," *The Journal of Social* Psychology, 89 (Feb., 1973), pp. 15-24.

27. Irving L. Janis, "Groupthink," *Psychology Today,* November 1971, pp. 43-46; 74-76.

28. Muzafer Sherif, O.J. Harvey, B.J. White, W.R. Hood, and C.W. Sherif, *Intergroup Conflict and Cooperation: The Robbers Cave Experiment* (Norman, Oklahoma: Institute of Group Relations, University of Oklahoma, 1961).

29. Jay Hall, "Decisions, Decisions, Decisions," *Psychology Today,* November 1971, pp. 51-54, 86-87. Hall developed the "Lost on the Moon" exercise and tested it with hundreds of subjects. In this article he reports upon 32 groups composed of 4 to 6 upper management personnel. Half of the groups who were given training on decision making averaged 26 errors as compared to 34 in the untrained groups. ¾ of the trained groups surpassed the score of the best individual score, whereas only ¼ of the untrained groups surpassed the score of the best individual score.

30. Kazuo Nishiyama, Japanese Quality Circles' 31st Annual Conference of the International Communication Association, Minneapolis, 1981.

Project Eight-1

Observing Process

A sociomatrix provides a way to ascertain who talks to whom. Such information enables researchers to describe more objectively group interaction. It also provides data for individual members each to reflect upon his own contributions. Learning to use a sociomatrix is not complicated but does necessitate some practice.

Step 1. Prepare a chart with the members' names arranged both across the top and along the left side of the chart: Note that this is just an example. The chart should be as large as a whole page in order to give you room enough to keep a tally of contributions in each box.

	John	Dale	Sue	Beth	Les	All	Totals
John	X						
Dale		X					
Sue			X				
Beth				X			
Les					X		
Total						X	

Step 2. Assign yourself a code for marking a contribution. For example, you might work out the following operational definition: a slash (/) will be placed in the column of the member who is spoken to on the row of the person speaking. The sign that a person is addressed is that his name is used, or that the speaker looks at him more than any other person in the course of his remarks. If he looks at several persons, the slash (/) will be placed in the "All" category. More detailed tally may be used. For example, a smile ($\smile$) might designate a contribution which attempts to build harmony. A frown ($\frown$) might designate a contribution which belittles an idea or another member. A question (?) might be designated when a contribution asks for information or an opinion.

Step 3. Tally the contributions for each member and the total for the group. Then calculate percentages. You can thus produce data which demonstrates who talked most to least, and who were recipients of the contributions from most to least.

Step 4. Discuss what communication patterns are revealed by the matrix and why. What *feelings* do each of the group members have about the data? Does the data tell you something you did not know about yourself and others? How might you change the interaction?

Project Eight-2

Teambuilding

   Every organization is concerned about the commitment of its employees to the mission of the organization. In the mid-seventies many companies launched programs titled Organizational Development. The B.F. Goodrich Corporation was one such company. At one of the training sessions to gear up for their Organizational Development efforts, John Ong, president of that corporation pledged his support to these efforts.

What symbolic significance does this presentation have?

_____

_____

_____

What specific subordinate purposes might this presentation have accomplished?

_____

_____

_____

_____

_____

John D. Ong is president of the B.F. Goodrich Company and a member of the company's board of directors.

B.F. Goodrich Management and Organization Development Conference

J.D. Ong
Kent State University
June 22, 1976

I would like to spend just a few minutes — and believe me I will make it a few — talking to you about the subject that brings all of us together tonight; the subject which, over the next few days — and I guess the next few months — is going to occupy those of you who are the initial members of our network, namely organization development. In management today we have a great number of mechanisms which we can use in order to array people against the tasks that we have to perform to achieve our objectives and in order to motivate them toward the accomplishment of those tasks. Organization Development is simply one of the mechanisms that we have; but I think it's a broad and flexible one and one which, regrettably, our Company has not utilized in the past but which happily I think we are beginning to utilize and utilize most effectively. We hope to expand its use in the future.

There have been many trends and fads in the behavioral sciences as applied in practice to the business world over the last 25 or 30 years. These seem to come and go with considerable speed and some of them have had little, if any impact on business organization. Others have had at least some passing influence. I think that some of the approaches that we have seen in the past have not been valid; perhaps not intellectually valid, and certainly invalid in terms of application. But organization development as that term is commonly understood in business today does seem to constitute a method for approaching the broad problems of human motivation which has proven effective in any number of very pragmatic applications. We think it's so important in our management at B.F. Goodrich that we have enshrined it, if you will, in a recent statement of our corporate philosophy, objectives and principles.

This is a document trying to state succinctly what our Company's philosophy is, what its principal objectives are in very broad terms and what some of the financial and operating principles are and that we are going to observe as we create our strategic plans and manage our businesses. We feel that such an important part of our effectiveness relates to the people within the organization that it was necessary in this statement of philosophy to pay heed to what our principles would be with regard to their treatment. I would just like to read you the very brief paragraph which describes the first of our operating principles:

This first operating principle is entitled:

Quality of Personnel and Organization Development — To meet the Company's objectives, the recruitment, retention and promotion of highly-motivated individuals with superior performance capability will be required. Therefore, systems for recruitment, training, and development will include carefully developed criteria and rigorous selectivity and be consistent with the company's commitment to provide equal employment opportunities to people regardless of race, sex, or ethnic origin. In addition, the company will stress management and organization development with specific focus on interpersonal relationships among individuals and business groups.

I quote that only to underscore the fact that the management of our Company—those of us in corporate management and the heads of all of our operating and support divisions—working together in framing this statement of our principles and objectives, fastened upon this as the first and thus the priority principle that we have as we approach our task of planning and execution. We feel this way not because organization development is the current fad, but because we have seen in other organizations and more recently in our own the effectiveness of this kind of approach to problem solving and human motivation.

I won't bother to quote the statistics to you or even cite a lot of examples, although many come to mind, of the way in which various organization development techniques and programs have had a direct and quantifiable impact on the operations of companies in the private sector. There are many such examples, and before our organized effort to develop organization development thinking in our company began, some of us, myself included, did quite a lot of reading and research and talking with others to try to gain a feel for what the experience had been; and our conclusion was that the experience had been very good. Pitfalls, of course; difficulties in execution, but the value seems to be there, and as I say, our rather preliminary and tentative experience to date within our own organization tends to confirm what we have learned elsewhere.

We have within the last year under Roger Howe's auspices, conducted a great number of efforts of various kinds; quite a variety of techniques and approaches and programs in every one of our operating divisions—we have six for those of you who are not familiar with the Company—and in all our corporate support divisions. I have monitored these very closely because I consider myself, along with Pete Pestillo, a kind of brooding mother hen in this effort, and I have been quite anxious to get immediate feedback and see what the impact was, and I must say I have been delighted and a little surprised too by the fact that the reaction has been massively favorable. We have had little negative reaction, and in fact your presence here tonight I think is as good an attestation as any I could cite of the fact that this kind of approach, this sort of thing, has spread rather rapidly and gained great credibility throughout the Company.

I think that Pete Pestillo mentioned we are very fortunate in having several years ago established the sort of relationship that we have through IPD with Kent State University. I must admit that both sides perhaps had ulterior motives going into our arrangement and perhaps neither of us quite understood the ultimate value of the experiment that we were undertaking. I will admit I have been surprised by the impact this IPD experiment has had on the organization. I am very pleased with the results—with having this kind of relationship and having developed it far more broadly and far more repaidly than I had thought possible.

We are in a good position to allow the University to help us in this task of preparing ourselves for the broader practice of organization development throughout the company. I have been most pleased as Pete and Roger have explained to me some of the developments that have resulted as this particular program was prepared to learn of the cooperation that has been evidenced by the University and particularly by those of you from the University who are with us tonight. We are delighted by the fact that we are going to be able to conduct this program at least in part as a part of the curriculum of the University. This, I think, is a credit to our own people; it is obviously a great motivation for those of you from Goodrich who are participating, and I hope that the University will find the program beneficial as well.

I think that joining the kinds of talents our two institutions possess in pursuit of specific goals — and certainly this program has some specific goals — we are going to be able to come up with something far superior to anything which B.F. Goodrich could manage to do by itself. I am just happy to be here tonight and to have this opportunity, more or less at the outset of your first module, to encourage you to pursue the program from the beginning to the end. I think you will find it personally rewarding, and I can assure you that the capabilities you are going to carry back to your particular part of the B.F. Goodrich Company are capabilities we need and capabilities we have every intention of utilizing in the future.

Thank you.

Appendix

General Interview Appraisal

Instructions: Rate each party to the interview by placing a check mark on the continuum at the appropriate place. Take into consideration the items indicated in the center of the page.

Interviewer (who has initial responsibility for managing the interview)

Name_____

Rating: Ineffective   Fair   Adequate   Effective   Superior

I. UNDERSTANDING
- Did he attempt to understand the other?
- Did he attempt to establish common ground?
- Did he talk in terms of the other's wants and needs?
- Did he discover any "hidden agenda?" (Undisclosed information, negative feelings or attitudes, the story behind the story).

II. BARRIERS
Did barriers exist between the two, based on
- Differences in position or status?
- Different expectancies?
- Different backgrounds of knowledge and experience?
- Confusion in the use of language?
- A negative climate (Possibly created by one of the individuals)?

III. OUTCOMES
Was the outcome, satisfactory or unsatisfactory to one or both, determined in part by
- Effective or ineffective planning?
- Effective or ineffective structuring of the interview?
- Effective or ineffective close?

Interviewee (Who also wants to represent himself well)

Name_____

Rating: Ineffective   Fair   Adequate   Effective   Superior

IV. QUALITY OF INFORMATION PROVIDED

- Did the interviewee appear informed and able to describe his role positively?
- Did the interviewee demonstrate a cooperative attitude or appear resistant?
- Did the interviewee deliver his answers with:
  appropriate vocabulary?
  enthusiasm in voice and body?
  or appear inarticulate?

General Interview Appraisal

Instructions: Rate each party to the interview by placing a check mark on the continuum at the appropriate place. Take into consideration the items indicated in the center of the page.

Interviewer (who has initial responsibility for managing the interview)

Name_____

Rating: Ineffective   Fiar   Adequate   Effective   Superior

I. UNDERSTANDING
- Did he attempt to understand the other?
- Did he attempt to establish common ground?
- Did he talk in terms of the other's wants and needs?
- Did he discover any "hidden agenda?" (Undisclosed information, negative feelings or attitudes, the story behind the story).

II. BARRIERS
Did barriers exist between the two, based on
- Differences in position or status?
- Different expectancies?
- Different backgrounds of knowledge and experience?
- Confusion in the use of language?
- A negative climate (Possibly created by one of the individuals)?

III. OUTCOMES
Was the outcome, satisfactory or unsatisfactory to one or both, determined in part by
- Effective or ineffective planning?
- Effective or ineffective structuring of the interview?
- Effective or ineffective close?

Interviewee (Who also wants to represent himself well)

Name_____

Rating: Ineffective   Fair   Adequate   Effective   Superior

IV. QUALITY OF INFORMATION PROVIDED

- Did the interviewee appear informed and able to describe his role positively?
- Did the interviewee demonstrate a cooperative attitude or appear resistant?
- Did the interviewee deliver his answers with:

   appropriate vocabulary?

   enthusiasm in voice and body?

   or appear inarticulate?

Job Interview Appraisal

Instructions: Rate each party to the interview by placing a check mark on the continuum at the appropriate place. Take into consideration the items indicated in the center of the page.

*Interviewer Name*_____

Rating: Ineffective   Fair   Adequate   Effective   Superior

I. UNDERSTANDING
- Did he attempt to understand the other?
- Did he attempt to establish common ground?
- Did he talk in terms of the other's wants and needs?
- Did he discover any "hidden agenda?" (Undisclosed information, negative feelings or attitudes, the story behind the story).

II. BARRIERS
Did barriers exist between the two, based on
- Differences in position or status?
- Different expectancies?
- Different backgrounds of knowledge and experience?
- Confusion in the use of language?
- A negative climate (Possibly created by one of the individuals)?

III. OUTCOMES
Was the outcome, satisfactory or unsatisfactory to one or both, determined in part by
- Effective or ineffective planning?
- Effective or ineffective structuring of the interview?
- Effective or ineffective close?

*Interviewee Name*_____

Rating: Ineffective   Fair   Adequate   Effective   Superior

IV. IMAGE
- Did the candidate convey a positive image of him/herself by describing his/her assets? or appear uncertain?
- Did the candidate articulate clear career goals? or appear to be shopping around?
- Did the candidate demonstrate he/she had researched the prospective employing organization and ask appropriate questions, or appear to be disinterested?
- Did the candidate deliver his answers with relevant vocabulary? affirmative language? organized ideas and sentences? enthusiastic, confident voice and body? or appear non-communicative?

Job Interview Appraisal

Instructions: Rate each party to the interview by placing a check mark on the continuum at the appropriate place. Take into consideration the items indicated in the center of the page.

Interviewer Name _____

Rating: Ineffective   Fair   Adequate   Effective   Superior

I. UNDERSTANDING
- Did he attempt to understand the other?
- Did he attempt to establish common ground?
- Did he talk in terms of the other's wants and needs?
- Did he discover any "hidden agenda?" (Undisclosed information, negative feelings or attitudes, the story behind the story).

II. BARRIERS

Did barriers exist between the two, based on
- Differences in position or status?
- Different expectancies?
- Different backgrounds of knowledge and experience?
- Confusion in the use of language?
- A negative climate (Possibly created by one of the individuals)?

III. OUTCOMES

Was the outcome, satisfactory or unsatisfactory to one or both, determined in part by
- Effective or ineffective planning?
- Effective or ineffective structuring of the interview?
- Effective or ineffective close?

Interviewee Name _____

Rating: Ineffective   Fair   Adequate   Effective   Superior

IV. IMAGE
- Did the candidate convey a positive image of him/herself by describing his/her assets? or appear uncertain?
- Did the candidate articulate clear career goals? or appear to be shopping around?
- Did the candidate demonstrate he/she had researched the prospective employing organization and ask appropriate questions, or appear to be disinterested?
- Did the candidate deliver his answers with relevant vocabulary? affirmative language? organized ideas and sentences? enthusiastic, confident voice and body? or appear non-communicative?

Performance Profile

Name _____

Presentation Title: _____

Feeling/Belief or Behavior desired for listeners as a result of your presentation: _____

_____

Outline of Major Divisions in Presentation

I. _____

II. _____

III. _____

IV. _____

The Critic May Check Strengths of the Presentation:

- Adapts to audience and occasion
- Previews organization
- Supports credible
- Ideas are worth our time
- Images are vivid
- Conveys feelings
- Delivery is conversational

- Delivery is enthusiastic
- Language appropriate
- Pronunciation articulate
- Presentation recapped
- Questions handled well
- Attractive grooming

And Problems to Work on:

- Fails to adapt
- Organization fuzzy or confused
- Supports insufficient
- Language inappropriate
  - Imagery lacking
  - Grammar slips
  - Pronunciation mistakes
- Delivery lacks feeling
  - Stiff body
  - Eye contact evasive
  - Moving too much
  - Gestures weak or lacking
  - Grooming inappropriate
  - Notes overused
  - Voice too loud
  - Voice too low

Feedback Comments:

Performance Profile

Name _____

Presentation Title: _____

Feeling/Belief or Behavior desired for listeners as a result of your presentation: _____

_____

Outline of Major Divisions in Presentation

I. _____

II. _____

III. _____

IV. _____

The Critic May Check Strengths of the Presentation:

- Adapts to audience and occasion
- Previews organization
- Supports credible
- Ideas are worth our time
- Images are vivid
- Conveys feelings
- Delivery is conversational

- Delivery is enthusiastic
- Language appropriate
- Pronunciation articulate
- Presentation recapped
- Questions handled well
- Attractive grooming

And Problems to Work on:

- Fails to adapt
- Organization fuzzy or confused
- Supports insufficient
- Language inappropriate
  - Imagery lacking
  - Grammar slips
  - Pronunciation mistakes
- Delivery lacks feeling
  - Stiff body
  - Eye contact evasive
  - Moving too much
  - Gestures weak or lacking
  - Grooming inappropriate
  - Notes overused
  - Voice too loud
  - Voice too low

Feedback Comments:

Performance Profile

Name _____

Presentation Title: _____

Feeling/Belief or Behavior desired for listeners as a result of your presentation: _____

_____

Outline of Major Divisions in Presentation

I. _____

II. _____

III. _____

IV. _____

_____

The Critic May Check Strengths of the Presentation:

- Adapts to audience and occasion
- Previews organization
- Supports credible
- Ideas are worth our time
- Images are vivid
- Conveys feelings
- Delivery is conversational

- Delivery is enthusiastic
- Language appropriate
- Pronunciation articulate
- Presentation recapped
- Questions handled well
- Attractive grooming

And Problems to Work on:

- Fails to adapt
- Organization fuzzy or confused
- Supports insufficient
- Language inappropriate
  - Imagery lacking
  - Grammar slips
  - Pronunciation mistakes
- Delivery lacks feeling
  - Stiff body
  - Eye contact evasive
  - Moving too much
  - Gestures weak or lacking
  - Grooming inappropriate
  - Notes overused
  - Voice too loud
  - Voice too low

Feedback Comments:

Performance Profile

Name _____

Presentation Title: _____

Feeling/Belief or Behavior desired for listeners as a result of your presentation: _____

_____

Outline of Major Divisions in Presentation

I. _____

II. _____

III. _____

IV. _____

The Critic May Check Strengths of the Presentation:

- Adapts to audience and occasion
- Previews organization
- Supports credible
- Ideas are worth our time
- Images are vivid
- Conveys feelings
- Delivery is conversational

- Delivery is enthusiastic
- Language appropriate
- Pronunciation articulate
- Presentation recapped
- Questions handled well
- Attractive grooming

And Problems to Work on:

- Fails to adapt
- Organization fuzzy or confused
- Supports insufficient
- Language inappropriate
  - Imagery lacking
  - Grammar slips
  - Pronunciation mistakes
- Delivery lacks feeling
  - Stiff body
  - Eye contact evasive
  - Moving too much
  - Gestures weak or lacking
  - Grooming inappropriate
  - Notes overused
  - Voice too loud
  - Voice too low

Feedback Comments:

Performance Profile

Name _____

Presentation Title: _____

Feeling/Belief or Behavior desired for listeners as a result of your presentation: _____

_____

Outline of Major Divisions in Presentation

I. _____

II. _____

III. _____

IV. _____

_____

The Critic May Check Strengths of the Presentation:

- Adapts to audience and occasion
- Previews organization
- Supports credible
- Ideas are worth our time
- Images are vivid
- Conveys feelings
- Delivery is conversational

- Delivery is enthusiastic
- Language appropriate
- Pronunciation articulate
- Presentation recapped
- Questions handled well
- Attractive grooming

And Problems to Work on:

- Fails to adapt
- Organization fuzzy or confused
- Supports insufficient
- Language inappropriate
  - Imagery lacking
  - Grammar slips
  - Pronunciation mistakes
- Delivery lacks feeling
  - Stiff body
  - Eye contact evasive
  - Moving too much
  - Gestures weak or lacking
  - Grooming inappropriate
  - Notes overused
  - Voice too loud
  - Voice too low

Feedback Comments:

Index of Names

Index of Companies/
Corporations/Organizations

Index of Subjects